Different Wavelengths

Different Wavelengths

Studies of the Contemporary Women's Movement

Edited by
Jo Reger

Routledge
Taylor & Francis Group

NEW YORK AND LONDON

Published in 2005 by
Routledge
Taylor & Francis Group
270 Madison Avenue
New York, NY 10016

Published in Great Britain by
Routledge
Taylor & Francis Group
2 Park Square
Milton Park, Abingdon
Oxon OX14 4RN

© 2005 by Taylor & Francis Group, LLC
Routledge is an imprint of Taylor & Francis Group

Printed in the United States of America on acid-free paper
10 9 8 7 6 5 4 3 2 1

International Standard Book Number-10: 0-415-94878-9 (Hardcover) 0-415-94879-7 (Softcover)
International Standard Book Number-13: 978-0-415-94878-4 (Hardcover) 978-0-415-94879-1 (Softcover)

Library of Congress Cataloging-in-Publication Data

Different wavelengths : studies of the contemporary women's movement / edited by Jo Reger.
    p. cm.
  Includes bibliographical references and index.
  ISBN 0-415-94878-9 (hardcover : alk. paper) -- ISBN 0-415-94879-7 (pbk. : alk. paper)
    1. Feminism--United States. 2. Feminism--United States--History. 3. Feminists--United States.
I. Reger, Jo, 1962-

HQ1155.D545 2005
305.42'0973--dc22

2004030630

Taylor & Francis Group
is the Academic Division of T&F Informa plc.

Visit the Taylor & Francis Web site at
http://www.taylorandfrancis.com

and the Routledge Web site at
http://www.routledge-ny.com

To Faith, who is the future.

CONTENTS

ACKNOWLEDGMENTS

I am grateful to a number of people who helped with this project. Julie Voelck sparked the idea for this volume by sharing with me the bibliographies she has been compiling on third wave feminism. Julie has been an understanding "ear" and "eye" throughout the creation of this volume. Nancy Whittier encouraged me to take on this endeavor, gave me needed feedback, and has served as an intellectual touchstone, mentor, and role model for me throughout my entire academic career. Ilene Kalish, my first editor, got the idea of the book immediately and saw its potential, and I thank her for her enthusiasm. Heather Brewer worked with me to make this manuscript a reality. She always cheered me up when she came to my office.

I also would like to thank my colleagues, Margaret Willard-Traub, Gail McGuire, and Karen Markel for their feedback on various chapters. Abdi Kusow provided needed advice on the process of editing a book. The ideas in the introduction are the result of many stimulating conversations held with friends across the country. In particular, I wish to thank Megan Murphy and Kate Weigand, along with Nancy Whittier and Julie Voelck, in particular for taking time to talk about contemporary feminism and all its issues. I also would like to thank Verta Taylor for graciously moving from being my graduate school advisor to being one of the authors and co-authoring the foreword with Leila Rupp. Many of the questions this book addresses have been raised in her work and the work she has done with Leila.

I end by acknowledging my two best "girls." To Faith and Dawn, you make all endeavors worthwhile.

FOREWORD

Leila J. Rupp and Verta Taylor

In the mid-1980s, when we were researching and writing *Survival in the Doldrums*, our study of the U.S. women's movement in the 1950s, we kept trying to think of a metaphor that would describe the process of a small group of elite and aging activists maintaining their commitment to women's rights from the suffrage movement through the years in which mass feminist mobilization receded and there was widespread opposition to feminism. We thought about daffodil bulbs in the winter and the cocoons from which butterflies emerge, but we never did come up with a word that fit those processes. So we went with "doldrums," and then later Verta developed the concept of "social movement abey-ance," delineating the organizational and cultural processes that allowed a submerged network of feminists to continue to fight for gender equality in an inhospitable period.[1] We called into question the then prevailing orthodoxy that the U.S. women's movement mobilized through two intense waves of protest and virtually died in the interim years. We argued, instead, for a more continuous view of movements as having thresholds and turning points that scholars had previously mis-taken as "births" and "deaths."

At the time, there was no talk yet of a third wave of feminism, and we saw our work as challenging the notion of two waves. But now we think that the wave metaphor—whether ocean waves or radio waves—may have more utility than we thought, as long as we under-stand that the lulls between the waves are still moving, that, from a transnational perspective, there may be choppy seas rather than even swells, and that waves do not rise and crash independently of each other. The thoughtful considerations of the wave model in this volume, although not all coming to the same conclusion, contribute to this far more complex vision.

The articles in the brilliantly titled *Different Wavelengths* move us ahead in our understanding of the contemporary U.S. women's movement and its relationship to what has gone before. The big difference between first wave/second wave and second wave/third wave relationships is that there is plenty of dialogue—if not always so civil—between those from the 1960s generation who identify as second wave and young women who call themselves third wave feminists, in part because less time elapsed between the peaks of activism. One of the big disputes is how diverse the third wave is compared to the second. The authors in this volume, coming from a variety of disciplinary perspectives, attend to racial, ethnic, class, sexual, and gender difference, avoiding simple conclusions about which wave does difference better.

The generational approach to second wave/third wave relations in this volume, characterized by the mother–daughter metaphor, gets at the heart of the sometimes contentious dialogue across periods of white-hot mobilization. We were struck in our own work on the 1950s with how fervently aging feminists longed for young blood, yet how ill-equipped they were to attract young, not to mention women of color or working-class women, into their ranks. The same was true in the transnational women's organizations in the period between the world wars. Some of their laments about the younger generation sound all too familiar today. U.S. suffragist Anna Howard Shaw in 1910 grumbled to Dutch feminist Aletta Jacobs that "it is everywhere the same question—the young people come into the work with the greatest lack of respect for the older people; they think we have made great blunders all these years and have kept the work back; that now they are going ahead in their sweet and beautiful way."[2] Some even foreshadowed complaints about third-wave interest in appearance and new media. One U.S. National Woman's Party member in the 1950s found the younger generation "hopeless," "not interested in anything but cosmetics, T.V. and modern amusements."[3]

At the same time, there are far more productive actual and metaphorical mother–daughter ties, including teacher–student bonds. From that perspective, we take pride in the feminist scholarship and activism of Jo Reger, Verta's student, who conceptualized and edited this volume, and Stephanie Gilmore, Leila's student, for contributing an article that rethinks the relationship between the second and third waves on issues connected to sexuality. What seems to be key to the process of handing over the torch is the willingness to allow a new generation of activists to forge its own way. The articles here that deal with third-wave tactics suggest that contemporary feminists are finding innovative ways to further the goals of the movement, and it is up to us older feminists to appreciate that creativity.

Finally, *Different Wavelengths*, through sustained empirical research and analytical rigor, gives rest to proclamations of the death of feminism. We've all heard the death knells and read the obituaries, even as we marched by the hundreds of thousands, fought against toxic waste dumps in our neighborhoods, worked for reproductive choice, supported the organization of immigrant domestic workers, produced and read zines, set up rape prevention programs and battered women's shelters, fought for a living wage, staged lesbian kiss-ins at shopping malls, or engaged in any other of the thousands of kinds of activism that must be considered under the feminist umbrella. For years now, we have been conducting research on a movement announced as dead, gone, kaput, nada. Mary Hawkesworth, in a provocative analysis of the semiotics of the premature burial of feminism, juxtaposes the recurrent obituaries of feminism to the multiplying number of women who identify themselves as feminist and the global activism of women fighting for social justice and asks, why? Looking back at the ancient Roman practice of interring living vestal virgins whose sexual misconduct, whether real or not, seemed to be bringing down the wrath of the gods, Hawkesworth suggests that live burial, a state between life and death, erases the problem while distancing the killers from the killing. In that context, a book such as this is a breaking out of the tomb and a proclamation of life for feminism.

When we first started speaking to academic and community groups about our research on the 1950s, we worked to explain that in the aftermath of the suffrage victory, feminists had come to seem as old-fashioned as linen dusters and high-button shoes. For us, as part of the second wave, that seemed very odd. But by the end of the 1980s, we had come to realize that the young women in our classes didn't find that strange at all, for they, too, thought that feminism was as old-fashioned as, well, tie-dyed shirts and fringed leather vests. That shift suggests that, despite the institutional gains of the women's movement and continued activism on the part of a wide variety of women, there really was a lull, a dip of the sea, making space for the third wave in the 1990s to rise up to new heights. *Different Wavelengths* is exactly what we need to understand where we've been and where we're going.

NOTES

1. Verta Taylor, "Social Movement Continuity: The Women's Movement in Abeyance," *American Sociological Review* 54 (1989): 761–75.

2. Quoted in Leila J. Rupp, *Worlds of Women: The Making of an International Women's Movement* (Princeton, NJ: Princeton University Press, 1997), 62.

3. Quoted in Leila J. Rupp and Verta Taylor, *Survival in the Doldrums: The American Women's Rights Movement, 1945 to the 1960s* (New York: Oxford, 1987), 81.

INTRODUCTION

Jo Reger

In the mid-1980s, I took my first women's studies class and found not
only a source of empowerment and anger but also my scholarly calling.
Inspired by the feminist perspectives I had never come in contact with
anywhere else in my education, I set out to become an active feminist,
someone seeking to make a difference in the world. In addition to my
need to do something with the energy I felt as a college sophomore
exposed to women's studies, I was also a woman in search of a feminist
community—a place where people got "it"—a place to say what I was
really thinking. That search led me to groups like the National Organization for Women (NOW), the local Fan the Flames Feminist Bookstore Collective, Take Back the Night, and Stonewall Union gay pride
marches and a variety of other events and organizations. In my journey
I helped found Stone Soup, a cable TV production company consisting
of myself and my friend Susan Bader. I also made several trips to Washington, DC to participate in marches for my rights and the rights of
those around me. Along the way I became a part of multiple communities of women and men dedicated to an ideology of equality. It was
these communities that sustained me and served as the inspiration for
the work I now do as an academic.

As a graduate student, I continued my search for feminist community, this time in a more academic sense. In my research, I focused on
NOW chapters and how they continue and sustain themselves over
time, from the excitement of 1960s feminism to the backlash of the
1980s and 1990s. This academic journey began with the realization that
what I was studying about the women's movement was not, in fact, my
reality. NOW was not filled with conservative white women seeking

only to change the political climate and pushing for new legislation. Instead, my years as an activist in NOW, often characterized as second wave feminism having its roots in the 1960s, included activism I thought was radical, including abortion clinic defenses, feminist Jewish Seders, and sex toy education workshops. The women I knew were from a continuum of political and ideological stances: married (to men) political lesbians with multiple lovers, aspiring politicians in button-down shirts and navy blue suits, sadomasochistic lesbian artists, doc-toral students, and liberal legislative aides. Many of these women were white but women of color were a vital part of these groups and actions. In addition, race and diversity were a constant source of discussion as groups struggled to integrate and expand. These realizations sparked a question that became the focus of my dissertation: When I turn to grassroots activists to understand a movement, what will I find?

In the 1990s (and continuing into the twenty-first century) my activism shifted from mainly being vocal in a public protest arena (such as a march or a lobbying day) to a more everyday kind of femi-nism. My activism today focuses on teaching about gender and social movements, mentoring students on research projects, participating in projects such as *The Vagina Monologues,* working with women's studies and campus feminist groups, and trying to live my life in a way I feel is feminist. At the same time, I haven't turned away from earlier forms of my activism. For example, I have marched on Washington for gay rights, signed petitions and sent e-mails to my legislators on abortion, and monitored environmental policies.

In the last few years, as I read about contemporary feminism, I again feel a disjuncture between what I have been reading about the move-ment and what I have been experiencing. I feel feminist but do not fit into a second (i.e., starting in the 1960s and 1970s and continuing into the backlash 1980s) or third wave (i.e., argued by some as beginning in the 1990s) description. I am barely a baby boomer and too young for the second wave, and not quite a member of Generation X, making me too old for the third wave. Issues of race and diversity have not been resolved, and continue to be an issue in the groups around me. Women of color are present and vital but still in the minority. In sum, I see that there have been some changes in feminism since the mid-1980s, but there are still many similarities.

My research question then moves from my dissertation when I was asking questions about the unexplored realities of feminism in the 1980s and 1990s, to wondering, in my current research, what is hap-pening to feminism in the twenty-first century? The answer, I believe, starts with advice from Gloria Steinem, who suggests that if you want to know about young feminists, you should ask one. The authors in *Different Wavelengths* take this advice to heart, and a variety of scholars, from graduate students to full professors, from a variety of disciplines, investigate contemporary feminism. This question corresponds with a popular and scholarly interest in the third wave. The idea of a third wave exploded in academic and popular literature in the mid-1990s, presenting multiple views of contemporary feminism.[1] In some works, the third wave was perceived as solidly in existence. Others called for its emergence. All, however, agreed that young women had not denounced, rejected, or turned away from feminism. This was abundantly clear in the personal tone and stories of volumes like *To Be Real, Listen Up,* and *Colonize This!* While these personal and individualized stories were satisfying in that they established a vibrant feminism, I continued to search for work that could tell me something about the collective efforts of feminism. I wanted to understand what was going on with feminism on a larger scale. My questions included these: Were there feminist communities, networks, and organizations? Or had activism become so individualized that there was no unified activism?

Later more collective stories began to appear. Edited volumes such as *Manifesta* by Jennifer Baumgardener and Amy Richards, *Third Wave Agenda,* edited by Leslie Heywood and Jennifer Drake, *Catching the Wave,* edited by Rory Dicker and Alison Piepmeier, along with special issues of *Hypatia* and *Signs*[2] began to paint a broader picture, one beyond the individual. With some notable exceptions, however, most of these works focused on cultural analyses of contemporary feminism and less on empirical investigations of feminist communities. Hungry for "bigger pictures" I proposed this book. This collection of research focuses on feminism in the United States as an ongoing social movement, made up of collective actors who work on similar or related issues. The focus moves from individual stories and cultural analysis, to a sociological investigation of what is happening in this broad, diverse, yet coherent social change movement. *Different Wavelengths* illustrates that despite its complexity, and for all its differences, a feminist movement continues.

As I gathered the chapters that make up *Different Wavelengths,* the main themes of the volume emerged. I came to see that these themes are also at the heart of issues, contentions, and questions that challenge third wave feminism in the United States. Those themes center around three main ideas: divisions and inclusivity in contemporary feminism; identifying shifts in feminist ideology and strategy; and the origins and delineation of feminist "waves." I first discuss these themes in the contemporary movement and then describe how they shape the book's organization.

THIRD WAVE THEMES AND CHALLENGES

By portraying the ideas in this book as both themes and challenges, I intend to illustrate the complexity activists and scholars face in trying to express a diverse set of feminist ideologies, identities, and strategies that have permeated U.S. culture. As Baumgardner and Richards are often quoted, "feminism is like fluoride, it is simply in the water."[3] Fluoride, although invisible to the naked eye, is a substance shaping the idea of water, just as feminism has shaped politics, social dynamics, and popular culture. Scholars, activists, and the media are not able to agree on the current effects of feminism on society. The popular media and some political pundits have repeatedly declared that feminism is dead or in decline, what Jennifer Pozner labels the "False Feminist Death Syndrome."[4] According to Mary Hawkesworth, these death notices serve a larger goal, erasing the social justice efforts of women around the world, while preserving the status quo. She writes, "The recurrent obituaries of feminist activism can also be interpreted as a redrawing of community boundaries designed to accomplish far more than the exile of feminism, designed, in fact, to annihilate it."[5]

Scholars and activists respond to these obituaries in different ways. Some argue that feminism is still alive, yet suffering from a backlash[6] and continued through the efforts of "older" feminists and their organizations, institutions, and policies put in place in the 1960s and 1970s. Others argue that feminism has changed form and is now carried out in a different way by a new generation of activists.[7] By examining issues of divisions and inclusivity in contemporary feminism; shifts in feminist ideology and strategy; and the origins and delineation of feminist "waves," this volume provides a lens through which to comprehend the complexity of contemporary feminism.

DIVISIONS, INCLUSIVITY AND
CONSTRUCTING A HISTORY

The history often told of the second wave is that women of color were shut out of feminist organizations by white women who believed that the category of woman was universal and could link all women together. This experience of being defined by white women's perspectives led many women of color to articulate a need for a more inclusive way to understand the diversity of women's lives. From these experiences, a dialogue on intersectionality (i.e., the intertwined connections between race-ethnicity, class, and gender)[8] arose providing third wave feminists with an ideology and goal for the future. Many third wave writers, both scholarly and mainstream, argue that a third wave is needed to correct the racial–ethnic and class grievances of the past. However, the question of inclusivity and the accompanying critique of the second wave pose serious challenges for contemporary feminism. One aspect of that challenge is to create a feminist history that captures the complexity of feminism in the past. By repeating or learning a sim-plified history (i.e., women of color were not present in second wave feminism because of racism), young activists miss an opportunity to learn from the past. Or as Catherine Orr puts it, young women are accepting a monolithic, mainstream idea of the second wave as "real" versus seeing it as one representation.[9]

While the conception of intersectionality and of a matrix of oppres-sion are invaluable to feminist ideology, some scholars argue that tak-ing this "shut-out" perspective ignores the (albeit marginalized) contributions of women of color in building organizations, networks, and communities in the 1960s and 1970s. Benita Roth argues that the second wave was one of *feminisms* with women of color and white women working on similar feminist issues in organizationally distinct movements. She writes:

> [P]revious pictures of second-wave feminism have erased the early and substantial activism of feminists of color embedded in these movements … and scholarship has generally failed to cap-ture the genuine complexity of feminist mobilization in this era.[10]

Others have argued that the *whitewashing* (Roth's term) of the second wave creates a history shaped by hegemonic (i.e., dominant) feminism that "deemphasizes or ignores a class and race analysis, generally sees equality with men as the goal of feminism, and has an individual rights-based, rather than justice-based vision for social change."[11] This perspective ignores the role of race and women of color in the mobili-zation and emergence of organizations such as NOW, which is often portrayed as all white and all middle class. In addition, Becky Thomp-son argues that by tracing the activism of women of color and antira-cist white women an understanding of multiracial feminism as a movement emerges, and a competing and more complex vision of fem-inist history is revealed.[12]

As more accurate representations of feminist history are con-structed,[13] a related challenge is for feminists coming of age today to then build on this history. Young feminists have noted the difficulties of building a movement around a single identity, that of "woman," which ignores difference.[14] Yet, it remains to be seen whether contemporary feminist organizing is inclusive of all racial-ethnic identities. In addition to race and ethnicity, the need to include women of different social classes, sexualities, genders, and religions is raised by contemporary writers. As with race and ethnicity, other social locations such as social class are in danger of the same historical simplification. The challenge to the contemporary feminism is to have a solid grasp on the past as activists work for the future. The efforts of marginalized groups such as working-class and poor women, people of color, transgender people, gays, lesbians, and bisexuals helped build the foundation of U.S. feminist activism. To construct a history without them, even for the sake of drawing attention to their marginalization, is to weaken the foundation of feminism's future.

SHIFTS AND THE FUTURE OF PROTEST

Understanding the shift in ideology, practices, and strategy from the previous wave is the second theme emerging from the movement and from this book. Much of third wave writing argues that activism and ideology are now different. Naomi Wolf argues for a shift from second to third wave feminism in her call for power feminism versus the victim feminism of the past. Victim feminism, according to Wolf, focuses on women's disempowerment, while power feminism views women's lives in a more positive manner.[15] Other ideological shifts are called for by those who argue that the everyday is the location for political action versus more institutional structures such as a legislature or governing body, that individuals are the most important change agents versus formal organizations, and that more traditional strategies (i.e., lobbying, electoral work) have lost their efficacy. Third wave ideology and strategies are often viewed as overcoming the past mistakes of second wave feminists and forging ahead into more cultural and everyday life arenas.[16]

This change in ideology corresponds to a change in tactics with third wave activism characterized as computer generated, do it yourself (DIY), online, and in cyberspace.[17] The Internet teems with third wave feminist websites that offer advice, reading lists, calls for action, rants, and merchandise. In addition to this new virtual space, the everyday is also the site of feminist activism. Some third wave activists talk of doing feminism by playing with appearance through makeup, hair, clothing, and piercings as a way to construct and transmit a political message. One expression of this is "girlie feminism," labeled by Jennifer Baumgardner and Amy Richards, where activists seek to reclaim the femininity and joy they perceive as missing in second wave feminism by embracing "disparaged girl things [such] as knitting, the color pink, nail polish and fun."[18] Rita Alfonso and Jo Trigilio note that Riot Grrrl band members and their fans also play with appearance, performing gender by "dressing up in baby doll dresses, usually worn with combat boots, colorful but torn stockings, and any number of tiny plastic hair barrettes, but writing 'slut' on their bodies to preempt society's judgment of them."[19]

Along with playing with appearance, third wave writers and activists also talk of "playing" with sexuality and gender norms. Merri Lisa Johnson argues that the newest generation of feminists needs to fight against the feminist-imposed norms that define and limit appropriate sexual behavior and desire. She writes that although Generation X feminists struggle with "rationalizing our dildos," feminist writing on sex offers either the "critique or the clit."[20] The key, according to Johnson, is to press forward "sex-positive in a culture that demonizes sexuality, and sex-radical in a political movement that has been known to choose moral high grounds over low guttural sounds."[21] Therefore, in contemporary feminism, the everyday (and every body) becomes the palette for third wave political action.

If these characterizations are correct (and some authors dispute the notion that feminist waves have completely distinct and different forms of activism), then the challenge for contemporary feminism is to take a look at past waves (or at least campaigns, organizations, protests, and sit-ins) and uncover the relationship between the past and the present. Feminist history provides insight into the roots of current ideology and strategy. While the sense of "play" may be new, many of the "playgrounds" are not. Radical and lesbian feminists used sexuality as an everyday political statement against hegemonic heterosexuality. Works by authors such as Andrea Dworkin and Adrienne Rich were (and remain) catalysts changing the way many women viewed sexual relationships and desire.[22] Clothing norms in the second wave made appearance political, albeit in a different sense. For example, in 1968 feminists protested the Miss America pageant by tossing articles of restrictive clothing such as girdles and bras into a trash can, although contrary to myth nothing was burned. A sheep was then crowned Miss America, symbolizing the constraining roles available to women.[23]

In a precursor to the feminist zine (i.e., a self-produced magazine), second wave feminists wrote treaties, analyses, children's stories, and manifestos, mimeographed them, and sent them around the country. Susan Brownmiller recalls that writing was central to the creation of community and the spreading of ideas in the 1960s and 1970s. As a result women's newspapers sprang up around the country, largely published without access to printing presses. She describes one newspaper, *Plexus,* as "typed with ragged right margins on an IBM Selectric and pasted up with rubber cement."[24] As more women's words appeared in print, feminist bookstores arose bringing feminist books, newspapers, journals, and music to communities. The first feminist bookstore opened in 1970 in Minneapolis with more appearing in the 1980s until the rise of mega bookstores and online booksellers brought about their decline.[25] In sum, much of what appears to be new today in contemporary feminism has its roots in the past. Issues of reproductive rights, the role of sexuality in self-definition, the importance of women's electoral presence, body image, and the right to live without violence are a few of the issues that carry over from one generation to the next. This is not to say that there is nothing new about feminist activism in the twenty-first century. The information revolution gives feminist activists today the opportunity to reach more people than ever before. However, these new technologies are not equally accessible.[26] Poor people often do not have access to this technology or find their access limited. Along with understanding the past, an additional challenge to contemporary feminism is to find forms of protest and strategies that are available to all, or to make them available to all.

WAVES AND ORIGINS

The connection between second and third wave activism and ideology raises doubts for a number of scholars about the precision of using a wave model to delineate periods of feminist activism.[27] Packaging history into neat and differentiated decades and goals provides a way to teach and understand feminist activism, but this metaphor leaves out activists and forms of activism that do not fit neatly into this model. This model is often presented as the first wave was from the late 1800s to 1910 and focused on suffrage; the second wave was from 1960 to the 1980s and focused on women's equity; and the third wave, which began in the 1990s, has continued into the early twenty-first century and focuses on diversity and cultural challenges. In addition, the metaphor presupposes a clear beginning and ending to each "wave" of feminism, something difficult to determine, according to Cathryn Bailey. Instead she argues that our understanding of the feminism of the day should incorporate the ambiguity and contradiction that has been present in all the "waves."[28] For example, Leila Rupp and Verta Taylor document that feminism was sustained through the "doldrums" between the first and second waves and never completely disappeared.[29] Kate Weigand argues that from the 1940s to the 1960s the Communist Worker's Party provided a place to continue a dialogue about feminism, illustrating the murkiness of the discrete wave model.[30]

Even if we hold on to the concept of a third wave as different and delineated from the second wave, another challenge to the third wave is establishing its origins. Multiple stories exist of the beginning of the third wave. In 1991, Lynn Chancer called for a "third wave" feminism to signify a turn from the defensive posture of 1980s feminism and its backlash.[31] Some scholars credit the idea of the third wave to Rebecca Walker when she called herself "third wave" in the introduction to her anthology *To Be Real* in 1995. For others, the Riot Grrrl uprising in the Northwest in the 1990s signaled the reconceptualization of a new, punk-infused, generationally defined form of feminism.[32] Finally, many credit the rise of the third wave as having its origins in the challenges made by women of color to the second wave for its lack of racial–ethnic inclusivity.[33] Baumgardner and Richards take this approach and argue that, "The Third Wave was born of diversity realized by the latter part of the Second Wave."[34] While the reality is that each of the sources has contributed to the feminism experienced today, it is up to third wavers to understand the many sources of contemporary feminism and how each source adds an important dimension to the movement's goals and strategies.

THE BOOK'S ORGANIZATION

Learning from former schisms and divisions, defining what the movement is and is not, and constructing a future not subject to the same problems as the past, are all challenges faced by contemporary feminists. The authors in this book address these challenges by providing the reader with empirically generated insights into the diversity and complexity of contemporary feminism. The chapters are organized into four sections: Part I addresses one of the most problematic issues facing contemporary feminism, that of diversity. Part II examines the relationships between second and third wave feminists and asks the question whether this is a mother–daughter relationship or whether other dynamics are at play. Part III examines the tactics and strategies of contemporary feminism and looks at new forms of protest and community building arising in an information age. Part IV explores some of the implications of the third wave, in particular use of the wave model. Following Part IV is an extensive bibliography for those interested in reading more about third wave dynamics.

In part I, "Who is Third Wave? Issues of Diversity" the authors examine the idea that the third wave deals with issues of race-ethnicity, gender, and sexuality differently from earlier periods. In "Strongblackwomen and Black Feminism: A Next Generation?" Kimberly Springer investigates younger black women's relationship to feminism through an analysis of contemporary texts. By exploring the relationships the writers have to their history, self, and black men, Springer argues that rejecting the label *third wave* is not a rejection of feminist ideology but instead signifies a need for historical continuity. Like Springer, Florence Maätita illustrates the complexity of being a third wave feminist in "*Que Viva La Mujer*: Negotiating Chicana Feminist Identities." Maätita draws on interviews with young Chicanas to document how they come to negotiate their identities as both Chicanas and as feminists. She demonstrates how issues of ethnicity and familial relations have not been adequately addressed by third wave feminists.

Kristen Schilt also examines issues of race from the perspective of whiteness. In "The Punk White Privilege Scene: Riot Grrrl, White Privilege and Zines," Schilt tests the idea that white third wave feminists have acknowledged and dealt with their race privilege by examining zines written by Riot Grrrl generation feminists. She finds that contemporary feminist writings and ideas by white women are not completely successful in learning racial lessons from the past. The final chapter in part I, Sally Hines's "'I Am a Feminist but ....': Transgender Men and Women and Feminism," examines the pre- and posttransition experiences of transgender men and women involved in feminist communities. Hines finds that the "but" in the statement stems not from an unwillingness on the part of the individual to identify as feminist but on the resistance some transgender men and women meet as they enter into second wave feminist communities shaped by radical feminist thought. She then considers how the third wave may create a more open space for transgender people.

In part II, "Mothers and Daughters? Relations between the Second and Third Waves," the authors address the relationship between younger and older (or third and second wave feminists). Two of the authors (Gilmore in part II and Naples in her analysis later in the book) describe the 2002 Veteran Feminists of America conference and reveal how relations between young women and their older feminist counterparts have been contentious at times, with younger women feeling condescended to and older women feeling devalued and ignored. In part II, three authors address this relationship sometimes characterized as mother and daughter. In "Solitary Sisterhood: Individualism Meets Collectivity in Feminism's Third Wave," Astrid Henry argues that third wave feminists adopt a shared generational stance that focuses on individualism and diversity. Through an analysis of feminist texts, Henry argues that this generational stance is oppositional to the second wave, a position that can ultimately harm the movement.

Stephanie Gilmore addresses the question of a generational divide in her analysis of NOW and its history of activism. She argues in "Bridging the Waves: Sex and Sexuality in a Second Wave Organization," that despite conferences such as the Veteran Feminists of America, the issues of the third and second wave are not that distinct from each other and that "mainstream" second wave organizations such as NOW addressed and continue to address issues of sex and sexuality at the heart of many third wave actions. Susanne Beechey in "When Feminism is Your Job: Age and Power in Women's Policy Organizations," takes a different perspective on organizations started in the second wave and investigates how young women fare in large, formal feminist policy organizations. She suggests that issues of age may be overstated in descriptions of the dissension between different feminist generations and instead points to deeper power dynamics as the cause.

In part III, "What Brings Change? Tactics of the Third Wave," the authors look at strategies and protests new to the movement. In "Talking about My Vagina: Two College Campuses and *The Vagina Monologues*," Lacey Story and I examine the ways in which Eve Ensler's production of *The Vagina Monologues* has shaped campus activism. Comparing two different campuses, we discuss how reaction to the monologues is mixed, serving as a cornerstone for feminist organizing in one case and resulting in controversy in another. Barbara Duncan in "Searching for a Home Place: Online in the Third Wave" explores another new phenomenon, the rise of virtual communities through websites. She compares the magazines *Bust* and *Ms.* to investigate the similarities and the differences between the readers who write or post, and how this shapes political action. While both magazines embrace their readers' views and opinions, *Bust*'s Internet site allows women to form interactive communities, vital to third wave feminism.

Dawn Bates and Maureen McHugh continue this examination of new technologies versus established media. In their chapter, "Zines: Voices of Third Wave Feminists," they explore how zines have become a form of resistance to the mainstream magazines that feed girls' narrowly defined conceptions of bodies and beauty, and affect self-esteem. They argue that through self-produced zines, zine makers express their personal discontent while also making a collective statement through zine communities and networks. The final chapter in the section, "Third Wave Feminism and Ecofeminism: Reweaving the Nature/Culture

Duality," by Colleen Mack-Canty, analyzes the connections between second and third wave activism. Through her interviews with ecofeminists, she finds that although these women do not necessarily fit the generational model of a third wave, the activist work they do corresponds to the third wave goals of acknowledging the intersectionality of all life (including nonhuman) and works to break down the dualism of nature and culture.

While the majority of the chapters provide empirical data on aspects of third wave activism, part IV, "Into the Future: Implications of a Third Wave," engages in an analysis of the movement and particularly the use of the concept "third wave." Nancy Naples draws on her personal experiences as a feminist, her research on poor and working-class women's activism, and her work in the classroom to question the perception of the women's movement as a series of historical waves. She argues that by moving away from the wave model, a broader picture of feminism and feminist activism emerges. Ednie Kaeh Garrison in "Are we on a wavelength yet? On Feminist Oceanography, Radios, and Third Wave Feminism," also critiques the wave model, illustrating how our understanding of feminism is limited by the metaphor of the ocean wave. She argues that adopting both an oceanic and radio wave metaphor opens up the conception of feminism and provides a powerful shift in scholarly and activist thinking. The final section of the book is a selective bibliography by librarian Julie Voelck that provides readers with sources for further reading materials on these and other related ideas.

CONCLUSION

Although major themes emerge from this volume—the importance of considering diversity and intersectionality, the need to understand generational relations, and the problematic nature of the wave model—there are points of divergence: one being a matter of definition. When I began to talk to contributors for this volume, it was suggested to me that I should define third wave for the authors because if I did not, the definitions would be too nebulous and "nothing would stick." After some consideration, I did not provide a definition and that decision forged one of the most interesting aspects of the book. For some of the authors, the idea of a generation-based third wave is not problematic. They clearly identify contemporary feminism as something different from the past, made up of a certain age group. This view is popular in scholarly and mainstream writings. For example, Candis Steenberger, working with this generational definition, writes:

The third wave exists within the women's movement itself, a generation of young women actively attempting to address the complexities involved in women's everyday experiences and the personal and structural relations affecting them.[35]

Other authors find it more difficult to define third wave feminism. For some, such as Naples and myself, the use of a generational model leaves out women who are too young to be considered second wave and too old to be a part of the Generation X'ers often credited with carrying on feminism. For others, the generational definition of third wave is not problematic but finding those who identify with the label is. For example, Beechey notes that although all the young women she interviewed were feminists, very few identified with the label of *third wave.*

Depending on the chapter, the idea of a third wave is accepted, challenged, or rejected, illustrating the complexity of studying feminism. By not adhering to one definition of third wave, this volume addresses one of the most important challenges facing feminist activists and scholars today: How do you organize or study a movement where activists do not define themselves commonly (e.g., suffragist, women's lib, radical feminist)? Will an organization with "third wave" in its name screen out women who believe themselves to be too old (or too young) or those for whom the label has no resonance (women of color already distanced from the label *feminist*)? We are left to question then whether or not the term *third wave* is a scholarly invention and not an emergent label from the movement.

Another point of divergence is in where the authors locate their analyses. This is illustrated in the variety of (to borrow a sociological term) the *units of analysis* the authors are examining. Illustrating the importance of texts in shaping cultural and political ideologies, Springer, Schilt, Henry, and Bates and McHugh examine a variety of texts from the academic to the popular, and from the professionally produced to the do-it-yourself. This range in textual styles and forms illustrates the importance of words in shaping how feminists come to view the world and how easy sharing individual and collective perceptions of the world has become. However, these views of contemporary feminism are not limited to textual analysis, several of the authors engage in case studies and interviews with contemporary feminists involved in a variety of settings from formal organizations, to virtual communities, to feminist networks. By talking to feminists, Maätita, Hines, Beechey, Reger and Story, Duncan, and Mack-Canty illustrate the diversity of feminist thinking from the young women in women's policy organizations to transgender men and women in third wave communities.[36] It is interesting to note that not all of the interviews and case studies are based on college campuses but instead reach into communities to find the everyday, after-college reality of feminist life. Intertwined with the diversity of analyses is the range of regional representation, moving past an East–West Coast bias and including studies based in the Western states, the Midwest, and in the United Kingdom.

It is complexity of themes and challenges that gives this volume its title, *Different Wavelengths*. This volume began as a search for an answer to the question, where is contemporary feminism? But it finishes with no single (or simple) answer. Contemporary feminism is diffuse, diverse, and often fragmented, like earlier feminism. The picture of feminism today is a complex one with a variety of ideologies, strategies, and tactics in place. What these authors tell us in a unified voice is that to draw a "big picture" of contemporary feminism is to draw a simplified picture, leaving out many people and forms of activism. This is not to argue that contemporary feminism is floundering, adrift, hopeless, contentious, or apathetic. Instead, this volume provides ample evidence for the argument that feminism today is alive, vibrant, growing, and is a very interesting phenomenon to study and participate in. The ideas in *Different Wavelengths* also represent where I am with feminism. I am now more content to live with the debates, dissension, and general messiness of the feminism around me. This book serves as a reminder for me in my search for feminist community to keep an eye to the past, my heart to the future, and to open the door for all people and ideas to enter.

NOTES

1. See Rebecca Walker, ed., *To Be Real: Telling the Truth and Changing the Face of Feminism* (New York, NY, Anchor, 1995); Barbara Findlen, ed., *Listen Up: Voices from the Next Feminist Generation* (Seattle, WA: Seal Press, 1995); Leslie Heywood and Jennifer Drake, eds., *Third Wave Agenda: Being Feminist, Doing Feminism.* (Minneapolis: University of Minnesota Press, 1997); Jennifer Baumgardner and Amy Richards, *Manifesta: Young Women Feminism and the Future* (New York: Farrar, Straus, Giroux, 2000); Daisy Hernández and Bushra Rehman, eds., *Colonize This! Young Women of Color on Today's Feminism* (New York: Seal Press, 2002); Rory Dicker and Alison Piepmeier, eds., *Catching a Wave: Reclaiming Feminism for the 21st Century* (Boston: Northeastern University Press, 2003).

2. Jacquelyn N. Zita, ed., "Third Wave Feminism," *Hypatia* 12 (Summer 1997); Kum-Kum Bhavnani, Kathryn R. Ken, and France Winddance Twine, eds., "Feminisms and Youth Culture," *Signs: A Journal of Women in Culture and Society* 23 (Spring 1998).

3. Baumgardner and Richards, 17.

4. Jennifer Pozner, "The 'Big Lie': False Feminist Death Syndrome, Profit, and the Media," in Rory Dicker and Alison Piepmeier, eds., *Catching a Wave: Reclaiming Feminism for the 21st Century* (Boston: Northeastern University Press, 2003), 31–56;

for an example see Neal Conan's introduction of feminism for "Talk of the Nation," April 22, 2004, National Public Radio, http://web.lexis-nexis.com/universe/document?_m=3a78dc441d9d8cb0c763ba26291d910 (accessed LexisNexis May 28, 2004).

5. Mary Hawkesworth, "The Semiotics of Premature Burial: Feminism in a Postfeminist Age," *Signs: A Journal of Women in Culture and Society* 29 (Summer 2004): 961–86 (accessed InfoTrac OneFile, August 12, 2004), 14.

6. Susan Faludi, *Backlash* (New York: Anchor, 1991).

7. See Baumgardner and Richards.

8. I purposely leave off sexuality and sexual orientation/preference as many of the second wave articulations did.

9. Catherine Orr, "Charting the Currents of the Third Wave," *Hypatia* 12 (Summer 1997), 32.

10. Benita Roth, *Separate Roads to Feminism: Black, Chicana, and White Feminist Movements in America's Second Wave* (New York: Cambridge University Press, 2004), 2.

11. Becky Thompson, "Multiracial Feminism: Recasting the Chronology of Second Wave Feminism," *Feminist Studies* 28 (Summer 2002): 337–663 (accessed InfoTrac OneFile, August 12, 2004), 1.

12. Thompson.

13. See Thompson; Premilla Nadasen, "Expanding the Boundaries of the Women's Movement: Black Feminism and the Struggle for Welfare Rights," *Feminist Studies* 28 (Summer 2002): 27–59 (accessed InfoTrac OneFile, August 12, 2004).

14. See Veronica Chambers, "Betrayal Feminism," in *Listen Up: Voices From the Next Feminist Generation*, Barbara Findlen, ed. (Seattle, WA: Seal Press, 1995), 21–28; JeeYeun Lee, "Beyond Bean Counting," in *Listen Up: Voices From the Next Feminist Generation*, Barbara Findlen, ed. (Seattle, WA: Seal Press, 1995), 205–11; Lisa Weiner-Mahfuz, "Organizing 101: A Mixed-Race Feminist in Movements for Social Justice," in *Colonize This! Young Women of Color on Today's Feminism*, Daisy Hernández and Bushra Rehman, eds. (New York: Seal Press, 2002), 29–39.

15. Naomi Wolf, *Fire with Fire: The New Female Power and How It Will Change the 21st Century* (New York: Random House, 1993).

16. Heywood and Drake.

17. Rita Alfonso and Jo Trigilio, "Surfing the Third Wave: A Dialogue between Two Third Wave Feminists," *Hypatia* 12 (1997): 7–16.

18. Baumgardner and Richards, 80.

19. Alfonso and Trigilio, 13.

20. Merri Lisa Johnson, "Jane Hocus, Jane Focus," in *Jane Sexes It Up: True Confessions of Feminist Desire*, Merri Lisa Johnson, ed. (New York: Four Walls, Eight Windows, 2002), 6.

21. Johnson, 9.

22. The result of these critiques led to much debate in feminism. For an overview see Ann Snitnow, Christine Stansell, and Sharon Thompson, eds., *Power of the Desire: The Politics of Sexuality* (New York: Monthly Review Press, 1983).

23. Sara M. Evans, *Tidal Wave: How Women Changed America at Century's End* (New York: Free Press, 2003).

24. Susan Brownmiller, *In Our Time: Memoir of a Revolution* (New York: Dial Press, 1999), 188–89.

25. Kristen A. Hogan, "Defining Our Own Context: The Past And Future Of Feminist Bookstores," *thirdspace* 2 (March 2003), http://www.thirdspace.ca/articles/hogan.htm (accessed August 6, 2004).

26. Conrad L. Kanagy and Donald Kraybill, "How Will the Internet Change Society?" in *Mapping the Social Landscape*, Susan Ferguson, ed. (New York: McGraw-Hill, 2002), 634–41.

27. Both in this volume and published in other areas. See Garrison, Naples, Springer this volume for critiques. Also see Dicker and Piepmeier, "Introduction"; Myra Marx Ferree and Patricia Yancey Martin, eds., *Feminist Organizations: Harvest of the New Women's Movement* (Philadelphia: Temple University Press, 1995); Verta Taylor, "Sources of Continuity in Social Movements: The Women's Movement in Abeyance," *American Sociological Review* 54 (1989): 761–75.

28. Cathryn Bailey, "Making Waves and Drawing Lines: The Politics of Defining the Vicissitudes of Feminism," *Hypatia* 12 (Summer 1997): 17–28.

29. Leila J. Rupp and Verta Taylor, *Survival in the Doldrums: The American Women's Rights Movement, 1945 to 1960s*, (New York: Oxford University Press, 1987).

30. Kate Weigand, *Red Feminism: American Communism and the Making of Women's Liberation* (Baltimore, MD: John Hopkins University Press, 2000).

31. Lynn S. Chancer, *Reconcilable Differences: Confronting Beauty, Pornography and the Future of Feminism* (Berkeley: University of California Press, 1998), 265–76.

32. See Jessica Rosenberg and Gitana Garofalo, "Riot Grrrl: Revolutions from Within," *Signs: Journal of Women in Culture and Society* 23 (Summer 1998): 811–41.

33. See Heywood and Drake, 8; Dicker and Piepmeier, 9; Baumgardner and Richards, 77.

34. Baumgardner and Richards, 77.

35. Candis Steenberger, "Talking the 'Post' Off of Feminism: History, Sexuality and the Women's Movement's Third Wave (Carleton University, unpublished master's thesis, 1999).

36. In the case of Gilmore's analysis of NOW, it is not people she queries but organizational documents and histories.

Part I

Who is Third Wave?
Issues of Diversity

1

STRONGBLACKWOMEN AND BLACK FEMINISM: A NEXT GENERATION?

Kimberly Springer

The history of black feminist activism is one that has been, tradition-ally, obscured in histories of the women's movement, as well as in fem-inist theory. In reality, there was no shortage of black women writing about their gender and race concerns in a range of theoretical tradi-tions from liberal to Marxist and defining their own theoretical posi-tion rooted in black women's experiences in the public and private realms of U.S. society. Additionally, scholars began to insert narratives of black women's gender activism in the historical records of the civil rights and women's liberation movements from the 1980s into the early twenty-first century.

Beneficiaries of this second look at black women's activism were not only the women themselves, who deserved the long overdue recogni-tion of dramatically shifting how we discuss intersecting identities, but also the next generation of potential black feminists. Specifically, those young black women, mostly college educated, who are part of the Gen-eration X cohort, and were nurtured in a cultural milieu that included the historical legacies of Sojourner Truth, Anna Julia Cooper, Claudia Jones, Lorraine Hansberry, Ella Baker, and a host of other black women activists/scholars/thinkers.[1]

At the same time, we cannot underestimate the reticence with which some young black women approach the black feminist label. Arguments against black feminism are most definitely cultural hangovers that have haunted black women concerned with sexism in black communities for generations: accusations of "acting white" by engaging with feminism; claims that feminism detracts from the black struggle; homophobia; and often a lack of understanding of the goals of feminism as a political ideology.

Black feminists who came of age in the 1960s and 1970s continue to wrestle with gender dilemmas and strive to impart knowledge about the struggle for racial and gender justice.[2] Yet, younger black women are also joining the dialogue through their activism, music, and writing. This chapter asks three central questions about contemporary young black women's views on gender and race: Is there a third wave black feminist politic? What issues are contemporary young black feminists prioritizing? How do these young women contextualize their experiences and their politics?

I approach these questions of a third wave black feminism through writing because of literacy's important place in social change movements, as well as a legacy of literacy's power for African-American women's self-definition. Denied literacy as enslaved Africans, sometimes educated in secrecy but at great risk, African Americans have found ways to communicate a message of struggle and liberation through oral and written traditions. As demonstrated in emancipation narratives such as Harriet Jacobs's *Incidents in the Life of a Slave Girl*, African-American women have used their literacy as a weapon against racial and gender oppression as exacted by white supremacy since the early presence of African Americans in the United States.[3] Moreover, African-American women used that literacy to take to task intracommunity responsibilities, calling upon men and women to define themselves as African and American. Late eighteenth-century writings offer a compelling picture of African-American women's grievances as blacks and women, while demanding full inclusion in decisions impacting their communities, their families, and their personal integrity. Those imperatives remain apparent in the writing of contemporary generations of black feminists.

Three contemporary texts fall under the rubric of young black feminist writing: Lisa Jones's collection of essays *Bulletproof Diva: Tales of Race, Sex, and Hair*; Joan Morgan's essays, released in 1999, *When Chickenheads Come Home to Roost: My Life as a Hip-Hop Feminist* (hereafter known as *Chickenheads*); and Veronica Chambers's 1996 memoir *Mama's Girl*.[4] These texts stand out as they speak explicitly from or about young black feminist perspectives in the 1990s. Jones's and Morgan's essays effectively meld the third wave penchant for personal narrative with second wave theoretical underpinning, creating a case for interrogating the politics of style (i.e., lifestyle) and the style of politics (i.e., political issues). While second wave feminists, particularly cultural feminists, were accused, rightly or wrongly, of attending too much to feminism as lifestyle, Morgan and Jones attend effectively to popular culture, an increasingly influential concern among next generation feminists.

In other words, young black feminists might be reacting to stereotypes about feminism as reducible to whether one shaves one's legs when, in fact, feminism is about much deeper, critical political issues. These three texts have much to contribute to academic pursuits concerned with examining the daily functioning of interlocking systems of oppression. Moreover, as texts that examine popular culture, they convey valuable, transferable messages for activists working around gender, race, and class in U.S. black communities. With a politics of style, young black feminists address both politics and style, which can be interpreted as the impact of writers firmly embedded in the hip-hop generation as a movement of style and politics.

Young black feminists elaborate on three central themes that create a unique and updated position for black feminism in the third wave. The first to emerge is young black women's relationship to our personal and political histories. This history includes our relationships to past social movements and to our biological and political foremothers. The next theme is a persistent one in black women's writing: relationship to self. Morgan, Chambers, and Jones each tackle the myth of the "Strong Black Woman" and what it means for how we relate to our mothers, other black women, and ourselves. Finally, the authors write about black women's relationships to black men as biological brothers, brothers in the political sense, and fathers.

Young, contemporary black women continue creating feminist analyses of black life, but they are not necessarily claiming the label of *third wave*. Their reasons, however, are different from those of women who fear feminism as an ideology. These women share their life stories in the public forum as a way of asserting a contemporary black female identity that is mindful of historical context and community imperatives. Recuperation of the self in a racist and sexist society is a political enterprise and a black feminist one that deprioritizes generational differences in the interest of historical, activist continuity.

TENDING OUR MOTHERS' GARDENS

What is the relationship between black feminists of differing generations?[5] Does a generational rift exist between them? One aspect of the
generational tensions between feminists in general is the frustration
older feminists feel at watching younger women reinvent the wheels of
social change. Black feminist cultural critic Michele Wallace, in retro-
spect, recognized the irritation of her mother and other women of her
mother's generation. In her essay "To Hell and Back," Wallace writes of
the late 1960s:

> My thesis had been that I and my generation were reinventing
> youth, danger, sex, love, blackness, and fun. But there had always
> been just beneath the surface a persistent countermelody, ... what
> I might also call my mother's line, a deep suspicion that I was
> reinventing nothing, but rather making a fool of myself in pre-
> cisely the manner that untold generations of young women before
> me had done.[6]

Other than this autobiographical insight by Wallace, few sources
speak of generational conflicts or distinctions between black feminists.[7]

As beneficiaries of social movements that drastically altered the
sociopolitical landscape of racial and sexual politics, Jones, Morgan,
and Chambers each addresses the question of generation. They give
credit to the civil rights, women's, and black nationalist movements for
the opportunities these movements gave us to attain places of privilege
in the workplace and institutions of higher education. Yet, they also
recognize the complacency that such awe-inspiring sheroes and heroes
inspired in Generation X. Chambers recalls, as a child, watching docu-
mentaries about black history. She and her brother would boast of how
they would have resisted racist oppression had they lived in those
times, but the reprimanding look on her mother's face told her that, in
reality, "we had no idea what we would or wouldn't have done." Chambers continues, "Deep down inside, I wondered. As bad as those times
were, I wished sometimes that there was some sort of protest or something that I could get involved with."[8] Such melancholy nostalgia
reflects a falsely held belief that all of the meaningful struggles are over,
that all of the battles have been won. Or, alternately, for a generation
increasingly disenfranchised by the potential of American politics, the
belief that change is impossible.

Chambers lived with both parents until age ten when her father left
the family. At the time of Chambers's reminiscence, her parents provided the basics for her and her brother, and the fact that they had

always lived in a house with a yard is a significant marker of the class security she felt as a child. Chambers's parents instituted a "Black History Day" in their home before Black History Month came into existence, so their daughter had an early sense of the sacrifices they made, particularly her mother, but felt none of those barriers herself. Chambers's memories of contemplating what she would have done during the height of the civil rights movement, ultimately, is the luxury of a generation that benefited from that particular struggle.

Morgan takes a less fanciful approach and considers the lulling effect on Generation X of successful social movements, in terms of civil rights and women's liberation movement gains. In the introduction to her book, entitled *Dress Up*, Morgan recalls being jealous of her mother's generation, not because they had it easy but because of the burgeoning contemporary women's movement and the dissemination of ideas about independence and self-fulfillment. Her mother's generation also had the cultural explosion of black women's literature to affirm their existence and the circumstances of "being black, female and surviving."[9] Morgan was ten years old when Ntozake Shange's choreopoem *for colored girls who have considered suicide when the rainbow was not enuf* premiered in New York City. When her mother refused to take her, a young Joan tried every trick in her arsenal—from whining, to singing "the Five Stairsteps' 'O-o-h child things are going to get easier' over and over again—attitudinal and loud—until I was two seconds shy of an ass whooping."[10] It was only with coming into her own awareness of race and gender that Morgan understood that "the play held crucial parts of her [mother] —parts she needed to share with her husband and not her ten-year-old daughter."[11]

When she attends the twentieth anniversary run of *for colored girls* in Manhattan, Morgan hopes that it will reveal secrets of black womanhood that she thought her mother withheld. This was not the case. She realized, "As a child of the post-Civil Rights, post-feminist, post-soul hip-hop generation my struggle songs consisted of the same notes but they were infused with distinctly different rhythms."[12] In realizing that she was waiting for someone to write a version of *for colored girls* for her generation, Morgan calls to task her own complacency, as well as that of her generation. She cautions, "Relying on older heads to redefine the struggle to encompass our generation's issues is not only lazy but dangerous. Consider our foremothers' contributions a bad-ass bolt of cloth. We've got to fashion the gear to our own liking."[13] Linking generational style and politics, Morgan calls upon the hip-hop generation to create a language and culture that signifies more than a lifestyle but also a political stance worthy of definition. Far from dismissing the achievements of past generations, Morgan acknowledges previous generations of women who, whether they identified as feminist or not, made possible Morgan's self-described position as a hip-hop feminist.

Describing herself as a descendant of civil rights, feminism, and soul music does not imply that, as a society, we are finished with the struggle for civil or women's rights. The popular press's use of the term *postfeminist* implies a uniquely liberated, sexy, young woman who believes feminism is dead or all the battles have been won. Morgan uses the prefix *post-* to signal the end of a particular era of *tactics and action.* She in no way indicates that the goals or hopes of those movements were fulfilled or are no longer relevant to current generations. She does openly recognize a position as "the daughters of feminist privilege."[14] The "we" means college-educated, middle-class black girls who believe that there is nothing we cannot achieve because we are women, though sexism and racism might fight us every step of the way. Morgan attempts to craft a collective identity for a new generation of thinkers and organizers. This is a unifying move meant to reach out to women like Chambers who long for significant struggles like those of past eras, as well as those who feel as though the movements of the 1960s were failures due to conservative backlash, without taking into account our own lack of political vigilance.

Lisa Jones issues a similar call to action for the post–civil rights, postfeminist generation. Though the subtitle of her book only mentions race, sex, and hair, she is also class conscious, either explicitly or implicitly, in the forty-four essays that make up her book. About the differences between generations, Jones parallels Morgan in her observations of the cultural production of the 1970s:

> The renaissance of fiction by black women in the seventies, we caught that too. Those books made us feel less invisible, though their stories were far from our own lives as big-city girls; girls who took ballet and were carted off to Planned Parenthood in high school so as not to risk that baby that Mom, not Mama, warned would have "ruined our lives." College was expected. The southern ghosts of popular black women's fiction, the hardships and abuse worn like purple hearts, the clipped wings were not ours. We had burdens of our own. Glass ceilings at the office and in the art world, media and beauty industries that saw us as substandard, the color and hair wars that continued to sap our energy. We wanted to hear about these.[15]

As young white feminists are seeking to step outside of what they consider rigid lifestyle (e.g., stylistic and political) instructions of their feminist foremothers, young black women are attempting to stretch beyond the awe-inspiring, legendary work of women such as Fannie Lou Hamer, Myrlie Evers-Williams, Ruby Doris Smith Robinson, Barbara Smith, bell hooks, and Angela Davis. Their work is unparalleled. When Jones poses the question, "Do you know who speaks through you?" she poses a rhetorical question that recognizes the significance of history in giving current struggles meaning.[16]

Morgan and Jones exhort the post–civil rights, postfeminist hip-hop generation to pay homage to past struggles, but not to rest on our ivory tower degrees. Both recognize the class implications of being exposed to black feminists' texts as assigned reading in college-level courses. Morgan, while recognizing historical reasons for black women's lack of engagement with feminism—for example, racism in the women's movement, feminism's alleged irrelevancy to black lives—believes that, at the most fundamental level, black women are "misguidedly over-protective, hopelessly male-identified, and all too often self-sacrificing."[17] She interprets homecoming parades for Mike Tyson upon his release from prison after serving a sentence for sexual assault and blind support for conservative Supreme Court Justice nominee Clarence Thomas as knee-jerk reactions to centuries of racist violence. However, jumping to the defense of black men—even when black *women* are the victims of male violence—does nothing for current and future generations struggling against gender bias within the black community. Critiquing popular culture and writing openly from a black feminist perspective in periodicals, such as the hip-hop magazine *Vibe* and *The Village Voice*, Morgan and Jones most likely reach a mix of middle-class, college-educated or college-bound black and white readerships. Still, in their writings they reference a continuum of black and women's struggle, overlaying historical context onto contemporary manifestations of racism and sexism, that can be useful for articulating a vision for attacking battering, rape, and gender violence in the black community.

STRONGBLACKWOMEN AND BULLETPROOF DIVAS' RELATIONSHIPS

Morgan writes that we, black women, need to take an honest look at ourselves and then tell the truth about what we find.[18] Jones, Morgan, and Chambers want to tell the truth about, in part, the myths that circumscribe the lives of black women, but Morgan ups the ante by also raising black women's culpability in keeping these myths alive. All three women dissect external messages from white society about beauty and how these messages wreak havoc with black women's self-esteem.

These authors also pry apart the smothering layers of self-hatred that are heaped upon black women from within black communities. The solutions they offer all involve, to some degree, letting go of the past and opening up to a future as fallible human beings and not women of mythical proportions.

Morgan situates the standard of the Strong Black Woman in the history of slavery and the ways black women were expected to persevere under any circumstances. Referencing Michele Wallace's explanation of the myths of the superwoman, the mammy, the jezebel, and the sapphire, Morgan contends that these myths have metamorphosed into the contemporary figures of, among others, the "Ghetto Bitch ... Hoochie Mama.... Skeezer.... Too independent.... Don't need no man....[and] Waiting to Exhale" women.[19] She believes that the older myths created to justify whites' brutality against black women in the slave economy are the contemporary conservative welfare myths we have internalized and use to craft any type of identity for ourselves.[20] At one point in her life, Morgan begins to feel like she is suffocating under the burden of trying to always appear in control and strong. A friend diagnoses her as succumbing to "strongblackwoman" syndrome whose motto is, "No matter how bad shit gets, handle it alone, quietly, and with dignity."[21]

Morgan writes "strongblackwoman" as one word and abbreviates it to SBW, signifying the transformation of stereotype into an accepted and recognizable identity that black women are encouraged to embrace. This linguistic move solidifies the idea of "strong," "black," "woman" as nonseparable parts of a seemingly cohesive identity. In this title, there is no room for being just one of the three identities at any given time. There is the expectation in the black community that black women will be all three, *at all times*. Though black feminism is firmly entrenched in the inability to separate out race and gender, adding an adjective like *strong* is too prescriptive and constrictive.

The strong, black woman is not a new concept. Nineteenth- and early-twentieth-century crusaders trumpeted this model as the best route to community well-being, but Michele Wallace and contributors to Toni Cade Bambara's *The Black Woman* worked to break down this model in the 1970s.[22] Morgan continues to take apart the strongblackwoman image for what it is: a way for black women to deny emotional, psychic, and even physical pain, all the while appearing to keep it together—just like our mothers appeared to do.

Once when she was about thirteen years old, Veronica Chambers told her mother that she was feeling depressed. Her mother gave her a scolding about being ungrateful for all that she had; and she let

Veronica know that depression was something that only "white girls" experienced. Black women were strong, did not get depressed, and, her mother added, Veronica would not be able to count on the world to make her happy.[23]

As much as Chambers's mother warns against the realities of a racist and sexist world, she can never fully explain *why* these realities exist. This is not a personal failure, but the inability of adult, black Americans to explain a number of unpredictable social realities to their children. The worsening of poverty in black communities, the continued degradation of women, the rescinding of civil rights gained in the 1960s, and the lack of a clear course of action from black leaders (or the dearth of black leaders) are equally incomprehensible to children as to adults living in a so-called democracy.

After a series of achievements and struggles—including abuse at the hands of her father and stepmother, putting herself through Simon's Rock College (entering at the age of sixteen), recognition as one of *Glamour* magazine's Top Ten College Women of 1990, and several successful magazine internships—Chambers burns out. She goes through a period of not eating and not sleeping though she is exhausted. She keeps this information from her mother because she believes, "depression was absolutely not allowed." She likens black women to magicians, "masters of emotional sleight of hand. The closer you get, the less you can see. It was true of my mother. It is also true of me."[24]

It took a watchful aunt to alert Chambers's mother that something was amiss. When Chambers does open up to her mother about her exhaustion and depression, she learns that her mother always assumed everything was fine. Her mother was so busy worrying about her brother, who was not doing well in school, would later deal drugs, and end up in jail, that she was just happy not to have to worry about Veronica. This conversation, Chambers's "coming out" to her mother as *not* always strong, begins her process of letting go of the strong black woman image. She is aided in this process by a group of college sistah-friends with whom she can relax and speak freely, peppering her language with affectionate, "chile, pleases," "girl-friends," "sis's," and "flygirls."[25] Through them and a better relationship with her mother, Chambers is able to recapture a feeling she had not had since her childhood days of playing double-dutch jump rope in Brooklyn. Of those days she recalls, "There is a space between the two ropes where nothing is better than being a black girl. The helix encircles you and protects you and there you are strong. I wish she'd [Chambers's mother] let me show her. I could teach her how it feels."[26]

The solutions Morgan, Jones, and Chambers offer to fighting strongblackwoman syndrome are not unlike those offered by black feminists in the 1970s. In addition to fighting the racist and sexist implications of this myth, Morgan and Jones call for redefinition. Morgan calls it her "Memo of Retirement." In it she addresses white people, people in her life who are overdependent on her to comfort them, and men who expect her to support them unequivocally without having needs of her own. She resolves, "The fake 'Fine' and compulsory smile? Gone. Deaded. Don't look for it.... Some days I really am an evil black woman."[27] Ultimately, when Morgan has her bout with depression, she leaves New York and moves to San Francisco for the winter. There she allows herself to fall apart with people who are not afraid of her fragility and do not expect her to be SBW.

Many women, particularly women of color, do not have the resources to take a winter sabbatical like Morgan. Yet, the more accessible aspect of Morgan's cure for depression is "claiming the right to imperfections and vulnerabilities."[28] Across classes, black women are taught to hide their imperfections for fear of being a discredit to the race or vilified with any number of stereotypes that mock their blackness and woman-ness. Perhaps more challenging than finding the monetary resources to take a mental health break is finding those people, female or male, with whom a black woman can be less than strong.

Jones, though more casual in her approach, calls for redefinition of self as key to recuperating an image of black women that is not detrimental to our individual and collective well-being. She advocates the creation of the "Bulletproof Diva," defining not only what she is but also what she is *not*. I quote extensively from Jones to demonstrate the range of experience she allows for in this redefinition:

> Consider this a narrative in which we invent our own heroine, the Bulletproof Diva. A woman whose sense of dignity and self cannot be denied; who, though she may live in a war zone like Brownsville, goes out everyday greased, pressed, and dressed, with hair faded and braided and freeze-dried and spit-curled and wrapped and locked and cut to a sexy baldie (so she is all eyes and lips) and piled ten inches high and colored siren red, cobalt blue, and flaming yellow. She is fine and she knows it. She *has* to know it because who else will.... A Bulletproof Diva is not, I repeat, *not* that tired stereotype, the emasculating black bitch too hard for love or piety. It's safe to assume that a Bulletproof Diva is whoever you make her—corporate girl, teen mom, or the

combination—as long as she has the lip and nerve, *and as long as she uses that lip and nerve to raise up herself and the world.*[29]

Morgan's "Memo of Retirement" and Jones's definition of the Bulletproof Diva do not advocate dropping out of politics or individualism. Rather they remind us of the road black women have traveled to get to this point in our collective history. They open up the possibility of self-preservation and community activism as intersecting, reinforcing objectives on the road to black liberation.

The distinctions between a strongblackwoman and a Bulletproof Diva are dependent upon relationships to others, but also how one relates to one's self. The strongblackwoman is an externally defined role. Unlike the mammy stereotype and her role as caretaker of whites, the strongblackwoman is defined by how well a black woman takes care of blacks in the face of racist oppression. Morgan recognizes that by adopting this role, black women do themselves a disservice, so she abdicates this role because it only serves to drain her and other black women of the energy and resources needed to be real to one's self. Jones picks up where Morgan leaves off in advocating the role of the Bulletproof Diva: a woman whose confidence and self-esteem are based solely on how she defines herself, not how others define her. The Bulletproof Diva is a blend of a Western individualist position and an Afrocentric communal ethic; the Bulletproof Diva serves the black community and the world by serving herself and her own desires for fulfillment. The Bulletproof Diva is, by extension, the descendant of nineteenth-century black feminist Anna Julia Cooper who maintained that, "Only the black woman can say 'when and where I enter ... then and there the whole Negro race enters with me.'"[30]

Another aspect of black women's relationships is how black women relate to one another. Young black women writers both highlight the support they feel from other black women and bear witness to the misguided power black women, sharing similar experiences around racism and sexism, exert over one another to wound in unfathomable ways. Competition, vying for status, and degraded self-worth can be black women's worst interpersonal enemies. Morgan, Chambers, and Jones heed Audre Lorde's call in her essay "Eye to Eye" (1984) for black women to face how we treat one another and what that says about how we feel about ourselves.

Chambers recalls behavior that, while not unusual, emphasizes the ways African-American women try to hold one another back: from calling Chambers a "sellout" to accusing her of "talking white" because she takes her education seriously. Morgan, in her chapter entitled

"Chickenhead Envy," cogently calls out the behavior of said Chicken-heads.[31] To her credit, she is also self-reflective, exploring what so-called Chickenheads reflect back to black women who are independent and ambitious. What, for example, are the classist implications of middle-class, upwardly mobile black women using the term *chickenheads* to malign other black women they deem "low class?" Morgan is initiating much-needed dialogue about black women's culpability in our own oppression and how we oppress one another, especially in the areas of class, color, and sexual orientation. Morgan and Chambers, in fact, dis-rupt the notion that there is a unified black sisterhood. While that may be the ideal, these authors point out how black sisterhood is sometimes far from the reality of our relationships.

For all the emphasis on truth telling and exploring the totality of black women's lives, the writers explored here are noticeably silent on issues of heterosexism, homophobia in the black community, and black women's sexuality in general. Jones and Morgan cogently delve into the history of stereotyping black women as hypersexual and animalistic, yet there is no discussion of what a positive black female sexuality would look like. Instead, black women's (hetero)sexuality is alluded to in their musing on "fine brothers" and dating mores. Black women's sexuality is something to be repressed, except on a surface level of rela-tionships with black men. Then, vis-à-vis black men, Morgan advo-cates a use of "erotic power," advising "sometimes a short skirt and a bat of the eyes is not only easier but infinitely more effective" for women to overtake men in a battle of the sexes—a struggle that has no true winners.[32]

Chambers's only mention of her own sexuality, for example, dis-cusses her fear of an unwanted pregnancy derailing her educational and career goals. Her studious avoidance of premature sexuality was a legacy of her mother's markedly understated reaction to Veronica's first menstrual cycle. Rather than celebrating her step into young woman-hood, like many mothers, her mother makes sure Veronica knows how not to get pregnant. In her later potentially sexual encounters with young men, Chambers only has the experiences of friends raised by single mothers, as she was, and friends who were already single moth-ers to call upon. Of flirting and potential intimate involvements, Chambers says, "No guy ever said a word to me that didn't sound like a lie. The answer [to sex] was always no."[33] While access to her sexuality is by no means dependent upon engaging in sexual relations with anyone, blanket denials of her sexual self vis-à-vis young men also deny Cham-bers access to her own sexual agency. Even an avocation of abstinence would be an exertion of sexual agency.[34]

Given the abundance of writing by African-American lesbians and their influence on black feminist theory, the lack of attention to hetero-sexism is a step backward in moving a black feminist agenda forward. In her chapter on "The F-Word," Morgan declares her allegiance to feminism because she feels feminism claimed her; however, the most she says about lesbians or heterosexism is a toned down rebuttal to a man who said she must just need the right man, "as if I'd consider being mistaken for a lesbian an insult instead of an inaccuracy."[35] This observation, in hindsight, is the closest we get in the text to disavowing heterosexism. Yet, in the context of these three texts, examining hetero-sexuality as a construct is also ignored. Instead, within the texts it is a given that they are "black straight girls" concerned with "black straight girl problems": not being called a lesbian, a preoccupation with black men dating "skeezers" and white women, not getting pregnant, and not disappointing mothers.

The absence of frank discussions about sexuality is an odd repres-sion that barely even acknowledges the authors' own sexuality, much less the variability of human sexuality. This is a noticeable elision given the attention they give to the complexity of black women's identities. This omission, or tentative dance around black women's sexuality, leaves one to conclude that sexual stereotypes have been so debilitating that refuting them only results in the negation of a fuller spectrum for black female sexual expression. When black women, for example Alice Walker, Michelle Wallace, and Rebecca Walker, frankly discuss their own and black women's sexuality—be they heterosexual, lesbian, bisex-ual, or transgender—they run a constant threat of censure inside and outside the black community through the deployment of degrading, historically rooted stereotypes of licentious black female sexuality.

In "Toward a Genealogy of Black Female Sexuality," Hammonds makes critical note of black feminist theorizing on black women's sexu-ality. In particular, she observes that, "Historically, black women have reacted to the repressive force of the hegemonic discourse on race and sex and this image [black women as empty space] with silence, secrecy, and a partially self-chosen invisibility."[36] Hammonds later calls not only for intervention that disrupts negative stereotypes about black women's sexuality but also for critical engagement between black heterosexual women and black lesbians to develop a fuller black feminist praxis around sexuality.

In light of the historical, strategic use of silence around black women's sexuality by nineteenth-century reformers and the contempo-rary maligning in the political arena of black women such as law professors Anita Hill and Lani Guinier, it is not surprising that Morgan,

Jones, and Chambers skirt the issue of black women's sexuality. The challenge that comes from analyzing their work is, as Hammonds suggests, the disruption of stereotypes but also frank discussion of black women's relationship to their sexual lives through consciousness raising at all age levels.[37]

BROTHERS OF THE FLESH, BROTHERS IN POLITICAL STRUGGLE

The critical moment of tension in the relationship between black women and feminism is the implication for black male/female relationships. Many times, black feminists in the 1970s spent so much time reaffirming their commitment to black men and the black community that their gender critiques and actions to end sexism were deprioritized. Thus it is incumbent upon young black feminist writers to tread a line between—to apply the Combahee River Collective Statement to the present—struggling with black men against racism but also struggling with black men about sexism.[38] Chambers, Jones, and Morgan do this to varying degrees by writing about black men as fathers, as mothers' sons, as biological brothers, as spiritual/artistic brothers, as potential lovers, and as lifetime partners. In their examination of their lives personally and politically, these writers show that the love black women feel for black men is sometimes diluted by the mutual disrespect and mistrust engendered by slavery and kept alive through women's and men's sustained patriarchal notions about gender.

Black fathers make brief appearances in these texts. Both Morgan and Chambers's fathers left their families when they were young, and Jones's parents (writers Hettie Jones and Amiri Baraka, then Black Arts Movement poet/playwright LeRoi Jones) divorced. The emphasis that the black community and media have placed on black men's role in raising their sons has resulted, Morgan contends, in "precious little attention [being paid to] the significant role black men play in shaping their daughters' ideas about themselves and love."[39] More than a dismissal of the role of fathers, the pain these women experience around the father–daughter relationship slips in and out of their narratives. This pain is unresolved, and therefore unspoken and untheorized. Morgan, in her chapter entitled "babymother," does attempt to address men's rights to choose, or not to choose, fatherhood as a reproductive rights issue feminists must deal with if we desire equality. However, the reader is left to wonder how much of Morgan's anxiety about men's reproductive rights is linked to the emotional and political fallout of her own father's absence. Such a revelation would do much of the professed work of feminist theory by connecting theory and personal experience.

The physical or emotional absence of fathers in a number of black American homes allows both Chambers and Morgan to confront black women about the significant differences in the ways they rear girl children and boy children. Chambers knew from an early age that her mother and her mother's closest friends, also immigrants from Panama, prized their boy children while girls were an afterthought. "'And Veronica,' they would say eventually. 'She's fine. All A's as usual,'" her mother would say in a sad voice that Veronica interpreted as a display of her mother's overriding concern for her brother, Malcolm.[40] Malcolm began exhibiting behavioral problems after their father left. Chambers hints at the gender issues inherent in valuing boys over girls, but even when she later laments her brother's problems with drugs and jail, she remains resistant to the idea that her brother might also experience race and gender in the choices available to him as a young black man, despite growing up in similar circumstances to Veronica. The endangered black male trope of the late 1980s and 1990s was problematic, but a broader political analysis of black men's vulnerability and subsequent understanding of her brother's life under white supremacy are buried under Chambers's sibling rivalry for their mother's attention and concern.

Morgan offers a fuller analysis of the disparities in how black women love their sons and raise their daughters, perhaps because her examination focuses more on the connections between sons and the lovers/partners/husbands they become. This is the closest any of these authors comes to lobbing a generational grenade and assigning culpability for perpetuating the strongblackwoman and endangeredblackmale roles, which are compatible only in that they encourage an enabler/dependent relationship. Morgan wonders how older women can teach their daughters to be independent and ambitious and then accuse younger black women of being too strong-willed to be acceptable to any man. Morgan also notes that these are the same women who loved their sons, but did not teach young men about mutuality in relationships.

The doppelganger to this portrayal of black mothers is, according to Morgan, those women who maintain "all men are dogs."[41] This might be a defensive stance to pass on to daughters, but what message does this impart to their sons about self-worth and their expected behavior in relationships? And what behavior do mothers condone or abet if they think men are meant to have many girlfriends, to be "playas"? Women who believe their sons can *do* no wrong and those who believe their sons can only *be* wrong, and therefore need constant protection, pass along a fatalistic prophecy that ignores all the black men who are, Morgan notes, assuming familial, work, and community obligations, "taking care of their kids, working and contributing to their communities."[42]

The writers examined here clearly are conflicted about how black women and black men relate to one another. Jones recalls the black men who responded to her feminist performance group's work as artistic and intellectual compatriots. Yet in her chapter "Open Letter to a Brother," she ponders the ways that sexual liberation enabled black men to reinforce negative myths about themselves, resulting in what she calls "The Dog Syndrome." Offering much-needed critiques of black masculinity, Jones seeks to delve deeper into how black men's lack of access to political and economic power became so entrenched in obtaining sexual power. The Dog Syndrome is in fact, according to Jones, "black male impotence masquerading as power."[43] This observation begins the work of linking the interpersonal and the structural.

Jones's and Morgan's essays, read with Chambers's more personal backdrop, begin to offer a direction for open discussion in the black community about black masculinity and femininity, black men and black women. If feminist generational politics come into play for these women, it is in putting contemporary tensions into historical perspective. Rather than blaming the past for the distrust that plagues black women and men, younger black feminists are, read in conjunction, asking black men to forego atonement for the past and take responsibility for male privilege in the present.[44] Being a black man in U.S. society is much more complex than adopting a pose and maintaining it. Yet, critically, these black feminists, Morgan in particular, are offering complementary suggestions for black women to check their behavior and expectations of men and relationships. How do we participate in our own oppression and that of future generations? What is our stake in maintaining gender relations that can only lead to continued trauma?

CONCLUSION

There is undoubtedly a next generation of young black women engaging with feminist politics as they intersect with the politics of racial liberation. However, it is clear that numerically there are not as many young black women joining feminist organizations or taking women's studies courses. Though these are not the only markers of feminist consciousness, they are among the most visible.

Thus, it is necessary to turn to the cultural expressions of young black women to learn about what they have to say about gender oppression. While it is also possible to look at the music, poetry, and other expressions black women use, it is through the writing examined here that we can gain some perspective on the issues young black women find important in defining their place in the history of black feminism. Through their writings, we see the continued thought that it is only through personal well-being for each member of the black community that we will come to intracommunity and broader societal social justice.

Morgan, Chambers, and Jones are not inserting themselves into the third wave paradigm so much as they are continuing the work of a history of black race women concerned with gender issues. These three writers in particular also have in common with their ancestors the gift of literacy and the privilege of education. They are using those gifts to insure that the next generation realizes that the fight for an end to all forms of discrimination is far from over, and in fact we need to be ever vigilant for the ways in which white patriarchal supremacy retrenches and manifests itself in new power paradigms. But above all, the most important lesson that these writers gained, and that they pass on, is that in a discriminatory society that continues to marginalize the theorizing of women of color, who but ourselves will honor our words as we continue the legacy of struggle to end racism, sexism, heterosexism, ablism, and classism?

NOTES

1. Generation X consists of those born between 1961 and 1981. Unlike the wave model, this bracketing of generations adapts to the age of the members of the generation. That is, baby boomers, regardless of how old they are, remain baby boomers. Those born between 1961 and 1981, though getting older, remain within that particular social designation of GenXers.

2. For the most recent addition to this dialogue about black feminist legacies, see: Johnnetta Betsch Cole and Beverly Guy-Sheftall, *Gender Talk: The Struggle for Women's Equality in African American Communities* (New York: Ballantine Books, 2003).

3. Harriet Jacobs, *Incidents in the Life of a Slave Girl: Written by Herself,* ed. Jean Fagin Yellin (Cambridge, MA.: Harvard University Press, 1987).

4. Lisa Jones, *Bulletproof Diva: Tales of Race, Sex, and Hair* (New York: Doubleday, 1994); Joan Morgan, *When Chickenheads Come Home to Roost: My Life as a Hip-Hop Feminist* (New York: Simon & Schuster, 1999); Veronica Chambers, *Mama's Girl* (New York: Riverhead Books, 1996).

5. I use the "third wave" analogy throughout this chapter. Feminist activists and women's movement historians use the "wave" model to describe the phases of the women's movement in the United States. This model obscures the historical role of race and women of color in feminist organizing. If we accept the first wave as that moment of organizing encompassing woman suffrage and the second wave as the women's liberation/women's rights activism of the late 1960s, we effectively disregard the race-based movements before them that served as precursors for gender activism, such as gendered resistance to slavery or the modern-day civil rights movement taking shape in the 1950s. For a more extensive critique of the waves model, see my

article in *Signs: A Journal of Women in Culture and Society* 27 (Summer 2002): 1059–82. My thinking on this issue of waves was greatly influenced by Beverly Guy-Sheftall's teaching and theorizing in books such as *Words of Fire: An Anthology of African American Feminist Thought* (New York: The New Press, 1995) and *Traps: African American Men on Gender and Sexuality* (Bloomington: Indiana University Press, 2001), which offer an unremitting critique of the periodization of the first and second waves, as well as ample evidence of African-American contributions to a sustained black feminist analysis.

6. Michele Wallace, *To Hell and Back: On the Road with Black Feminism* (Brooklyn, NY: Olympia X Press, 1997), 11.

7. One of the few, but most memorable articles was: Kristal Brent Zook, "A Manifesto of Sorts for a Black Feminist Movement," *New York Time Magazine*, November 12, 1995, 86–89.

8. Chambers, 52.

9. Morgan, 19.

10. Ibid.

11. Ibid., 20.

12. Ibid., 21–22.

13. Ibid., 22.

14. Ibid., 22.

15. Jones, 133–34.

16. Ibid., 26.

17. Morgan, 55.

18. Ibid., 23.

19. Ibid., 100.

20. Sheila Radford-Hill makes a similar observation. In her book, *Further to Fly: Black Women and the Politics of Empowerment* (Minneapolis: University of Minnesota Press, 2000), she claims black women have been experiencing a crisis in identity since 1965, roughly coinciding with the publication of the Moynihan Report that demonized black women as the root cause of black "pathology."

21. Morgan, 72.

22. Toni Cade Bambara, *The Black Woman: An Anthology* (New York: New American Library, 1970).

23. Chambers, 72.

24. Ibid., 73.

25. Ibid., 145.

26. Ibid., 7.

27. Morgan, 85.

28. Ibid., 110.

29. Jones, 3; emphasis mine.

30. Cited in Dorothy Roberts, *Killing the Black Body: Race, Reproduction and the Meaning of Liberty* (New York: Vintage, 1998), 84.

31. Morgan, 185–86; A chickenhead is a woman who is a materialist, dresses in barely there outfits ("skankwear") and, according to Morgan, is adept at stroking the male ego (185). She is also calculating, cunning, and savvy when it comes to getting what she wants—all acceptable traits for men in a white, capitalist patriarchy, but wholly unacceptable for black women.

32. Ibid., 221–22.

33. Chambers, 70–71.

34. This failure to speak frankly about sexuality continues in Chambers's follow-up book, *Having It All?: Black Women and Success* (New York: Doubleday, 2003).

35. Morgan, 42.

36.   Evelynn Hammonds, "Toward a Genealogy of Black Female Sexuality: The Problematic of Silence," in *Feminist Genealogies, Colonial Legacies, Democratic Futures*, eds. M. Jacqui Alexander and Chandra Talpade Mohanty (New York: Routledge), 170–81.

37.   An addition to the literature on black women's sexuality is Tricia Rose's *Longing to Tell: Black Women Talk About Sexuality and Intimacy* (New York: Farrar, Straus & Giroux, 2003). Rose presents oral histories of black women—across age, sexual orientation, color, ethnicity—speaking openly about how they learned about their sexuality, as well as how what they learned has played out in their lives. Rose's book supplies the primary source documents we so desperately need to think about black women's sexuality outside dominant and black community stereotypes.

38.   Combahee River Collective, *The Combahee River Collective Statement: Black Feminist Organizing in the Seventies and Eighties* (New York: Kitchen Table Women of Color Press, 1996), 12.

39.   Morgan, 123.

40.   Chambers, 46–47.

41.   Morgan, 137.

42.   Ibid., 131.

43.   Jones, 217.

44.   Such a position runs counter to the Nation of Islam's yearly Million Man March, or Day of Atonement, which has resulted in questionable, if any, sustained political action.

2

QUE VIVA LA MUJER[1]: NEGOTIATING CHICANA FEMINIST IDENTITIES

Florence Maätita

In the 1960s and 1970s, Chicana feminism developed within the context of the Chicano nationalist movement, which centered on ending racial and ethnic oppression.[2] However, once Chicanas, like other women of color at the time, began to reconsider their roles within the movement by speaking out against sexism and male domination, others in the movement accused them of aligning themselves with white feminists or lesbians.[3] Simultaneously, Chicana feminists were concerned that other (i.e., white) feminists were not open to their concerns. Thus, from its onset, Chicana feminism was not only an attempt to eradicate racism and sexism; Chicana feminism is also premised on the idea that being Chicana—or a woman of color—and a feminist are not contradictory. As Ana Nieto Gomez wrote:

> I am a Chicana feminist. I make that statement very proudly, although there is a lot of intimidation in our community and in the society in general, against people who define themselves as Chicana feminists. It sounds like a contradictory statement, a *Malinche*[4] statement—if you're a Chicana you're on one side, if

23

you're a feminist, you must be on the other side. They say you
can't stand on both sides—which is a bunch of bull.... In fact the
statement is not contradictory at all, it is a very unified statement:
I support my community and I do not ignore the women in my
community (who have been long forgotten).[5]

Therefore, the concerns of Chicana feminists, along with other women
of color, about intersectionality, inclusivity, and negotiating seemingly
contradictory identities, laid the foundation for future feminist ideology and debate.

In the late 1970s, American mass media began to paint a picture of
the women's movements as dead and thus no longer newsworthy.[6]
However, scholars argue that feminism is very much alive and present
in the early twenty-first century, and it is now known by some as the
third wave.[7] Although many scholars agree that feminism is still alive,
the use of wave imagery is problematic and continues to obscure race
and ethnicity. As Kimberly Springer argues:

If we consider the first wave as that moment of organizing
encompassing woman suffrage and the second wave as the
women's liberation/women's rights activism of the late 1960s, we
effectively disregard the race-based movements before them that
served as precursors, or windows of political opportunity, for
gender activism.... In sum, as we learn more about women of
color's feminist activism, the wave analogy becomes untenable.[8]

In efforts to move beyond the age-based and generational approach to
feminism, there is a push to acknowledge waves in terms of how current and prior feminist activism overlap. One important overlap
between feminism's second and third waves concerns the role of race
and ethnicity (in addition to class and sexual orientation) in the movement. As Ednie Kaeh Garrison writes:

The emergence of the "Third Wave" owes a great deal to critiques
of the homogenization of the category "women" articulated most
directly in the political and intellectual work by radical women of
color, poor women, and lesbians dating from at least the Second
Wave. Their opposition to the perceived dominance of white feminism in the Second Wave is linked to critiques of racism, classism, and heterosexism within the 1960s and 1970s women's
movement.... It is now clear that feminist critiques of feminism
are part of the very origins of Third Wave feminism....[9]

Thus, in theory, the third wave is founded on what was lacking from the second wave, which is the ability to deal with race and ethnicity and how they intersect with gender.

In this chapter, I investigate the relationship between feminist and Chicana identities. I argue that young Chicana feminists' experiences illustrate issues of diversity that disrupted the second wave (i.e., 1960s and 1970s) of the women's movement and continue to trouble the third wave. I find that young Chicana feminists are largely ignored in academia, with much of the literature focusing on women who participated in or were directly affected by the women's movements of the 1960s and 1970s. This lack of attention, in part, is the result of a false assumption that all young women today, regardless of race-ethnicity, are neither interested in feminism nor do they identify themselves as "feminist."[10] Such beliefs are thought to pertain to young Chicanas who purportedly reject feminism because of the whiteness it implies.[11] Existing literature on young Chicanas also indicates that they reject the label *feminist* without taking into consideration whether they may be—and are—adopting this label in certain contexts. Moreover, research assumes that young women of Mexican descent readily accept the label *Chicana* just as easily as they reject the label *feminist*.[12] In effect, the literature seems quick to generalize the experiences of young women of Mexican descent to suggest that they *passively* accept a Chicana identity as they *actively* reject a feminist identity. Thus, extant literature ignores continual ways that young women negotiate identities of Chicana and feminist.

Decisions to accept or reject feminist identities are ultimately rooted in the various meanings young women associate with these labels, in addition to the contexts in which such meanings exist. More important, the complexity of this identity development and negotiation has significant implications for the inclusiveness of third wave feminism for young Chicanas. Such complexities point to issues that third wave feminism must address in order to be fully inclusive. Specifically, not only must third wave feminism acknowledge the intersectionality of race-ethnicity and gender, but it must also address how familial and cultural expectations continue to affect how women come to feminism.

This analysis is based on interviews with twelve young women of Mexican descent. During three trips to the West Coast in 1997, I contacted an all-Chicana student organization at a California university, from which I gathered a snowball sample. In total, I interviewed twelve women of Mexican descent.[13] The women in this study are between the ages of nineteen and twenty-five, with an average age of about twenty-two.[14] Ten of the twelve women are first-generation Americans; Spanish is the first language for nine of the women. Seven were currently in school full-time (four as undergraduate students, two as graduate students, and one in junior college). Only one did not continue formal schooling after high school. Nine of the women are the first in their families to continue formal schooling after high school. Because my original research intentions involved active rejection or passive acceptance of Chicana feminist identities, I did not limit my sample to those women who specifically identified as Chicana feminists. Seven of the twelve respondents explicitly identified themselves as feminists. However, others aligned themselves with feminist ideologies while embracing terms other than *feminist* for reasons that I will discuss below. As most of the respondents attend or have attended college, they spoke to the effects of their education on how they arrived at these identities. Yet, they recognized how their understanding of Chicana feminism was incompatible with familial and cultural expectations. How respondents negotiated such identities vis-à-vis cultural expectations informs our understanding of third wave feminism.

NEGOTIATING CHICANA FEMINIST IDENTITIES

The interviews illustrate a more complex process of becoming a Chicana feminist than existing literature suggests. On the one hand, these women indicate the possibility that they actively accept identities as Chicanas as they actively accept identities as feminists. However, the women engage in these processes differently when they are at school and when they are with their families. In both contexts, the women distance their understanding of feminism from what they consider the province of whiteness. Given that (relative to prior waves) third wave feminism is supposedly a more inclusive movement, this distancing points to problems that have yet to be addressed. I first address how the women came to adopt the identity of Chicana before discussing their adoption of a feminist identity.

Becoming Chicana

The women in this study are of Mexican descent, but they did not necessarily grow up identifying as Chicana. They revealed that they had heard the term before, but more often than not, the term had negative connotations. While most of these women grew up associating the terms *Chicana* or *Chicano* with *cholos*,[15] they did not develop a positive understanding of "Chicana" until college or their involvement in Chicana student organizations.[16] As Sara,[17] a twenty-year-old undergraduate, said:

I didn't start calling myself Chicana until I got to college. I started taking classes and I joined [this Chicana student organization], and I was with all these other *mujeres*[18] that knew about all this stuff and I just didn't know. So I'd always ask questions, "Wait a second. What does this mean?" and this and that. And when I realized what [Chicana] meant, that it's a pride in our indigenous roots and you're acknowledging the fact that... I don't know how to explain it.... You're politically aware of how you're being placed in society. And it's just like, "Yeah, I agree with that." That's when I first started calling myself Chicana.

Through her involvement in her organization, Sara was able to associate the label *Chicana* with a sense of pride. This association enabled her to feel "politically aware" and, in turn, embrace the label for herself. Her being politically aware was much like what Denise, a twenty-four-year-old undergraduate, referred to as reaching "a level of consciousness." Both reaching a level of consciousness and becoming politically aware, according to respondents, entailed pride in ethnic and cultural roots.

In addition to associating the label *Chicana* with an ethnic and cultural identity—much like activists in the 1960s and 1970s did[19]—respondents recognize that identifying as such is empowering. Identifying as Chicana gave them the power to ask questions and claim a voice. Eva, a nineteen-year-old undergraduate, expressed this view when she discussed what it means to call herself Chicana:

Chicana.... Just empowerment, coming to voice. That's how I came to voice. I never spoke in class that much. I hardly raised my hand, yet I was always full of ideas. And I always questioned, "Why the hell can't I speak?" I never got the opportunity at home. ...Just coming to voice. ... That's where you come out and you start, "Why?" This is mine, you can't take this from me. This was always mine. And I didn't have it. Or I had it, I possessed it. I possessed my voice. However, why couldn't I speak it? Why couldn't I express it? But now I can, so fuck you. Fuck you, I'm going out. And I kick the doors open, "¡*Vamonos!*"[20]

While most respondents were not as candid as Eva, they did have similar experiences in discovering what it means to identify as Chicana. Most important for those women, identifying as Chicana distinguished them from those they considered white. Rejecting a white identity, claiming a voice, and embracing a group identity as Chicana ultimately empowered these young women to confront racism and sexism simultaneously.

Becoming Feminist

A feminist consciousness arose out of the Chicano Nationalist Movement, from the late 1960s until the 1970s, when Chicana activists began to feel that their issues as women were not adequately addressed in that movement.[21] The women in this study developed a feminist consciousness through their involvement with student organizations. Feminism helped them label their experiences with sexism. Many women knew that they were treated differently because they were girls. For many, being a girl meant not being able to spend the night at friends' or cousins' homes, being expected to serve the men in the household and clean up after them, and being told to wear dresses instead of shorts or pants. While these women acknowledged how they were treated, they were quick to point out that they did not like the treatment that they received. However, until they got older, they were not exposed to the word *feminism* and what it implied. It was then that respondents' focus on feminist ideals became a salient part of their identities.

Most of the interviewees were exposed to feminism primarily through their student organizations and in history and women's studies courses. Being exposed to feminism entailed finding a vocabulary for unnamed feelings and realizing that other women shared these feelings. Jessica, a twenty-four-year-old college graduate, for instance, discussed this exposure:

> I had read some small stuff in high school, about women getting the right to vote. But it wasn't until I took [the professor's] class that I started getting more and more into and more interested in feminism. It seemed that I was having these same ideas as other women. For me, it was very powerful and moving.

Her experience is reminiscent of what writers call the "click," in that women readers "clicked" upon recognizing "that sexism was the explanation for a particular experience."[22] Despite what Jessica considers a "powerful and moving" experience, these women identified three significant barriers they face: the whiteness of the movement; negative images of feminism; and familial and cultural expectations. I will discuss these barriers in turn.

The Whiteness of the Movement

Interviewees' definitions of feminism illustrated a distinction between Chicana feminism and what they considered white feminism. However, some pointed out that Chicana feminist issues were the same as white feminist issues. For instance, respondents claimed that both Chicana and white feminism want women to be treated and recognized as equal to men. Yet, the main difference respondents saw between themselves and other feminists (i.e., white feminists) was that they were Chicanas and other feminists were not. Thus, for respondents, their feminism could not be separated from the fact that they were Chicana and not white. Eva addressed this point when she explained what Chicana feminism meant for her:

> Chicana feminism.... It's not man-hater or whatever. I think it's coming to a term of consciousness where once you're at that consciousness, you have to do something about [what's going on with Chicanas today]; you have to take responsibility.... You're just as guilty as the person next to you who hasn't done anything about it. You study it. You critique other male patriarchal societies or systems. Except that I'm *mujer*.

Challenging patriarchy and being active are defining elements of feminism, regardless of whether it is Chicana feminism, African-American feminism, or white feminism. However, the only difference in this case is that Eva and other respondents are *mujer* and other feminists are not.

While Eva identifies how she distinguishes herself from other feminists, other respondents discussed how other feminists have excluded them and other women of color. For instance, Sara stated that in a woman's studies course, she learned that feminists "were very selective in who they allowed into the feminist movement."[23] Because of their selectivity, she considers feminism to be "very white-oriented." Moreover, in her experience she has not witnessed much progress in including women of color in feminism. She told of a rally she helped coordinate to illustrate this point:

> [We] had a rally [at school] ... and we wanted to have women of color speakers speak and talk about how the women's movement is not just about white women and how we have to take into consideration our race and class. It's all intermixed, right? And it was mostly the sororities that were saying, "Why are you trying to divide us if we're all women?" They wouldn't get the point.

For Sara, having women of color as speakers was a way to present feminism as not only a white, middle-class women's issue. To her, having women of color would have acknowledged differences and diversity among women and feminist agendas, which is a sentiment that the rally co-organizers did not understand.

Seeing feminism as only a white women's issue prompted two interviewees to reject *feminist* for other terms that integrated their Chicana
and feminist identities. Sara, for one, discussed the problems she saw
with calling herself a feminist:

> I don't call myself a feminist.... If you mean feminism in the
> forms of just realizing that women are oppressed—all women,
> not just white women—and trying to strive for equality and equal
> opportunity then I guess I am [a feminist]. But to me, the term
> *Chicana* already encompasses that 'cause it's a political term
> where you're realizing what's going on. And part of that is as a
> Chicana, it's incorporated. You're not just talking about your
> brown-ness. You're talking about your woman-ness, you, your
> everything. So, to me, Chicana says it all.

Denise, a twenty-four-year-old undergraduate, saw similar problems
with the label *feminist* when she discussed how she came to find a label
that suits her. After much searching, she settled on calling herself a
xicanista, a term Ana Castillo coined to "redefine (not categorically
reject) [Chicanas'] roles within our families, communities at large, and
white dominant society."[24] Denise said:

> I remember reading somewhere about womanists and I thought
> that I would consider myself a womanist. I was at a conference
> and I was talking to some Black girl and I told her I was a woman-
> ist. She was all, "You can't be a womanist. 'Womanist' is for Black
> women." Then I thought, "Okay, maybe I'm not a womanist after
> all because I'm not Black." Then I heard about Ana Castillo's
> *xicanista*. I read a little about it and I guess I would call myself a
> *xicanista*. I'm not a feminist. I'm not a womanist. I'm a *xicanista*.
> That to me says that I'm for women and I'm *mujer*. I guess that
> makes me *xicanista*. I like that word better anyway.

How Denise went from feminist to womanist to *xicanista* indicates
some problems other women have finding the language to connect
their brand of feminism and their racial-ethnic identity. Moreover, her
story indicates how other women—and not just white women, in this
case—are affected in terms of whether they embrace feminism.

Negative Images of Feminists

The whiteness associated with feminism was not the only way that
respondents qualified their feminism because negative images of

feminists also affected their understanding of feminism. Respondents identified themselves as prowoman without wanting to identify themselves or have others identify them with media-constructed images of feminists as angry, bra-burning male-bashers. Most of these women distinguished themselves from such images with some variation of "I'm not hard core, but...." For instance, when I asked Lourdes, a twenty-three-year-old college graduate, to explain what she meant when she used the term *hard core*, she responded:

> By hard core, I mean, I don't go out marching in the streets, burning my bras or anything. That to me is hard core. Being out and vocal and angry. Male-bashing and stuff. I don't do that.

Denise, the *xicanista*, discussed what she meant by hard core in a similar way:

> I wouldn't say that I was hard core. That means that I wasn't in the streets yelling at people. I see hard-core feminists burning bras, not shaving their legs, and yelling and stuff. I believe in equality for women, but I ain't about to not shave my legs!

Most respondents associated hard-core feminism with an antimale stance, a stance they thought they could not embrace by virtue of their being Chicana. For women such as Jen, a twenty-one-year-old undergraduate, intrinsic in their definition of *Chicana* is a continuous alliance with the men in their community. For example, while Michelle, a twenty-five-year-old college graduate, acknowledged the possibility of being feminist without being angry, her definition of feminism was rooted in the need to include her *hermanos*, her brothers.

Michelle: I would call myself a feminist, although I'm not hard core.

Florence: What do you mean by hard core?

Michelle: To me, hard core feminists are in-your-face and they are angry at men. As *Raza*, I think we all have to stick together, so I can't be angry at my hermanos.

Thus for Michelle and others identifying as hard core was contrary to the Chicana/o ideology.[25] In essence, they thought it was possible to be a feminist aligned with the men in the community rather than a feminist who separated herself from men, which is a common perception of feminists and, accordingly, how the interviewees define hard core.

Familial and Cultural Expectations

Respondents discussed how they negotiate the barriers that the whiteness of feminism and the negative images of feminism present for them within their involvement in student organizations. Conflicts also arise as newly embraced Chicana and feminist identities challenge (and even disrupt) traditional expectations when respondents are with their families. Respondents address this conflict by distancing their Chicana feminist identities with the expected role of the "good daughter." How interviewees address this conflict suggests a great deal about the familial and cultural expectations respondents confront and, in many ways, accept.

Most respondents said that they were reared in traditional households.[26] One way that most interviewees—especially those who are first-generation American—define tradition is by its separation of the public and private domains. For instance, Jen elaborated on this definition when she said:

> Traditional ... just very ... that the woman is in the home, in the kitchen. She has to take care of all the cleaning. She has to take care of all the cooking. And the dad's the one who's working outside and making all the decisions. My dad, as soon as they got married and they bought their house, my dad didn't want my mom to work anymore.

Jen also pointed out that her mother tried to teach her that staying home and having dinner ready for her husband when he comes from work "was what a good woman does." She and other respondents recognized that expected duties within the private domain define women in Mexican culture. Moreover, interviewees did not think that women in their families had power, especially the power to use their voices. In effect, for most respondents, women relinquishing control and power to men were part of how they defined tradition.

Growing up, respondents realized that they did not like what was expected of them, such as serving the men in the family and cleaning up after them. Yet, they still did what was expected out of respect for their fathers. For instance, Jessica discussed her family, but did what was expected out of respect for her father:

> I remember seeing things in my family; the women would serve the men and I'd have to ask my father's permission to do things

like go to the movies or go over at (sic) [Michelle's] house. I would always think to myself that it wasn't fair, but I did it because I was taught to respect my father.

Others shared Jessica's sentiment, explaining that had they defied their fathers, they would have risked losing their titles as the "good daughter." Interviewees defined the "good daughter" as someone who obeyed her father and respected his home, a feeling they still held once they had grown up and left for college.

As respondents came of age, college and student organizations provided them with a multitude of opportunities and viewpoints that were not available to them with their families. Much of what they were exposed to at this time in their lives challenged how they previously saw themselves as women and as Mexicans. According to interviewees, this resocialization was evidenced in how identifying as Chicana and/or feminist involved "coming to voice," as I discussed before. Many explicitly discussed how "coming to voice" meant finding a voice that they were not allowed to use at home, thus respondents were better able to negotiate identities for themselves as Chicana feminists when they were away from their families. Yet, experiences in school offered different opportunities, challenged (and disrupted) respondents' ways of thinking about themselves and the culture, and, most notably, challenged what they considered traditional.

Upon returning to their homes, interviewees face a great deal of conflict as they attempt to balance expectations and their newly formed identities as voiced Chicana feminists. Many explained how they had to separate their Chicana feminist identities and their "good daughter" identities, as the two were incompatible. These perceptions, in turn, affected their relationships with other family members because many did not think they could share their new experiences with their family. Despite their inability to share new insights with their family, their need to retain good standing in the family was a priority. For instance, though she recently moved out of her parents' home, Renée still wanted to be considered the good daughter. She said:

I used to rebel when I was little. I was a tomboy and I didn't want to wear dresses. But now, although I don't like it, I clean up after my little brothers, 'cause [my dad] tells me to. I know that this is his home and I have to be respectful to him when I'm in my father's home. I don't like to, but I do it anyway. I have to be the good daughter when I'm in his home.

Her need to be the good daughter superseded the fact that she did not want to do what was expected of her, which entailed going against her feminist principles.

Silencing their voices in their parents' homes was another way that respondents substituted their Chicana feminist identities for the "good daughter" identity. For instance, Jessica, who recently moved back in with her parents, discussed how she had to silence herself out of respect for her parents:

> It's a lot different now that I'm back in [Southern California] and I'm living with my parents again. I can't stand it! I can't understand what goes on there with my mom and dad. I want to yell at them, "Don't you understand?" But I just keep my mouth shut because I have to respect them. And I don't want to be homeless.

Because of the identity that she formed for herself outside of her parents' home, now that she has returned, she has become more critical of their relationship. However, while she wanted to challenge them, she consciously chose to silence her voice out of respect for her parents.

Interviewees posited how they not only silenced their voices out of respect for their families, but also did so out of respect for the Mexican/Chicano culture. Teresa spoke of how she had to be careful not to be "outspoken" while visiting her family in Mexico. She said:

> I just came back from a trip to Mexico and I guess it's the first time I actually went back that I was older and I could really realize what was going on. I noticed right away the women having to serve the husbands. The women having to have everything set for them. Ugh! Even passing the bread, which was right next to them on their plate. Part of me was like, "Can't you get up and get it yourself?" And I had to catch myself a couple of times trying not to be outspoken. I understood it was their culture and their way of living.

Because she was older and had gone away to college, she was more critical of the power relations and gender roles she was exposed to in Mexican culture. However, she did not speak out against it out of respect, even if that meant silencing her own voice, the voice that she found when she became a feminist.

Like Chicana feminists before them, most of these women embrace an identity as feminist—or at least identified with feminist principles without adopting the label—after embracing an identity as Chicana.

Identifying as Chicana feminists entails a great deal of pride and a sense of empowerment as they confronted racism and sexism simultaneously. Yet they still encounter significant barriers, not only in terms of whether they embrace such an identity, but in what context they embrace that identity. They discussed the persistent notions that feminism is the province of whiteness and of feminists as hard-core women who seek separation from men. Moreover, they discussed how they and their families still deem being Chicana and feminist contradictory. Regardless of such obstacles, these women engaged in a complex negotiation process wherein they neither passively accepted a Chicana identity nor actively rejected a feminist identity. Instead, they actively negotiated identities as Chicana and feminist that were not contradictory. Thus, how they found meaning in and eventually embraced these identities speaks to shortcomings of third wave feminism.

IMPLICATIONS FOR THIRD WAVE FEMINISM

In this chapter, I examined how young Chicanas come to third wave feminism and how their perceptions of this feminism present problems for a successful racially and ethnically inclusive movement. First, the women in this chapter identified how they perceive feminism to be the province of white women. If third wave feminism is more racially and ethnically inclusive than previous waves, why do these women distance their feminism from what they consider white and hard core? Also, how can we understand the problems that women have finding language that acknowledges their feminism and their sex, race, ethnicity, and cultural heritage? In other words, the associations these women make between feminism and whiteness do not correspond to a racially and ethnically inclusive movement.

We can certainly attribute the problems with feminism that the women I spoke with identify to central criticisms of the second wave of the women's movement. Women of color who found second wave feminism problematic maintained a need to move beyond the "ampersand problem" by acknowledging the intersectionality of gender, class, racial, and ethnic oppression.[27] For these women, they could neither separate their race, ethnicity, and gender, nor could they acknowledge these attributes independent of one another. Yet, the women in this study indicated that feminism still suffers from the same shortcomings. Specifically, much of their discussion about feminism rested on the very critique of the second wave that other women of color before them made. As Garrison[28] and the women in this study maintained, third wave feminism is premised on the idea that second wave feminism did not address intersections between race, ethnicity, and gender. This point is evident when we acknowledge how the women in this study distance their understanding of feminism from what they consider white, for instance. Moreover, this critique is evident when respondents like Sara discuss how they learned that second wave feminists "were very selective in who they allowed into the feminist movement."

Drawing on a foundation that is critical of the second wave, the third wave should be relatively more inclusive than prior expressions of feminism. Yet, as the women in this study suggest, there is a long way to go before feminism as a movement and a consciousness addresses all women equally. Hence, not only did these women suggest that their understanding of feminism is a critique of what was lacking in the second wave, but they are quick to point out that current interpretations of feminism still do not acknowledge race and ethnicity. This notion relates to concerns about how overlooking race and ethnicity weakens any "wave" analogy, which Springer raised in her discussion of third wave black feminism.[29] Thus, as these women are aware of such "wave thinking," they are also aware of what such thinking continues to overlook: race and ethnicity. For example, this awareness is apparent when Sara discusses difficulties she had organizing a campus rally. When she wanted women of color to participate, other organizers "wouldn't get the point" when they accused her of being divisive.

Despite such limitations, some of these women were able to embrace identities as Chicana and feminist that were not different from how other (i.e., white) women come to feminism. For instance, experiences at women's studies and history classes, involvement in Chicana student organizations, and familiarity with (and resistance to) negative images of feminism certainly affected how the twelve women in this study came to an understanding of Chicana feminism. Such experiences— college courses, student organizations, and techniques for managing negative images of feminism—were not necessarily unique to how these women experience feminism. What was most unique, however, was how their families and their families' culture affected how and where they embraced Chicana and feminist identities. It is clear that feminism has yet to be accepted in Mexican and Chicano cultures. At the same time, if third wave feminism wants to include Chicanas—and other women of color, to be sure—it needs to speak to family relations and traditions.

Third wave feminism should be what it claims to be. In other words, it must make women of color central and visible, allowing for the combination of family, culture, and feminism. Once this wave addresses these issues and understands the intricacies of identity formation for young women, then it can be a successful, open, and inclusive movement for all women. Until then, these women—and others like them—will continue to promote a type of feminism that accounts for the intersections of race, ethnicity, class, sexual orientation, and gender. As Eva said at the end of our conversation, "*Que viva la mujer.*"

NOTES

1. "*Que viva la mujer*" literally means "Long live the woman."
2. For a review of early Chicana feminist writings, see Alma M. García, ed., *Chicana Feminist Thought: The Basic Historical Writings* (New York: Routledge, 1997).
3. bell hooks, *Ain't I a Woman: Black Women and Feminism* (Boston: South End Press, 1981); bell hooks, *Feminist Theory: From Margin to Center* (Boston: South End, 1984); Patricia Hill Collins, *Black Feminist Thought* (New York: Routledge, 1990); Esther Ngan-Ling Chow, "The Development of Feminist Consciousness among Asian American Women," in *The Social Construction of Gender*, ed. Judith Lorber and Susan A. Farrell (Newbury Park, CA: Sage, 1991), 255–68.
4. *Malinche* was an Aztec Indian slave who served as an interpreter for Hernan Cortés, the Spaniard who led the full conquest of Mexico in 1521. Because of her relationship with Cortés, many people consider her to be a traitor. For Chicana feminist interpretations of the Malinche story see: Norma Alarcon, "Traddutora, Traditora: A Paradigmatic Figure of Chicana Feminism," *Cultural Critique* 13 (1989): 57–87; Adelaida R. Del Castillo, "*Malintzín Tenepal:* A Preliminary Look into a New Perspective," in *Chicana Feminist Thought*, ed. Alma M. García (New York: Routledge, 1997), 122–26.
5. Anna Nieto Gomez, "Chicana Feminism," in *Chicana Feminist Thought: The Basic Historical Writings*, ed. Alma M. García (New York: Routledge, 1997), 52–53.
6. Myra Marx Ferree and Beth B. Hess, *Controversy and Coalition: The New Feminist Movement Across Three Decades of Change*, rev. ed. (New York: Twayne, 1994).
7. Claire Renzetti, "New Wave or Second Stage? Attitudes of College Women toward Feminism," *Sex Roles* 16 (1987): 265–77; Virginia Sapiro, "Feminism: A Generation Later," *Annals of the American Academy of Political and Social Sciences* 515 (1991): 10–22; Verta Taylor and Nancy Whittier, "The New Feminist Movement," in *Feminist Frontiers III*, eds. Laurel Richardson and Verta Taylor (New York: McGraw-Hill, 1993), 533–48; Nancy Whittier, *The Feminist Generations: The Persistence of the Radical Women's Movement* (Philadelphia, PA: Temple University Press, 1995); Rose L. Glickman, *Daughters of Feminists* (New York: St. Martin's Press, 1993); Barbara Findlen, ed., *Listen Up: Voices from the Next Feminist Generation* (Seattle, WA: Seal Press, 1995); Rebecca Walker, ed., *To Be Real: Telling the Truth and Changing the Face of Feminism* (New York: Anchor Books, 1995); Leslie Heywood and Jennifer Drake, eds., *Third Wave Agenda: Being Feminist, Doing Feminism* (Minneapolis, MN: University of Minnesota Press, 1997).
8. Kimberly Springer, "Third Wave Black Feminism?" *Signs: A Journal of Women in Culture and Society* 27 (2002): 1059–82. See also Springer, chapter 1.
9. Ednie Kaeh Garrison, "US Feminism—GRRRL Style! Youth (Sub)Cultures and the Technologies of the Third Wave," *Feminist Studies* 26 (2000): 141–51. See also Garrison, chapter 13.
10. As noted by Renzetti; Sapiro; Taylor and Whittier; Whittier.
11. Elizabeth Martinez, "In Pursuit of Latina Liberation," *Signs: A Journal of Women in Culture and Society* 20 (1995): 1019–28.
12. See Martinez.

13. Two interviews were conducted in the office of a Chicana student organization. Another two were conducted in the homes of mutual friends. Three interviews were held in the respondents' homes. When it was not possible for me to conduct a face-to-face interview, I set up a telephone interview upon my return to school. Five interviews were conducted over the telephone. Each interview lasted between one and two hours.

14. I do not mean to promote an age-based/generational understanding of feminism. Rather, their brand of feminism is about acknowledging continuity throughout feminist history. Such continuity and overlap entails acknowledging the historical and current presence of women of color in feminist movements. Addressing how these women make sense of the critiques out of which third wave feminism was born is the purpose of this chapter.

15. *Cholos* are commonly known as gangsters with "deep urban roots in the 'zoot suiters' of the 1940s and 1950s." See Irene I. Blea, *Researching Chicano Communities: Social-Historical, Physical, Psychological and Spiritual Space* (Westport, CT: Praeger, 1995).

16. A number of respondents told me that they "stumbled upon" or actively sought out these organizations when they began college because they needed the comfort of being around *Raza*, which is a reference to "the people." For many women, going to college was the first time that they were away from home and in an environment that was not mostly made up of brown faces. The need to find these organizations and become involved grew from a sense of culture shock. Said one interviewee, "Until I got here, I'd never been around so many white people before!" Thus, in many ways, these organizations served as safe havens for new Chicana college students.

17. All of the names are pseudonyms.

18. *Mujeres* refers to women. The term *mujer* refers to a woman.

19. See Garcia; Marta Cotera, *The Chicana Feminist* (Austin, TX: Information Systems Development, 1977); Gloria Anzaldúa, *Borderlands/La Frontera: The New Mestiza* (San Francisco, CA: Aunt Lute Books, 1987); Irene I. Blea, *La Chicana and the Intersection of Race, Class and Gender* (New York: Praeger, 1992).

20. *Vamonos* means "Let's go."

21. See, e.g., Theresa Aragon de Valdez, "Organizing as a Political Tool for the Chicana," *Frontiers* 5 (1980): 7–13; Cherrie Moraga and Gloria Anzaldúa, eds., *This Bridge Called My Back: Writings by Radical Women of Color* (Watertown, MA: Persephone Press, 1981); García, *Chicana*; Alma M. García, "The Development of Chicana Feminist Discourse, 1970–1980," *Gender & Society* 3 (1989): 217–38; Denise A. Segura and Beatriz M. Pesquera, "Beyond Indifference and Antipathy: The Chicana Movement and Chicana Feminist Discourse," *Aztlan* 19(1992): 69–92.

22. Ferree and Hess, 79; see also Amy Farrell, "Like a Tarantula on a Banana Boat: *Ms.* Magazine, 1972–1989" in *Feminist Organizations: Harvest of the New Women's Movement*, eds. Myra Marx Ferree and Patricia Yancey Martin (Philadelphia, PA: Temple University Press 1994), 53–68.

23. For more on race and what is learned in women's studies classes, see Henry chapter 5.

24. Ana Castillo, *Massacre of the Dreamers: Essays on Xicanisma* (New York: Plume, 1994), 40.

25. See Irene I. Blea, *Toward a Chicano Social Science* (New York: Praeger, 1988); Blea; Castillo; García, *Chicana*.

26. As ten of the twelve respondents were first-generation Americans, the "tradition" to which they referred was the Mexican culture. In this section, I will only refer to the Mexican culture when I speak of "tradition."

27. Elizabeth V. Spelman, *Inessential Woman: Problems of Exclusion in Feminist Thought* (Boston, MA: Beacon Press, 1988); also Cotera; hooks; García; Collins.

28. Garrison.

29. Springer.

3

"THE PUNK WHITE PRIVILEGE SCENE" [1]:
RIOT GRRRL, WHITE PRIVILEGE, AND ZINES

Kristen Schilt

The specter of racism has haunted white feminists since the inception of the U.S. women's movement. Historical research has shown that early suffragists used racist tactics to win the vote for white women at the expense of black women.[2] In more recent years, feminists of color have written extensively on their alienation and exclusion from second wave feminist agendas. Early attempts at racial inclusion in the second wave movement failed, often boiling down to little more than "add color and stir," rather than facilitating an understanding of how different oppressions often work together. These attempts failed in part because many white feminists saw racism as secondary to the "real enemy," which was sexism. The inability to address how a white feminist political agenda reflected race and class interests made the formation of racially inclusive feminist coalitions difficult. While white feminists in the 1980s made greater attempts at incorporating women of color's experience, bell hooks argues that most of the discussion was simply "lip service" to the idea of diversity and did not lead to sustainable strategies of communication that were not exclusionary or racist. [3]

The emergence of new waves of feminist action in the late 1980s and early 1990s offered a chance for young feminists to learn from past generations and make a feminist community that incorporated and addressed the racial critiques of second wave feminism. Riot Grrrl was one such emergent feminist group. Positioned between "postfeminism" and what some labeled *third wave feminism*, women and girls involved in Riot Grrrl challenged the stereotype of young women being apathetic to feminism, and attempted to bring the idea of sisterhood and connection between women back into focus with some new twists.[4] Through subcultural media, such as punk music, zines,[5] and performance art, many of the white women and girls involved in Riot Grrrl sought to acknowledge and begin to address and dismantle their race privilege in order to move away from the lack of racial awareness that plagued second wave feminism.

To explore the success of these attempts to address race and privilege, I analyze discussions of feminism, race, and privilege in a selection of Riot Grrrl-associated zines produced in the early 1990s.[6] I maintain that, despite a heightened awareness of white privilege, many of the zines I examined were unable to move past discussion of feminism as a "women's issue" to see the ways in which race and class also affect women's lives. Yet, as with second wave feminism, the critiques women of color leveled at the group did lead to greater race cognizance for a small portion of white zine makers. Additionally, these critiques opened up a discussion about whiteness and white privilege in the discussions about punk rock that surfaced in punk zines, and aided in the formation of new feminist coalitions that were more racially diverse. Analyzing the struggle to address whiteness in these feminist zines illustrates how feminist activists still grapple with issues of whiteness. However, this analysis suggests possibilities for developing ways to investigate how race and gender intersect, rather than relying on the fiction that all "women" can organize successfully around a universal "womanhood."

To conduct this study, I performed a textual analysis of Riot Grrrl-associated zines in my personal collection[7] that had been traded with girl zine makers in the early 1990s or ordered via zine distributors. I began with one hundred zines and eliminated zines with a single focus; for example, poetry zines and music zines. I also eliminated personal zines not focused on feminism. I included all zines that I classified as Riot Grrrl-associated, meaning they referenced Riot Grrrl, debates over Riot Grrrl, Riot Grrrl-associated bands, or explicitly stated that they were Riot Grrrl zines. While women and girls associated with Riot Grrrl were not the only individuals producing feminist zines during this time period, I limit my focus to Riot Grrrl-associated zines, because talking about whiteness was a central theme of early Riot Grrrl ideology. At the end of the selection process, I had a group of forty zines. Examining these forty zines, I pulled out passages that dealt with general themes of feminist politics, Riot Grrrl, and race or racism. After analyzing these passages, I broke these sections down more specifically to fit codes I had developed: feminist awakenings, racial awakenings, discussions of white privilege, discussions of racism, and critiques of Riot Grrrl.

Zine making is mainly a middle-class phenomenon because it requires access to time and resources. Most of the printing costs are absorbed by the editor, as are the costs of paper, layout, and distribution. Zines are also largely produced by white people, as they emerged from the predominantly white punk subculture. Additionally, it is mainly an adolescent format, as teenagers in general have more leisure time than adults. For these reasons, girl-zine editors tend to be white, young, and middle class. As my sample reflected these same demographics, I argue that this research contains fairly representative examples of zines made by adolescent girl-zine makers in the United States in the mid-1990s. However, it is possible that there were other Riot Grrrl-associated zines that I did not have in my collection that used different strategies for discussing race and whiteness. However, while the findings should not be generalized to all Riot Grrrl-associated zines or all white, feminist zine makers, this data does give insight into how a specific group of young feminists grappled with moving feminist race politics forward through attempting to address white privilege.

TALKING ABOUT WHITENESS

White studies, or critical race studies, have generated a large body of scholarly work since the mid-1990s. Ruth Frankenberg's *White Women, Race Matters*[8] is one of the groundbreaking books on how white people perceive their race. Based on her interviews with white women, Frankenberg argues that white people do not perceive themselves as having a racial identity, which essentializes whiteness as a natural, unmarked category. Richard Dyer similarly writes that while white people do not think of themselves as raced, he argues, "most of the time white people speak about nothing but white people, it's just that we couch it in terms of 'people' in general."[9] Dyer argues that most white people do not see the privilege that comes with being a member of the hegemonic racial category and feel that their successes and achievements stem from their special abilities, not privilege associated with being white. He maintains that the problem is that whiteness is constructed as normal, which leaves out the power behind it. He writes: "White power nonetheless reproduces itself regardless of intention, power differences and good-will."[10] Only when white people begin to see themselves as "white peo-ple" rather than just "people" can white power and privilege begin to be dismantled.

During the second wave of feminism, Frankenberg argues that dis-cussions with women of color often faltered as white women had a pervading fear of not knowing the rules of nonracist discourse. This fear led toward an avoidance of talking about race in favor of focusing on "women" as a rallying point. Feminist theory and scholarly work, emerging from the second wave, exacerbates the problem of "whiteness as the norm." Aida Hurtado notes that academic production takes time and money, something that people living in poverty (who are predom-inantly people of color) do not have, thus privileging white women.[11] This limits what types of women's experiences are discussed in feminist theory. She argues that many white feminists gloss over the differences between white women and women of color and maintains that while white feminists have been helpful in breaking new ground in feminist theory, they have not been able to deconstruct or recognize the blind spots that exist in their relationships to women of color.

In order to allow more open discussion of race, Dyer argues that it is a necessity for white people to move past their guilt over racism and start finding more productive strategies for opening up discussions about whiteness and how white privilege operates as an unmarked category.[12] Hurtado maintains that feminist work by women of color threatens the reality construction of many white feminists who see all feminism as rooted in the commonalities of experience.[13] Yet, while new feminist discourses have emerged from these critiques, Franken-berg argues that white women still find it difficult to move past defen-siveness and apologia in order to participate in coalitions and effective discussions with women of color.[14] As a bridge between second and third wave feminism, then, Riot Grrrl offers both a glimpse into how new generations of feminists began to incorporate the critiques of second wave feminism by women of color and a way to explore how effective these new generations are in finding productive ways to talk about white privilege.

RIOT GRRRL, WHITENESS, PUNK ROCK, AND PRIVILEGE

In order to discuss the rhetoric of whiteness employed in Riot Grrrl-associated zines, a brief account of the background of the Riot Grrrl subculture is necessary. Riot Grrrl began around 1991 when a group of women from Washington, D.C. and Olympia, Washington, came together to discuss making a music magazine. The discussion that followed led to the realization that they were interested in forming a more direct-action feminist collective. Through music, zines, and performance art, Riot Grrrl gave girls the tools to become what Mary Kearney terms "cultural producers" rather than passive recipients of negative media messages.[15] Riot Grrrls learned to question the images of feminism they received from the media and produce media that placed their own experiences at the forefront. Through these subcultural media, Riot Grrls critiqued sexism in the larger society and the punk scene to which many belonged, and attempted to unpack race, racism, and white privilege.

Many of the white women involved in the founding of Riot Grrrl had worked in feminist organizing and taken women's studies courses. They had read *This Bridge Called My Back* and bell hooks;[16] they knew that second wave feminism had failed to adequately address the whiteness of the movement. Drawing on this knowledge, many early zines produced by white women associated with Riot Grrrl did attempt to investigate the whiteness of Riot Grrrl. For example, *Bikini Kill*, a zine from 1991–92, contains a list of the top ten male responses to charges of sexism. Number ten is "At least you don't have it as bad as a) women used to b) people of color c) women in other countries."[17] The author of the article calls into question this ranking of oppressions, writing:

> See, I talk/write about girlstuff so much cuz I am a whitegirl and I am not really into trying to speak for other people or species although I am becoming a better and better listener. I mean, me writing about this stuff in this zine doesn't mean I think girl oppression is any more important or pressing than racial or species or sexual oppression. It is just that I need to organize around what I know and support others to do the same cuz I can't speak for everyone but I do see all this shit as connected.[18]

Yet, while zines like *Bikini Kill* exhibit awareness of the issues that surround the creation of a hierarchy of oppressions or speaking for all "women," there is still an element of the "organize around your own oppression" second wave tactic, a tactic that was denounced by women of color as a way to avoid confronting racism head-on.[19]

Critiques of the whiteness of Riot Grrrl and the lack of appeal of punk rock feminism to women of color began to surface in zines made by women of color associated with Riot Grrrl. For example, the editor of *Gunk*, who was one of the few African-American girls to be a part of the first emergence of Riot Grrrl, writes about attending the first Riot Grrrl convention in which there was a panel on racism. She mentions that it was not very effective because it was created and run by white girls and had mainly white participants. She writes:

> This sounds kinda snotty but I see Riot Grrrl growing very closed to a very chosen few i.e. white middle class punk girls. It's like it's some secret society, but then there are some who feel that a secret society is what we need. I constantly don't feel comfortable with this cuz I know so many girls that need to hear this shit, but weren't [at the convention] cuz they would feel intimidated cuz they don't look punk.[20]

Sisi, a Latina involved in the early Riot Grrrl movement, also notes the exclusiveness of the feminist subculture. She maintains that Riot Grrrl in Los Angeles remained predominantly white because girls who were not into punk music or the punk look had a hard time relating to the movement.[21] As Riot Grrrl emerged from predominantly white middle-class punk scenes, however, it continued to attract women and girls who fit those demographics, as a result of their access to zines and Riot Grrrl-associated bands through their punk networks.[22]

Despite the awareness of the white background of Riot Grrrl, however, many young feminists of color initially felt very supportive of Riot Grrrl because it brought the sexism in the punk scene under close scrutiny. This attraction ended quickly, brought to a close by white girls' failure to investigate their own whiteness, address the critiques leveled by women of color, and discuss how racism and classism often work in concert with sexism. Additionally, many white girls involved in Riot Grrrl felt threatened by discussions of how "revolution girl-style now" might be racist. This led many nonwhite girls to feel that their experiences were devalued in the subculture. Leah, in *Patti Smith*, notes that she had to leave Riot Grrrl behind because it did not "understand or respect my colored girl ... self."[23] Lauren, writing in *You Might As Well Live*, says, "Where's the riot, white girl? And yeah some of you say we are 'out to kill white boy mentality' but have you examined your own mentality? Your white upper-middle class girl mentality? What would you say if I said that I wanted to kill that mentality too?"[24] These critiques show that despite early attempts to address race and whiteness in zines, white privilege remained largely unaddressed by white women. To examine why, I turn now to an analysis of the rhetoric employed in Riot Grrrl-associated zines for discussing feminism, privilege, and whiteness.

RHETORICAL STRATEGIES FOR
DISCUSSING WHITENESS

My content analysis yielded three predominant patterns, which I have termed "feminist awakenings," "racial awakenings," and "race cognizance." Riot Grrrl was a feminist movement that attracted girls as young as twelve, so the majority of the zines fell into the feminist awakening pattern, as these predominantly white young women dedicated most of the space in their zines to talking about their newfound feminist identity. As white zine makers got older, however, their zine content often shifted to display racial awakenings or, in rare cases, race cognizance. Zines produced by girls of color, on the other hand, show race cognizance at an early age, which demonstrates that in the Riot Grrrl movement, women and girls of color were still positioned as having to teach white women and girls about white privilege.

Feminist Awakenings

The first pattern I label "feminist awakenings," which bell hooks describes as [white] women's realizations that the gender oppression they face in their personal lives is a larger, political issue.[25] Twenty-eight of the zines I analyzed fell into this category. The main narrative of these zines is the experience of girls who have never been exposed to feminism before (much less the punk rock feminism of Riot Grrrl) suddenly beginning to recognize how gender and sexism affect their lives. They tend to focus on debates about feminism, deconstructing the stereotypes of women in society, and spreading the word about feminism to other girls and women. These zines tend to be produced by younger (ages 13–16) white, middle-class teenage girls[26] who do not dedicate much space to interrogating their position in the racial hierarchy. For example, the editor of *Succubi* zine writes about the media stereotype of a Riot Grrrl, saying:

> I have read about ten definitions of what "grrrl" is, and none of them are the same. If anything, I'm a wanna be grrrl. I doubt that I am a true grrrl because according to the media, a grrrl is a feminist who loves Bikini Kill and all the other "riot grrrl bands of choice." Well, I am a feminist and I like Bikini Kill and I hate most guys and I write all over my epidermis with permanent marker and I wear barrettes and I do a zine and I wear Docs and I buy my clothes used. But I don't go to Riot Grrrl meetings. I think I am a grrrl if I follow my own definition.[27]

Nowhere in her zine does Leslie discuss that a "grrrl" is also thought of as being white, revealing what Adrienne Rich has called "white solipsism," which is tending to "think, imagine, and speak as if whiteness described the world."[28] Some zines in this category do acknowledge the image of Riot Grrrl as white, such as *Riotempresses*, a zine by Riot Grrrl Kentucky, which states "You don't have to be militant, you don't have to be punk rock, you don't have to screech, you don't have to be white" to be a Riot Grrrl.[29] However, this statement does not lead to any further discussion of whiteness or white privilege.

The situation changes when looking at a zine produced by a girl of color. The editor of *Gunk*, an African-American punk, mentions race in almost every article of her zine. She even includes a poll, entitled "More Scary Proof That Americans Are Racist":

-62% of non-blacks believe African Americans are more likely to "prefer to live off of welfare."
-56% of non-blacks believe African Americans are more violent than whites.
-53% of non-blacks believe African Americans are less intelligent than whites.[30]

Seeing the world from the perspective of a black girl, the editor chooses to use the term *non-black* when talking about white people. As a woman of color, she has deeper analysis of race than the white editor of *Succubi*, who lives only a few miles away in New York. White girls producing feminist awakening zines are so focused on the newly found politics of feminism and gender oppression, they do not reflect on the ways in which sexism might affect girls from different racial and ethnic backgrounds differently. This lack of racial awareness supports hooks's point that feminist awakenings are a very white middle-class phenomenon, while women of color and poor women often grow up with the knowledge of how race, class, and gender oppression intersect.[31] Being insulated from this knowledge by their race and class privilege, many young, white Riot Grrrls were able to assume that their experience was the "everygirl" experience, rather than imagining that girls of color or working-class girls might have a different perspective.

Interestingly, this white solipsism appears to exist only in the area of talking about women. Many zine makers in this category discuss white men at great length while ignoring their own whiteness. Like many white second wave feminists, white zine makers who had just been introduced to feminist ideas, as evidenced by their discussion in zines of suddenly realizing they were feminists, believed that what was oppressing them was the same as what was oppressing girls of color: white males. Discussing the oppression caused by white men allowed white Riot Grrrls to feel that their issues were relevant to all girls. This is evinced in feminist awakening zines that invoke the slogans "Every girl is a Riot Grrrl" and "Revolution Grrrl-Style Now." The idea behind these slogans was that the same tactics could "free" all girls from oppression, regardless of race or class.

Racial Awakenings

Feminist awakening zines did exhibit in some cases the ability to merge into a new pattern, racial awakenings, which I found in five (12%) of the zines I analyzed. This pattern particularly was noticeable when I was able to analyze several issues of one zine. One example is *Out of the Vortex*, a zine made by two white girls. Both editors were involved in NOW and other mainstream feminist organizations. Early issues of their zine deal with many topics relevant to feminism, saying little about race. However, in issue seven, one editor writes about being accepted to Yale and Oberlin and the decision process of selecting one over the other. She mentions nothing in the article about the privilege behind having the choice of two prestigious universities until the last page. She writes:

> I'm uncomfortable with all the unexamined privilege I see in what I've written for this issue. Actually it's in every issue, but it's only embarrassingly recently that I've become aware of it. When I am writing about the choice I have between Oberlin and Yale, am I conscious of the economic, intellectual, and class privilege that this choice implies? When I write about girls, am I writing only about white girls' experiences without even thinking about it? I think I live my life from a standpoint of countless unexamined privileges (white middle class educated skinny "gifted" able bodied the list goes on), and it's completely not enough merely for me to admit this.[32]

This article illustrates how zine editors were able to take feminist awakenings a step further to begin to think about race and power. While the critique of privilege was only half a page in *Out of the Vortex*, the same editor went on to produce a different zine while in college, *Kusp*, with more in-depth critiques of whiteness and race privilege. Therefore, in some situations, moments of racial awakenings can be a step on the way to learning how to address race and power in more effective ways.

In most zines I analyzed, however, racial awakening narratives identify whiteness, but the discussions about white privilege are token in nature. There is frequently an element of power evasion, in which some zine makers recognize the privilege inherent in being white but refrain from discussing what it means. This power evasion, then, can be seen as a disclaimer tactic. For example, in *Glitter* zine, the editor writes in her introduction: "I don't think it matters much what I look like but I am white and I am middle class and I am educated and I am ablebodied and I have skinny privilege." She goes on to say:

> I'm not asking you to say ok I forgive you your privileges and I'm not asking you to take me by your hand and lead me along cos I may be privileged but I can tell whats fucked but I am asking you to think about how your own privilege or lack of privilege is used, how it affects others and how it affects yrself. I am asking you to call me on any shit you think is not ok cos sometimes we need to be reminded and sometimes we need to be educated. [33]

However, this introduction is the only mention of whiteness or privilege in the zine, as if this disclaimer alleviates power differentials. Thus, while racial awakenings reveal a budding awareness of how whiteness operates as the norm and the privilege associated with being white, they do not always develop into fully developed deconstructions of race and power.

Race Cognizance

The third pattern I identified was race cognizance, a term I borrow from Frankenberg.[34] In this pattern, which I found in six zines (15%), the zine editors recognize the power inherent in being white and engage in a critical analysis of white privilege. *Smile for Me*, a zine made by a white girl, exemplifies this awareness of race and whiteness. In one article, the editor relates a story about her "white racism." While waiting for the bus, a Latino man approaches her and asks her for directions. Her immediate suspicion is that it is a scam because he is working class and not white. She writes, "Why did I not believe he was really asking for directions. I've given directions to people (incidentally yeah right white well-off people) plenty of times before. Why did I think he was obviously trying to pull something? I think it is pretty clear why."[35] A few pages later, she discusses her article and questions whether talking about her racist thoughts is simply "commodifying" the issue. She adds, "It's difficult to admit the ways I'm racist (oh poor me), it's easier just to say 'I know I have racism' and not go beyond that, do you know what I mean?" These sentences sum up the problem that many white feminist zine makers had: they knew they were not free from racism but they didn't know what to do about it or how to successfully discuss their newfound awareness.

Other race cognizant zines take up this question of what to do with whiteness and racism, particularly in the microcosms of punk rock and Riot Grrrl scenes. In *The Nerdy Grrrl Revolution,* one editor writes:

> I could live my entire life without ever confronting this issue. Even in the most liberal of circles, it is so safe to be white. The dominance of men in the punk scene is nothing compared to the white dominance of the punk scene. Why is this not addressed? Do we need the oppressed to come and point it out to us? If so, then I am sorry. It isn't happening. Admittedly, it is not solely our place as whites (god I'm writing as if I'm speaking only to the white community! racismracismracism) to integrate the punk scene. I cannot force anybody to become a part of a scene that they don't feel comfortable in, but I can at least do my part in acknowledging the problem and opening the door.[36]

Smile for Me has a similar critique of the punk scene being too white. However, the author takes the idea of getting "non-whites" involved in punk to task and calls for punks to try to branch out, to join "non-white based activities." She maintains that the only way to meet "non-white" people is to sacrifice the comfort of the punk scene and try to join another group.

The first example in *Nerdy Grrrl* appears to boil down to the same tactic tried by second wave feminists: add color and stir. This idea suggests that white privilege will be erased if people of color simply join the punk movement. It ignores, however, that white privilege operates even within oppositional subcultures such as punk. While white punks think of themselves as fighting hegemonic values, their rebellion is given more leeway because they are white. The editor of *Gunk*, a black girl, points out that African-American punks experience a kind of double stigma:

> White kids in general regardless if they are punk or not can get away with having green mohawks and pierced lips 'cause no matter how much they deviated from the norms of society their whiteness always shows through. For instance, I'll go somewhere with my friends who all look equally as wierd [sic] as me, but say we get hassled by the cops for skating or something. That cop is going to remember my face alot clearer than say one of my white girl friends. I can just hear him say now, ... "Yeah there was this black girl w/ pink hair and two other girls.[37]

She points out that, despite their outward appearance, white punks would be seen as less of a threat to the police than punks of color. Her account illustrates both the point that people of color can see white privilege more clearly than white people and that white people passively benefit from being white.

The second strategy outlined in *Smile for Me* appears to be more useful, for it calls for white people to leave their privileged location and join racially diverse organizations, a reversal that could be seen as "add white and mix." This ignores that adding white "lightens" or alters political agendas, as inherent in white privilege is the assumption that the white perspective is the normative or "correct" perspective. People of color, then, may not be thrilled at the idea of white people, with no recognition of how they act as oppressing agents, joining their political groups. Additionally, many white people do not even know how to talk about race to people of color. The editor of *Nerdy Grrrl* exemplifies this position, writing:

> Do the words that I use offend you? If so, TELL ME. I want to know. I know that words DO mean something, and I am ignorant to the nuances of racial terminology. It is not my prerogative to decide which words are okay in this situation. It has to do with the fact that words have socialized meaning, and the people who are affected by them need to be in control of that. So I'm really serious. Let me know, okay?[38]

While this is obviously an attempt at addressing the meaning of whiteness, the most likely audience for this zine coming out of Olympia, Washington, was other white girls. Thus, as well-meaning as these critiques are, they do not offer plausible solutions for change.

A handful of zines do manage to lead to deeper investigations of whiteness, however. *Girl Germs*, a zine compiled by a racially diverse group of women, contains many discussions of white privilege. In one issue, Allison Wolfe, the singer of the Riot Grrrl-associated band Bratmobile, discusses a song she recorded in Thai.[39] However, she had begun to realize that singing in Thai was just an example of her privilege as a middle-class white girl, who had the privilege of living in Thailand as an exchange student and learning another language. Realizing this, she felt embarrassed about the song and wished she had not recorded it. Through this critique, white readers are confronted with the idea that their race contributes to their achievements and has meaning in the larger racial hierarchy in the United States.

The fact that race cognizant zines with deep analyses of race and whiteness, such as *Girl Germs*, are rare, speaks to the difficulty of moving whiteness out of an unmarked location, making its effects visible. Young, white Riot Grrrls found a voice in zines that spoke about feminist awakenings and were able, at times, to move their awareness of sexism into a critique of the white solipsism they observed around them. However, they had a difficult time finding a way to address and effectively talk about whiteness. As shown, the majority of race cognizant zines remain bogged down in apologia and guilt over "white girl racism." Yet, these critiques issued in Riot Grrrl-associated zines were not unproductive because they generated debate and critique within the movement, particularly by girls and women of color associated with Riot Grrrl. These discussions and critiques generated their own form of feminist action, which I will discuss in the next section.

"IT STARTED ME ON MY JOURNEY": WOMEN OF COLOR, RIOT GRRRL, AND PUNK ROCK

As with second wave feminism, it was critiques by women and girls of color that finally created a more effective discourse about the "punk white privilege scene." Hurtado argues that this pattern exists because white feminists are unable (or unwilling) to delve into how their whiteness affects their relationships with women of color. She writes, "Although white feminist writings have been very helpful in breaking new theoretical ground, they have not been as helpful in deconstructing white women's 'blind spots' in relationship to women of Color [sic]."[40] Hurtado argues that people of color are better able to articulate what whiteness and white privilege mean because they are constantly thinking about it. This perspective places a double burden on people of color, however. Not only are they oppressed by whiteness but they also are responsible for educating white people about their white privilege. While Frankenberg has shown that white women often gain race cognizance from forming racially diverse relationships, there is still the question of whether taking on this role of race moderator is beneficial to nonwhite women.[41]

In the case of Riot Grrrl, many girls of color ultimately decided not to take on the role of educator and left the movement. This abandonment of Riot Grrrl was not done in an entirely negative fashion, however. While nonwhite girls remained critical of Riot Grrrl, they were quick to point also to how important it was as a stepping stone to the formation of other feminist coalitions. Zine maker/academic Mimi Nguyen says:

> Riot Grrrl is the best thing that ever happened to punk. It is amazing that all these young (mostly white) women have decided to redesign the whole world according to the architecture of their

private-made-public traumas and promises of "girl love" wish fulfillment. Riot Grrrl is amazing in so many ways: as confrontation, as education, as performance, as aesthetic, as support, as theory, as practice etc. But it is important for me as a feminist of color to criticize Riot Grrrl for the ways in which it has (or hasn't) dealt with differences of race and class. In that aspect, rather than presenting an alternative, Riot Grrrl totally parallels "mainstream" Euro-American feminism.[42]

She adds, "I've met a lot of women who were once involved in Riot Grrrl and punk and have since moved on to other subcultural spaces (or created their own), and that's been amazing."[43] Many women were also able to see that Riot Grrrl had helped them develop a sense of themselves as a feminist. Leah, in *Patti Smith*, says, "I will always remain grateful to grrrl-punk and zine culture for teaching me to speak the truth, love my freakishness and make my own freedom. It started me on the journey."[44]

New feminist coalitions did begin to emerge from Riot Grrrl. Sisi from *Housewife Turned Assassin* formed Revolution Rising, a collective that produces zines, stickers, and spoken word tapes that express the need for social change and racially diverse coalitions. Compilation zines by zine makers of color, such as *Evolution of a Race Riot* and *Yello Kitty*, began to surface. These zines include articles by white women as well, illustrating that young white feminists were beginning to find more fruitful ways to discuss their privilege. Moreover, work like this by feminists of color has forced the punk scene to begin taking whiteness and white privilege seriously. *Punk Planet*, one of the main punk magazines, ran an article by Nguyen in the December 1998 issue, entitled "Looking for Race in Punk," showing that punk as a scene is beginning to confront its whiteness.[45] Traditionally, punk has taken a color-blind approach, invoking a common community, "we are all punk" idea. Many see being punk as something that transcends race, gender, and class. Nguyen points out that in order for people of color to fit into punk, they are expected to leave behind their racial, class, or sexual identity. She writes, "Color-blindness suggests that race is only skin deep; that beneath is something more fundamental. It's a typically power-evasive move, one that pretends that individuals don't operate within the context of uneven social relations."[46] These discussions show that while white girls in Riot Grrrl were not always able to create a punk rock feminism that addressed the experience of all girls, it did provide girls with the tools to investigate whiteness and white privilege in alternative feminist movements.

CONCLUSION

Valerie Amos and Pratibha Parmar argue that inclusive feminism cannot emerge until there is a "critical engagement with challenging racism" on the part of white feminists.[47] While Riot Grrrl is only a microcosm of Western feminism, analyzing its attempts at addressing white privilege speaks to the larger issue of whether intersectionality, or the way that gender intersects with other social locations like race, class, or age, will ever be a starting point for Western feminist movements. Like the radical feminists of the 1960s, white girls involved in Riot Grrrl, while aware of white privilege, often were not able to move past being defensive or apologetic about their whiteness. The few who did gain race cognizance often were unable to find ways to form multiracial coalitions. Thus, it is possible to see Riot Grrrl as another white-dominated feminist movement that failed. A different, and more positive way to position Riot Grrrl, however, is as a movement that began to incorporate this intersectionality as part of a crucial step toward racial awakening and race cognizance for young white feminists, a step on a feminist journey rather than a destination.

While the discussions of whiteness in Riot Grrrl-associated zines were not always successful in moving past apologia or defensiveness, the analysis raises many interesting points about how a racially diverse feminist coalition may emerge. It is difficult to imagine how young, white girls will grow up in the suburbs with critical formulations of the mechanisms of whiteness and white privilege without some race awareness education or interactions with people of color. The feminist awakening pattern I found in my analysis appears typical for this group of girls. This pattern begins with the process of seeing how one fits into the world as a woman, a category that is often most salient for women in dominant race and class positions. It is through these feminist awakenings that racial awakenings and race cognizance can begin to emerge, as I documented in the few cases where I could track progressive issues of the same zine. That this racial awareness emerged mainly after critiques by women of color shows the importance of interactions with diverse populations for members of hegemonic class and race categories. While this still placed women of color in the position of having to educate white people about their racism, looking at the different forms of activism that emerged from these critiques, both in the arenas of feminism and punk rock, illustrates bell hooks's point that conflict does not have to be negative or detrimental to a feminist movement but rather can be the basis for a racially diverse feminist agenda.[48] It is when feminist awakenings do not develop into an awareness of the intersectionality of race and class with gender or when white people refuse to acknowledge that they too have a race category, that activism and progression come to a halt.

Recent third-wave feminist texts appear to have made a jump from the necessity of the color-blind stage of feminist awakening to taking intersectionality and white privilege as starting points for activist work. In *Third Wave Agenda*, Leslie Heywood and Jennifer Drake note that their conception of feminism realizes that what oppresses one woman may not oppress another and that white women may actually be a part of what oppresses women of color.[49] To the authors, all these contradictions are what make up third wave feminism, a feminism in which whiteness and white privilege are examined alongside of the experiences of women of color. The racially diverse authors included in *Third Wave Agenda* do not dedicate a great deal of space to agonizing over whether they are part of an oppressive system of whiteness; they recognize that being white gives them an inherent privilege and begin to deconstruct those privileges. To them, the need to address white privilege is a given in any feminist coalition, showing that the idea of white privilege has entered into a great deal of feminist discourse.

As evidenced in books like *Third Wave Agenda*, white women involved in third wave feminism have begun to take on the role of educating other white women about their racism and race privilege. Much of this discourse stems from the discussions that surrounded Riot Grrrl and the ensuing spin-offs of different, more racially inclusive forms of feminist action. Thus, while Riot Grrrl might not have been the right format for reaching out to feminists of color or deconstructing white privilege, the critiques leveled at Riot Grrrl opened up a discourse on race and whiteness led by young feminists of color and Riot Grrrl discontents. One of the biggest contributions that Riot Grrrl made to youth feminism was in providing white girls with information about sexism and racism. While many needed critiques by women of color to show them the meaning of this information, the resulting activism that sprung up from the discontent speaks more to the necessity of creating a form of feminism that encompasses change than to the failure of Riot Grrrl. Being involved in Riot Grrrl gave girls and women the tools to continue their activist pursuits, even after their exit from the movement. Looking at texts such as *Third Wave Agenda* reveals how some women have been able to create a type of feminism that examines whiteness and privilege alongside the experiences of women of color, and suggests that feminist awakenings for young women may more quickly be followed by race cognizance.

NOTES

1. The title for this paper comes from the song "Axemen" by Heavens to Betsy (Heavens to Betsy, *Calculated*, compact disk, Kill Rock Stars, 1994).

2. Paula Giddings, *When and Where I Enter: The Impact of Black Women on Race and Sex in America* (New York: William Morrow, 1984); Dorothy Roberts, *Killing the Black Body: Race, Reproduction and the Meaning of Liberty* (New York: Vintage Books, 1997).

3. bell hooks, "Feminism: A Transformational Politic," in *Theoretical Perspectives on Sexual Difference*, ed. Deborah Rhode (New Haven, CT: Yale University Press, 1990), 185–196.

4. Early Riot Grrrl had little connection with other third wave feminists, such as Rebecca Walker, in the early 1990s. Walker, who employed more traditional feminist activism strategies, such as voting drives, had a close tie to second wave feminism. Due to the media construction of Riot Grrrl as bratty teenagers, the women involved were often viewed as apolitical or threatening when they wanted to take part in more second wave forms of activism. For an example of this treatment, see *Bust* magazine article, in which Gloria Steinem acknowledges that *Ms. Magazine* should have been more open to Riot Grrrl and that the group did a great deal of important feminist work that was ignored in their coverage on third wave feminism. Celina Hex, "Fierce, Funny, Feminists," *Bust* (Winter, 2000), 52–56.

5. "Zines," short for fanzines, are homemade magazines with limited distribution. They are usually typed or handwritten and then photocopied. Zine makers trade zines with other writers mainly through the mail, at zine conferences, and punk shows. For more on the history of zines, see Bates and McHugh, chapter 10.

6. The name *Riot Grrrl* was a media label attached to feminist activism that was taking place in Olympia, Washington, and Washington, D.C. in the early 1990s. Not all women and girls who were labeled *Riot Grrrl* actually chose that name. Therefore in this article I use the term *Riot Grrrl-associated* to make clear that the authors of these zines may or may not have taken the label for themselves but were nonetheless associated with the political sentiments of Riot Grrrl.

7. Zines are not formally published and there is no central location, such as a zine library, to access all zines produced, so collecting a random sample of girl-zines would have been impossible.

8. Ruth Frankenberg, *White Women, Race Matters: The Social Construction of Whiteness* (Minneapolis: University of Minnesota Press, 1993).

9. Richard Dyer, *White* (London: Routledge, 1997), 272.

10. Dyer, 279.

11. Aida Hurtado, *The Color of Privilege: Three Blasphemies on Race and Feminism* (Ann Arbor: University of Michigan Press, 1996).

12. Dyer.

13. Hurtado.

14. Frankenberg.

15. Mary Kearney, "Producing Girls: Rethinking the Study of Female Youth Culture," in *Delinquents and Debutants: Twentieth Century American Girls' Culture*, ed. Sherri Inness. (New York: New York University Press, 1998), 285–310.

16. Cherie Moraga and Gloria Anzuldua, eds., *This Bridge Called My Back: Writings by Radical Women of Color* (New York: Kitchen Table Press, 1983); bell hooks, *Feminist Theory: From Margin to Center.* (Boston: South End Press, 1984).

17. *Bikini Kill* zine, circa 1991.

18. Ibid., circa 1991. Note: Quotations from zines retain the original grammar and spelling.

19. See hooks, *Feminist Theory*, for a critique of this approach.

20.   *Gunk* zine, circa 1992.

21.   V. Vale, *Zine,* Volume 1 (San Francisco: V/Search, 1996).

22.   This is not to say that working-class white women were not involved in Riot Grrrl. Many of the original "founders" of Riot Grrrl D.C. were working class. However, as younger girls across the country became involved, it became largely middle class.

23.   Karen Green and Tristan Taormino, *A Girl's Guide to Taking Over the World: Voices From the Girl Zine Revolution* (New York: St. Martin's Griffin, 1997), 3.

24.   *You Might as Well Live* zine, circa 1995.

25.   hooks, *Feminist Theory.*

26.   I am extrapolating these demographics from the content of the zines.

27.   *Succubi* zine, circa 1994.

28.   Adrienne Rich, *On Lies, Secrets, and Silence* (New York: Norton, 1979), 299.

29.   *Riotempresses* zine, circa 1995.

30.   *Gunk* zine, circa 1992.

31.   hooks, *Feminist Theory.*

32.   *Out of the Vortex* zine, circa 1995.

33.   *Glitter* zine, circa 1995.

34.   Frankenberg.

35.   *Smile for Me* zine, circa 1993.

36.   *Nerdy Grrrl Revolution* zine, circa 1994.

37.   *Gunk* zine, circa 1992.

38.   *Nerdy Grrrl Revolution* zine, circa 1994.

39.   *Girl Germs* zine, circa 1992.

40.   Hurtado, 87.

41.   Frankenberg.

42.   V. Vale, *Zines: Volume Two* (San Francisco: V/Search, 1997), 67.

43.   Vale, Volume 2, 63.

44.   Green and Taormino, 4.

45.   Mimi Nguyen, "Looking for Race in Punk," *Punk Planet,* (November/December 1998): 80–83.

46.   Nguyen, 81.

47.   Valerie Amos and Pratibha Parmar, "Challenging Imperial Feminism," in *Feminism and Race,* ed. Kum-Kum Bhavnani (Oxford: Oxford University Press, 2001), 17–32.

48.   hooks, *Feminist Theory.*

49.   Jennifer Drake and Leslie Heywood, eds., "Introduction," in *Third Wave Agenda: Being Feminist, Doing Feminism* (Minneapolis: University of Michigan Press, 1997), 1–20.

4

"I AM A FEMINIST BUT…": TRANSGENDER MEN AND WOMEN AND FEMINISM

Sally Hines

Women's studies, coming out of second wave feminism, was one of the first academic fields to respond to the growing public awareness of contemporary Western transgender practices.[1] During the decades of what has come to be known as third wave feminism, feminist theorists have retained a high level of interest in transgender. *Transgender* is used here as an umbrella term to denote a diversity of identities that challenge the binary categories of male and female and which may (or may not) relate to body modifications through the use of hormones or surgical procedures. Transgender practices include movement across (e.g., transsexual reassignment from male-to-female or female-to-male), between (e.g., male or female drag), or beyond (e.g., gender queer) gender categories and challenge the understanding of the terms *sex* and *gender* as biologically fixed. Additionally, transgender practices problematize a straightforward correlation between "sex" and "gender," raising complex questions about how these categories are constructed. Although these issues have long been central to feminist thought, on a theoretical, political, and cultural level, second wave feminism has been largely hostile to transgender practices. Trans women (i.e., born men) have been seen to reinforce stereotypical femininity, while trans men (i.e., born women) have been viewed as renegades seeking to acquire male power and privilege. In 1998, Stephen Whittle posed the question, "How can feminism accept men with women's bodies (or is that women with men's bodies)?"[2] Whittle's question remains central to feminist debates and the controversial relationship between transgender and feminism.

With such questions in mind, this chapter draws upon the second and third waves to explore the relationship between feminism and transgender. I first examine radical feminist writing from the 1970s through the 1990s and address how this perspective affected an anti-transgender sensibility within second wave feminism. I then locate poststructuralist feminist and queer theories, which have been integrated into third wave feminist ideologies and practices, as models through which contemporary feminism can account for transgender. To do so, I draw on a recent qualitative study to analyze the relationship between feminism and trans masculinity and trans femininity. I interviewed thirty transgendered men and women over nine months. All of the participants are residents of the United Kingdom. Thirteen participants are trans men (born women), and seventeen are trans women (born men), ranging in age from twenty-six to seventy-five years old. A little over half of the sample lived in rural towns or villages with the rest in urban cities. Fifteen identified themselves as heterosexual, while fifteen identified themselves as either gay, lesbian, bisexual, or queer. Eight participants were single, while the remainder were in relationships; and seven were parents. In addition to interviews, I also communicated with participants by telephone, e-mail, and written correspondence. While some participants used pseudonyms, others wished to be known by their own names.

Drawing on the data, I investigated how trans men and women participants articulate their experiences of second wave feminism and explored the ways in which they relate to contemporary feminism. I found that the majority of trans men participants had an involvement in feminist or lesbian communities and particularly within queer subcultures, before or during transition,[3] though they largely view second wave feminism as socially and politically problematic. Many have a continued involvement within feminist politics and queer communities, however, and locate contemporary feminism as a less hostile personal and political space than that of second wave feminism. I also found that trans women were rejected by radical feminist communities, which refused to accept their female identity. Many trans women, however, demonstrate a heightened awareness of feminist critiques of trans femininity and consciously attempt to construct gendered expressions that are in contrast to stereotypical models of femininity. I conclude by suggesting that third wave feminism is relevant for an understanding of gender dynamics as illuminated by the stories of transgender people and argue for a comprehensive incorporation of trans experiences into future gendered analyses.

THEORETICAL DEBATES ON TRANSGENDER

The publication of Janice Raymond's thesis *The Transsexual Empire*[4] established a radical feminist perspective on transgender that was to significantly affect the dominant feminist position for succeeding decades. Raymond's argument is that sex is chromosomally dependent and thus secured at birth. From this perspective, gender is seen as an expression of biological sex with the categories of sex and gender connected. This leaves transsexuality to be read as a genetic male practice fashioned by a patriarchal medical system to construct servile women. Raymond's position is absolute; trans women are not, nor can they ever be, "real" women. Her fiercest criticisms are directed at trans women who identify as feminist and lesbian:

> The transsexually constructed lesbian-feminist may have renounced femininity but not masculinity and masculinist behaviour (despite deceptive appearances).... It is significant that transsexually constructed lesbian-feminists have inserted themselves into positions of importance and/or performance in the feminist community.[5]

Her analysis presents a restrictive model of gender, which negates expressions of masculinity within lesbian or feminist identities. While Raymond views trans women as "deviant males,"[6] trans men are seen as treacherous women.

In 1994 *The Transsexual Empire* was republished with a new foreword by Raymond. This update can be read as a response to the developing field of transgender studies and trans activism. The decade and half between the publications witnessed considerable shifts in the experiences of trans people and in theoretical approaches to transgender, which were being developed by trans academics themselves. Significantly this period saw the increased visibility and activism of trans men. Nonetheless Raymond merely repeats her earlier denunciation of trans men as "the tokens that save face for the transsexual empire."[7] This argument was reinforced when, in 1997, Sheila Jeffreys offered explicit support for Raymond's position in her article "Transgender: A Lesbian Feminist Perspective,"[8] which refueled the feminist attack on transgender. Departing from the prevailing feminist focus on trans femininity, Jeffreys's key point of contention is trans masculinity. She views trans masculinity as a "modern invention," thus erasing historical female to male (FtM) transitions, and urges that it is "*now* imperative for lesbian communities to pay attention."[9]

Rather than reviewing radical feminism as a fringe perspective, it is important to recall that during the 1980s and early 1990s, radical feminist theory held widespread popular appeal within feminist and lesbian politics. As radical feminism infused cultural battles around sexuality, debates around sexual imagery and practice dominated second wave feminist and lesbian concerns. As I will show, trans men and women frequently became the focus of community contests of inclusion and exclusion. Transgender practices raise key questions about the construction of gender identities and the authenticity of "sex." A radical feminist response to these complexities has been to reinforce a gender and sexual binary model in order to regulate gendered belonging. Moreover, in recent years a radical feminist critique of transgender can be seen to have moved beyond those who directly identify as radical feminists and into a mainstream feminist agenda, as illustrated by feminist author and scholar Germaine Greer's public outing of a trans female colleague at Cambridge University, U.K.[10]

Despite its influence, I do not wish to position radical feminism as *the* analytical framework of the 1980s and 1990s. During this time poststructuralist and postmodern feminists, queer theorists and transgender academics were developing fierce critiques of an essentialist approach (i.e., one that equates gender and sex as connected) and producing alternative theoretical models of gender and sexuality. In the late 1980s and throughout the 1990s, the rhetoric of radical feminism gave way with nonnormative gender and sexual identities such as S/M, butch dyke, lesbian boy, drag butch, and drag king influencing feminist perspectives that attempted to move away from viewing transgender as suspect.

Alongside the experiences of queer communities, academic feminists were beginning to argue for a politics of sexual diversity through theorizing gender and sexuality as distinct though overlapping categories. Judith Butler thus argues that a binary model has restricted feminist understandings of sex and gender:

When the constructed status of gender is theorized as radically independent of sex, gender itself becomes a free-floating artifice, with the consequence that *man* and *masculine* might just as easily signify a female body as a male one, and *woman* and *feminine* a male body as easily as a female one.[11]

Here we can see the ways in which a feminist framework can be used to understand gendered identities and expressions that are not fixed to sex. This model provides a more nuanced understanding of trans identities; where erotic desire does not automatically fit preconceived binary identities of either gender (man/woman) or sexuality (homo/hetero). It additionally allows for divergence between self-gender identity and bodily appearance; as exemplified by those who identify as gender queer and who reject surgery, or by trans people who due to negative psychiatric evaluation, lack of funding, or lengthy waiting lists do not have access to the surgery or hormone therapy they desire.

The influence of poststructuralism and queer theory upon strands of feminism (and vice versa) during the 1990s led to a more explicit engagement with transgender. The emphasis upon difference within these approaches allows us to go beyond the prevailing notion of trans people as a homogenous group, to recognize distinct trans identities. Queer theorists have shown how traditional lesbian and gay theory and politics have been (and often remain) exclusive toward those whose identities fall outside of that which is deemed to be "correct" or "fitting"; a frequent theme reflected in the experiences of participants in this project. In viewing all gendered and sexual identities as socially constructed, queer theory aims to dissolve the naturalization and pathologization of perceived minority identities. This approach may be incorporated into a third wave feminist understanding of transgender that accepts a multiplicity of gendered identities and representations that are not fixed to sex.

Theoretical approaches to gender and sexuality are relevant here due to the influence of theory on social movements, in particular feminist movements. In the following sections I draw on interview data to address these themes further. First, I consider how the influence of a radical feminist perspective within second wave feminism affected attitudes toward transgender, and address the impact of this upon the experiences and understandings of trans men and women. Second, I explore how the attention to difference within poststructuralist feminist work and queer theory may be linked to third wave feminist ideologies which are more receptive to gender diversity.

LIVING THROUGH THE SEX WARS:
NARRATIVES OF TRANS MEN

As attention during the 1980s focused upon sexuality, feminist politics became dominated by fierce debates around the meanings of lesbianism and lesbian sexual practices. These debates cut through many contemporary trans male narratives. In interviews with thirteen trans men, I identified themes of pretransition inclusion in feminist and lesbian communities and posttransition exclusion from these communities within second wave feminism. I find that for some trans men after transition there is a continued involvement within contemporary feminist and particularly queer communities.

Pretransition Involvement

Many participants have talked about their involvement in feminism, though they were keen to point out that they were not "radical feminists." Although members of feminist communities, trans men's involvement was not without controversy. Political and cultural debates within second wave feminism frequently focused around stylistic expressions and gendered images. In talking about his pretransition involvement during the 1980s within feminist and lesbian communities, Philip remembers arguments over appropriate fashion. He said:

> I used to wear lots of different costumes and I always used to play around with image, and one of my images was miniskirt, high heels, and fishnets, and that was at a time when lesbian feminists were saying women shouldn't wear makeup, so therefore I went and did all that to annoy them.... Some of what I was doing was a reaction to that attitude, 'cuz I was in the gay scene. So I was part of the people who wanted to wind the radical feminists up basically....

In sum, while still living as a woman, Philip was aware of the constraints of radical feminist thought. Part of this awareness was the way in which trans people were understood in the stand-offs between radical feminist and feminist and lesbian communities. Philip continued:

> That's reminded me of something that happened in the '80s.... There was the Fallen Angel, one of the first gay pubs that existed, in Islington, and on Tuesday night or something it was women only, and "S/M Dykes" decided to go down there and all these women knew we were coming and we had a transsexual with us, 'cuz we happily included trans women, and we walked in and it

was full of women and they were all silent and there were only about six of us. And this woman stood up and said something like "Will all women who object to the presence of these women now leave" and they all stood up one by one and filed out, it took about ten minutes. And that was also directed at the presence of this transsexual as well.

Just as participants were a part of feminist communities, they also related their former experiences within lesbian communities. However, many qualified their involvement by saying they identified as "dyke" or "queer," rather than as "lesbian," once again distancing themselves from radical feminism. Svar recalled his pretransition decision to identify as a "dyke" versus a "lesbian." He said:

I think the first time I fell in love it was with a woman.... That was when I was fifteen, so I was a baby lesbian for a while and then when I came up to London to go to art school, when I was eighteen, then I just started hitting the gay scene and I have quite an extensive dyke history you might say, in the London scene.... I'd say more dyke than lesbian. I was never really one of these, you know, goody-goody sort of wholesome shoes, sort of lesbian as such, I was always... I always considered myself more as a dyke. I was never a lesbian separatist, sort of like man-hater, angry.... Even though I was at Greenham Common[12] all those years ago (he laughs).

Thus many of the trans men interviewed distanced themselves from feminist communities and some aspects of feminist identity, preferring to identify with queer subcultures before their transitions from women to men. That sense of distancing continued after many of them had made their transitions.

Posttransition Exclusion

Gayle Rubin's discussion of a hierarchical valuation of sex acts illustrates how certain sexual practices are privileged above others. Her sliding scale of social and political privilege places cohabiting heterosexuals at the higher end, closely followed by other heterosexuals. Gay men and lesbians in long-term partnerships are placed above promiscuous gay men and lesbians, who in turn, are just above the lowest groups within the sexual hierarchy; "transsexuals, transvestites, fetishists, sadomasochists, sex workers such as prostitutes and porn models, and the lowest of all, those whose eroticism transgresses generational boundaries."[13] While Rubin's schema does not take account of trans identities beyond those of the transsexual and transvestite, her discussion of a Western system of sexual stratification illustrates the ways in which feminist thought has traditionally failed to address all levels of sexual and gender discrimination. Indeed, as Phillip's account of the Fallen Angel bar shows, feminist and lesbian communities frequently employed their own systems of sexual and gender stratification.

Exclusion based on a social ordering of sexual and gendered practices appears as a frequent theme in trans men's stories. Paul discussed the reactions of feminist and lesbian friends after his transition. He said:

> I kind of had mixed reactions from the lesbian community. They almost kind of laughed in my face. I remember one girl who just couldn't deal with any of it and that's when I'd already been on hormones six months, so, you know, I thought, "Well, bye, bye."

Others had similar experiences and often heard the critique of trans masculinity as an unethical way of women accessing male power and privilege:

> Svar: There was actually from the dyke feminist scene, there was quite a lot of opposition to female to male transsexuality.... I mean one friend did actually say to me, "Oh I see... so you're abandoning the female race then...."
>
> Sally: So did you experience problems around acceptance from within the lesbian community?
>
> Svar: With some, but then I'd just say, "I'm not doing this to myself to create a master race or something...." But yeah, there was some accusations, you know, "You're trying to have power, get power." And it was kind of quite shocking really, when you say, "Look, I've made this decision because I'm trying to deal with something in myself and I can do without all that, I can do without that attitude, what I could do with is your support here, you know, how can you say these things?"

Del's experiences of exclusion mirrored Svar's and illustrated how feminist critiques collapse trans masculinity and patriarchal white male identity. Del said:

> I've had experiences fairly recently where close friends who are dykes.... I realized, after five years, that they were having a problem

with my gender identity and that they really didn't understand where I was coming from and they were presuming that I was like this kind of straight white man and you know, a magazine that I have contributed to since its beginning, didn't want my work anymore and I was really shocked… you know that group of people, who had the magazine, I go way, way back with them and I was shocked, absolutely shocked that they would do this. And there [are] clubs that friends of mine are going to and I want to go to and I can't and this is something that's a real hold over from lesbian separatism in the 1970s and 1980s in this country, it's ridiculous. And it's funny because people who probably weren't even born then are forcing these boundaries. I see it as lesbians still feel[ing] very much under threat, so instead of building bridges they're erecting barricades.…

Although exclusion from feminist and lesbian communities is a recurring theme, some of the same participants expressed an ongoing professional and personal involvement within lesbian and queer cultures, as illustrated by Del. He said:

I feel that there's a filmmaking community, a queer filmmaking community that I feel part of. I'm still on the lesbian photography show touring around. I'm on the lesbian artist news group that I've always been on. That's part of my history and that's part of who I've been and I've produced a lot of work within those communities, I don't see any reason to leave them.

The importance of belonging to established networks is further reflected when Del contrasts his experiences of exclusion from British lesbian cultures with continued acceptance whilst working for lesbian magazines in the United States. He continued:

I'd been in America working for lesbian magazines and taking pictures for them and it was great 'cuz in California I was… I didn't feel any separation… I was working for "On Our Backs" and I did a porno shoot with these four young dykes, one of whom is a transgendered butch, or might become transsexual I don't know, but it was kind of like a butch/femme photo shoot and, you know, they were getting down to it and I had no sense that there was any.… They were absolutely not uncomfortable with me, you know, I was still a role model for them and my gender seemed not to matter. I seemed to get a lot of respect from the youngsters, like from teenage to thirty years old, they weren't having any problems with me.

Del's story indicates that *despite* dominant transphobic rhetoric, some trans men were able to find a home, and indeed were often key players, within feminist and lesbian communities before, during, and, in some cases, following transition. Thus, although the men interviewed tended to distance themselves from radical feminist communities and ideologies both pre- and posttransition, some are able to maintain networks, primarily in queer feminist communities.

Becoming Feminist Men

Writing about the invisibility of trans men within feminist theory, Jason Cromwell argues that, "Feminists should be concerned that male-dominated discourses have made female-to-male transpeople virtually invisible."[14] In this study, I suggest that trans men are also primary subjects for feminist study because many continue to identify *as* feminists. Del said:

> Women feel betrayed, or that I've left them, or that I think there's something wrong with being a woman, which I absolutely don't think that there is… I am totally… I mean what my work is about is female empowerment…. I will always be a feminist.

Judith Halberstam points out that historically, FtM transition has often represented social and economic mobility, and gender and sexual conservatism.[15] Halberstam rightly cautions against the supposition that female-to-male transition per se is an indicator of gender and sexual radicalism. Nevertheless, in talking about identity, politics, values, and relationships, many of the men I spoke with articulate masculinities that are in some way distinct from traditional notions of male power or privilege. As Del notes, the interaction of a feminist trans masculinity with a more traditional masculinity can be troubling to trans men. He said:

> And then of course there's the way in which men don't guard what they say when they're with someone they think is a man. I've had…. Even my hairdresser, who knows, my barber, he's told me about rape, you know, rapes that he's committed when he was a kid, you know getting the girls drunk….

Jacob Hale argues that "for some ftms (female to male transgenders) one of the more disconcerting aspects of social and medical transition is the extent to which we become privy to displays of nontranssexual men's sexism as our gender presentations and embodiments come to elicit attributions as men, fellows of our fellows."[16] A similar tension may arise when trans men examine their intimate relationships with women.

Del: It's hard … I am in a relationship now that I feel like the man, I'm getting things that men get and it makes me wonder would I get these if I hadn't taken testosterone?

Sally: What sort of things?

Del: Would I be in this kind of relationship? Would someone be doing my laundry? I've never had anyone doing my laundry before. And now, is it just a coincidence or.…

Sally: Is that problematic for you?

Del: It is problematic yeah, as a feminist it's problematic.…

Similarly, Svar says of his relationship with his partner:

[S]he treated me sometimes a bit too like a guy and since then we've actually talked about this and I've had to say, you know, "I am not one of 'these' men, I am not like that, I am not a man's man. You seem to forget that I actually was a female human being far longer than you have been a female human being, so don't treat me like that."

These stories show that trans men are not simply adopting traditional masculinity as claimed by feminist critiques of female-to-male transition. Moreover, many have been active members of feminist and lesbian cultures and articulate masculine identities informed by feminist concerns. Del clearly distinguishes his masculinity from normative masculine models. He said:

You have to understand that someone like me is never going to be able to access real male privilege. I found that out when, even though I was wearing a suit and a tie, when I was traveling back from LA to London and I wanted to get an upgrade, well … I'm not an alpha male. You have a six foot man come next to me, stand next to me, and we are [each from different] species. And I can't even really impersonate that kind of man. So, I will always be beta male or epsilon male or whatever.

Del's comments clearly challenge the idea that trans people seek to ape traditional gender roles. Correspondingly, interviewees reflect on the distinguishing characteristics of trans masculinity, as shown by Dan. He said:

> Dan: I would describe myself as FtM as opposed to straight male.... Because of my background and my upbringing it gives me more depth than just being bio male and I think that's an important distinction. So whilst I want to be perceived and understood and taken totally as male, I will never be 100 percent male because of my background....
>
> Sally: Can you tell me more about that distinction?
>
> Dan: I suppose there's a lot greater awareness.... It's to do with female conditioning, being brought up in a gentler society, a more caring environment ... being more aware of people, what they're doing, how they're feeling, if something's wrong ... a greater intuition, which I can also observe with other FtMs that I can't see with bio men.

Dan's narrative shows how trans masculinities may challenge dominant ideas around what constitutes a male sensibility. While Dan notes how trans masculinity is acted out differently from nontrans masculinities, William contrasts reflexive understandings of gender amongst trans people with a perceived lack of gendered awareness in nontrans people. William said:

> The trans thing ... there's a lot more of a blurring of these boundaries of what men and women are. A lot of people in the world don't think about their own identity enough, and outside of the trans community there's a lot of people who don't think about gender.

Theorists of masculinity have problematized the exclusion of men from feminism by exploring how their involvement in feminism requires personal and political transformations that can be seen to disturb the concept of a unitary masculinity.[17] Similarly, a central theme expressed by the majority of trans male participants is not to behave or be seen as "typical" men. While it is important to live and be seen as male, a key area of concern raised is to be understood as being *different* men.

In sum, I have shown how many trans men participants had involvement within feminist and lesbian cultures prior to transition. The decades of second wave feminism, however, are articulated as problematic because the influences of radical feminism frequently affected hostility toward trans men. Alongside experiences of exclusion, some trans men were able to find a home within feminist and queer communities during and following transition. My findings counter the argument that trans men routinely seek to imitate patriarchal masculinity. Rather, many participants articulate masculinities that are in tune with third wave feminism and are a contrast to hegemonic (i.e., dominant) masculinity.

RIDING THE WAVES: TRANS FEMALE NARRATIVES

As we have seen, the impact of a radical feminist critique on transgender practices was both personally and politically problematic for trans men. Similarly trans women frequently found themselves excluded from feminist and lesbian communities. At the core of feminist discussions around trans femininity is the concept "woman." In explaining the marginalized histories, experiences, and social and political demands of women, the women's movement applied "woman" as a fixed category, which was distinct from "man." As Judith Butler writes:

> For the most part, feminist theory has assumed that there is some existing identity, understood through the category of women, who not only initiates feminist interests and goals within discourse, but constitutes the subject for whom political representation is pursued.[18]

For trans women, not being born biological female (i.e., fitting the category "woman") led to their exclusion from feminist and lesbian communities. In addition, as men undergoing transitions to trans women, they faced pressure to conform to traditional ideals of femininity by gender identity clinics. However, some were able to find acceptance in third wave feminist communities.

Women Born Women Only

Because the definition of "woman" became inextricably tied to biological sex, trans women experienced difficulty as they attempted to define their gender and sexual identity and fit into lesbian or feminist spaces, or both. Echoing the narratives of trans male participants, many trans women speak of rejection from second wave feminist and lesbian communities. Rebecca said:

> I have come up against … I'm a clubbing animal and there used to be a club in Liverpool that was very gay friendly that I used to

go to. And a lot of gay women went to it and I was.... How can I put it? They didn't want to engage. I know that has been the experience of a lot of people.

Gabrielle tells a similar story when talking about her attendance at an early Gay and Lesbian Pride event:

I remember Jubilee Gardens even though I wasn't relating as queer then, except maybe internally, but I just went and it was great. But I do remember feeling like it wasn't my day, it was for gay and lesbian people and we were not viewed necessarily with inclusiveness by the community, and weren't made to feel as though they wanted us to be part of the community.

She continues:

I'm not really happy with spaces for, what did they used to say, "women born women only." I'm not pleased about that. But at the same time I would never force myself. I would never oppress anyone, but at the same time I don't want to be oppressed either. And as I said earlier, who's policing the boundaries, the borders of these things? You know the protest outside the Michigan Womyn's Festival,[19] it's the most extreme feminist separatists who are being allowed to police who comes in and who doesn't and these fine trans people, and other people of course, nontrans people who are sympathetic, have been working to try and change the attitudes of the women who run the festival, and that's great, and all strength to them.

Gabrielle reported having a similar difficulty negotiating the boundaries of identity. She said, "I suppose, I mean, words are really tricky... I'd say I'm a trans lesbian, but I don't know, you know, because it's like, as they say, "Who controls the boundaries of what is anything?""

The experiences of Rebecca and Gabrielle show how trans women found themselves rejected by radical feminist ideologies and communities because they are not women born women. Questions around the position of trans women within feminism cut to the heart of discussions around the constitution of "woman." Anna's narrative explicitly illustrates how the identity of "woman" has been fiercely defended:

Lesbians tend to steer clear [of trans women] 'cuz they don't know what they're dealing with. When you stake a claim on a lifestyle, if someone threatens that, you rebel against them, and they see that I make a mockery out of it. And people who you'd expect to be the most understanding 'cuz they've had a difficult ride as well, turn out to be the least accepting sometimes.

In addition to feeling excluded from feminist communities, trans women also faced pressures to conform to traditional femininity, despite their feminist ideologies.

The Pressure to Conform

Contrary to the claims that trans women ultimately exemplify problematic masculine behavior, many of those interviewed employ feminist critiques to reject what they view as "unacceptable" attitudes in other trans women. In this way Gabrielle describes the dynamics within a gender identity clinic. She said:

There were some trans women who were very sexist behaving and had a mindset of very sexist men and we really took them to task, a few of us, and said, "Listen, you better go and sort yourselves out because from where I'm sitting you're really an outrage and I'm insulted by what you say and your attitudes towards women."

Finding acceptance in a community posttransition could be complicated, as illustrated by Rebecca. She said:

I sometimes wonder … I try to be understanding of people's needs … I think that there are trans people who because of their need to be accepted push too hard and that puts anybody's hackles up. I'm not saying there are not gay and lesbian people who will say "We don't like you," because I know that there are people who do that, but sometimes it's more complicated.

Similarly Gabrielle was sympathetic to feminist challenges to stereotypical modes of femininity sometimes displayed by trans women. She said:

And perhaps it would be arguable that with the loss of our privilege, trans women might be prone to certain compensations that might not be particularly constructive, you know…. Trans people often overcompensate at certain times…. Excessively exteriorly feminine behavior amongst trans women…. And I think a lot of trans people become a lot more balanced as they go through transition and become people who are mature in their trans experience after having transitioned and then it becomes a lot more balanced.

Overcompensation is exacerbated through psychiatric practices, which frequently demand that trans women model an outmoded feminine style before being accepted for hormone therapy or surgery. Several women, Rebecca, Amelia, and Dionne, discussed this in their interviews. Rebecca said:

> I find it highly insulting that someone, usually a man, will tell someone how to behave as a woman. And anyway, in contemporary Britain, what is a woman? It has changed greatly and thank goodness. You know, what is femininity? What is feminine dress?

Likewise Amelia challenged the restrictive dress codes within gender identity clinics:

> It's an interesting personal experience.... Presenting myself there was none of.... I suppose because I'd come up through the feminist era, there was none ... I am me and black leather looks good on a man or a woman. I used to live in black leather. Clothes were not the issue, they never were the issue. These idiots in the gender identity clinics say, "You can't be a woman if you don't wear a skirt." Who dares say that? How dare they say what makes a woman and what makes a man? And to me, if I took this dress off and put on my partner's suit, I'd still be me.

The following comments from Dionne provide a strong critique of expectations of traditional feminine presentation, and illustrate her developing agency as she rejected the correlation of femininity and female identity. She said:

> If a butch dyke wants to present as masculine she's still mostly seen as a woman. But if I'd have gone in butch, or even in a pair of jeans, they (psychiatrists at gender identity clinic) wouldn't have treated me. I had to go in as feminine. And initially I had to present as heterosexual. I wouldn't have said I liked women. And why do women have to dress in a certain way? It's wrong.... And I've started to realize that and now I hardly ever wear a skirt. I've realized that you don't have to be feminine to be a woman, you can have short hair.... But if I'd gone in at the start and said, "I want to be a butch woman, a butch dyke," they wouldn't have

treated me. I felt I had to be very feminine. And that's all to do with how society perceives women, which is something women have fought for a long time and I'm just finding it all out.

Here we can see trans women employing feminist critiques of the beauty myth, wherein women face societal pressure to conform to an idealized standard of beauty, to confront conventional forms of gender presentation. Thus the basis of "real life" within the "real life test," which is central to psychiatric evaluation determining whether a person is granted access to hormone treatment or surgery, is radically questioned. Experiences of sexism during transition then, can be seen to bring about a feminist identity for trans women.

FINDING A PLACE

The all-embracing notion of "woman" began to fracture through a series of challenges from feminists who argued that their experiences remained unarticulated in a predominately white, middle-class, and educated movement. By the start of feminism's third wave then, it was more appropriate to talk of a range of feminisms than to discuss a uniform body of feminist thought. While some theorists and activists welcomed the destabilization of a politics of identity which was characterized by a universal narrative of women's experience, others took a more defensive attitude to these ruptures. In third wave feminism, multiple female identity positions are recognized and attention is paid to the ways in which women's identities are constructed in relation to difference (e.g., class, race and ethnicity, sexuality, location, and age). This focus on diversity parallels the reflections on difference within poststructuralist feminism and queer theory. Corresponding with the narratives of trans male participants, trans women have frequently located contemporary feminism as a more welcoming space than second wave feminist communities. Emma said:

There has certainly been an element of trans phobia within feminist and lesbian communities. Although recently I've got on very well with sections of that community and have been pretty well accepted as me....

Similarly Gabrielle reflects:

Having been to Pride for maybe ten years in a row and always feeling out of it 'cuz we weren't included and then we were

included and it was magical.... And yeah, I do feel included....
And I remember going to Pride and going in the women's tent
and it was fantastic, scary but fantastic, really exciting.

Gabrielle sees a positive shift in feminist attitudes toward transgender
and credits her friends for the support they gave her during early stages
of transition. She said:

And I've been lucky to know such wonderful people, 'cuz over the
years I've said stupid things, just in my naiveté, because I'd been
conditioned the way I was, I would say things in a blasé way,
which now I look back on and cringe, and they were very understanding and didn't pick me up on it, or beat me up, so one
learns. You just recondition yourself, well I hope you do. I always
considered that it was a really great privilege to do something in
society which a lot of people would never do, which is to revalu-
ate everything that you have been taught and that you accept and
that you've been conditioned [to], and to keep that which you
consider to be worthwhile and to chuck out and replace a whole
load of stuff that you don't [consider worthwhile].

Here we can see how trans women were able to find third wave feminist
spaces that accept them. Gabrielle links the previously explored relationship between trans men and feminist and lesbian communities to
broader changes in attitudes toward transgender. She said:

But I think it's a really interesting thing, 'cuz obviously you've got
a lot of trans men who came through a lesbian community and
were affiliated to very much a sense of community through that
'cuz there is a strong sense of community and having come
through that they keep their friends with them, they may be
rejected by some, but they keep quite a lot of those friends. And
quite a lot of those women work through their issues with the
trans thing and quite a lot resolve it and come out ok, which is
really good. So there are quite a lot of lesbian women who are
supportive and I've felt really supported.

Despite experiencing alienation from some feminist communities then,
Gabrielle, like other trans men and women, largely speaks positively
about her relationship with current feminist and queer communities.
However, while celebrating an increased feminist engagement with transgender, it is important not to portray a linear account of a theoretical or

cultural trajectory from radical feminism to queer. Rather, the complexities within these narratives show that the arguments of radical feminism continue to inform feminist theory and cultural politics. Although the impact of radical feminism may live alongside queer movements, I suggest that the influence of poststructuralist theory and queer politics has encouraged third wave feminism to pay greater attention to gender variance.

CONCLUSION

This chapter has explored the dynamics of gender diversity in relation to second and third wave feminism. First, I show that the gender of transition impacts upon participants' understandings of feminism. As social groups, trans men and women have different experiences and understandings of feminism prior to transition. Second, gender has considerable bearing on the divergent experiences within feminist communities for trans men and women during and after transition. Many of the trans men rejected aspects of radical feminist thought yet found acceptance within feminist or lesbian communities. Trans women, on the other hand, experienced pretransition exclusion and struggled to belong posttransition. In sum, trans men and women encounter distinct feminist challenges, which in turn, impact upon the different levels of acceptance they experience within feminist and lesbian communities. There are, however, many common themes between the narratives of trans men and women. In particular both draw on experiences of rejection from second wave feminism, while more positive stories are told about relationships with contemporary feminism as informed by queer ideology.

In attempting to forge stronger links between feminism and transgender, I do not want to fall into what Henry Rubin terms an "ideal feminist identity paradigm,"[20] in which feminist identity is based upon female sex. This dynamic locates trans men as the "good guys" who, because of female socialization and experience, possess a degree of understanding about what it is to be a woman and as such may be perceived as feminists. Although this liberal hypothesis differs from biologically centered theory, which reduces gender to sex, it continues to employ biology as a reflector of "true" identity and negates the self-identities of trans men. Moreover, if we transfer this paradigm to trans women, by turn, they must inhabit a male sensibility and are not feminists. In contrast to an identity paradigm, Rubin proposes an "action paradigm" in which feminist identity arises out of political commitment rather than female biology. He argues that "'Womanhood' is no longer a necessary, nor sufficient qualification for feminist identity. A feminist is one who acts in concert with feminist ideals."[21] Thus political practice rather than gender or sex lies at the heart of feminist identity. We can add on to this that a feminist viewpoint need not depend upon feminine socialization in order to enable the feminist voices of trans women to be heard. Emi Koyama's discussion of trans-feminism, which expresses the feminist concerns of trans women, shows how trans politics may enable contemporary feminism to move beyond the confines of second wave feminism.[22] In conclusion I suggest that, if attentive to gender diversity, third wave feminism may provide a collective arena through which our differences may produce a more extensive feminist knowledge.

NOTES

1. Hird links increasing public awareness to the high-profile media coverage of Christine Jorgensen in the 1950s. See Myra J. Hird, "Out/Performing Our Selves: Invitation for Dialogue," *Sexualities* 5 (2002): 219–38.

2. Stephen Whittle, "Guest Editorial," *Journal of Gender Studies* 7(1998): 2.

3. I do not wish to suggest that this is the case for all trans men. I acknowledge Namaste's point that a key methodological problem within studies of transgendered identities concerns the way in which they have been "conceived as a function of lesbian/gay identity politics." Vivienne K. Namaste, *Invisible Lives: The Erasure of Transsexual and Transgendered Lives* (Chicago and London: University of Chicago Press, 2000), 64. I am aware that many trans men have not been aligned personally or politically with either feminist or lesbian communities. However, the majority of trans male participants in this project did articulate these previous connections and this may be a specific reflection of the British cultures where this research took place.

4. Janice G. Raymond, *The Transsexual Empire: The making of the she male* (London: Women's Press, 1979).

5. Raymond, 1979, 10.

6. Ibid., 5.

7. Janice G. Raymond, *The Transsexual Empire* (London: The Women's Press 1994), xxv.

8. Sheila Jeffreys, "Transgender Activism: A Feminist Perspective," *The Journal of Lesbian Studies*, 1 (1997): 55–74.

9. Jeffreys, 68; my emphasis.

10. This event took place in 1997. As a member of the governing body, Germaine Greer publicly objected to a trans woman being admitted as a Fellow to the all-female college.

11. Judith Butler, *Gender Trouble: Feminism and the Subversion of Identity* (New York and London: Routledge, 1990), 6.

12. In 1981 a women's peace camp was set up outside the U.S. air base at Greenham Common, near Newbury, Berkshire, U.K., as a protest against the location of Cruise missiles at the base. The camp was active for nineteen years until the year 2000.

13. Gayle Rubin, "Thinking Sex: Notes for a Radical Theory of the Politics of Sexuality," in *Pleasure and Danger: Exploring Female Sexuality*, ed. C.S. Vance (London: Pandora Press, 1992): 267–319.

14. Jason Cromwell, *Transmen & FTMs: Identities, Bodies, Genders and Sexualities* (Urbana and Chicago: University of Illinois Press, 1999), 9.

15. Judith Halberstam, *Female Masculinity* (Durham, NC and London: Duke University Press, 1998), 168.

16. C. Jacob Hale, "Tracing a Ghostly Memory in My Throat: Reflections of Ftm Feminist Voice and Agency," in *Men Doing Feminism*, ed. Tom Digby (New York and London: Routledge, 1998), 198.

17. Samuel Adu-Poku, "Envisioning (Black) Male Feminism: A Cross Cultural Perspective," *Journal of Gender Studies* 10: (2001): 157–67.

18. Butler, 1.

19. In 1991 two trans lesbians were removed from Michigan Womyn's Music Festival (MWMF) due to their "womyn-born-womyn-only" policy. Further evictions of trans people followed in subsequent years. Gender activists such as Lesbian Avengers and Transexual Menace have organized "Camp Trans" outside the festival as a protest at MWMFs discriminatory policy.

20. Henry S. Rubin, "Reading Like a (Transsexual) Man," in *Men Doing Feminism*, ed. Tom Digby (New York and London: Routledge, 1998), 308.

21. Ibid., 308.

22. Emi Koyama, "Transfeminist Manifesto," in *Catching a Wave: Reclaiming Feminism for the 21st Century*, eds. Rory Dicker and Alison Piepmeier. (Boston: Northeastern University Press, 2003): 244–59.

Part II

Mothers and Daughters?
Relations between the Second and
Third Waves

5

SOLITARY SISTERHOOD: INDIVIDUALISM MEETS COLLECTIVITY IN FEMINISM'S THIRD WAVE

Astrid Henry

A third wave of feminism has emerged in the United States since the mid-1990s, grounded in the distinct generational experiences of women who have come of age after feminism's second wave. As Jennifer Baumgardner and Amy Richards describe in *Manifesta*, "For anyone born after the early 1960s, the presence of feminism in our lives is taken for granted. For our generation, feminism is like fluoride. We scarcely notice that we have it—it's simply in the water."[1] Coming of age after the social and political gains of the second wave—and thus living in a world where women's equality seems at least somewhat secured—third wave feminists assume a certain level of individual and political freedom. Barbara Findlen stresses the historically unprecedented nature of this relationship to feminism when she notes that it is "the kind of experience *only* a woman of this generation could have had. We are the first generation for whom feminism has been entwined in the fabric of our lives."[2] Taking feminism for granted, however, has seemingly led to a more ambivalent relationship to it: while third wavers see feminism as "our birthright," to quote one commentator, when compared to the second wave feminists who came before us we seem much less secure in our ability to affect real political change, particularly if such change is premised on collective action.[3]

Self-described third wave feminists have used the term as a way to distinguish themselves, both generationally and ideologically, from second wave feminists, the generation of feminists who came of age in the late 1960s and 1970s. The publication of a number of anthologies since the mid-1990s has helped to further define what is meant by third wave feminism.[4] The feminism that has emerged from these texts makes clear that positing a shared "sisterhood," in the second wave sense of the term, has not been a major priority for third wavers. Rather than arguing for a feminism based on the shared identity "woman" or on shared political goals, as the rhetorical gesture of sisterhood once suggested, younger feminists today seem to find their collectivity mainly through a *shared generational stance* against second wave feminism and second wave feminists. As I have discussed elsewhere, third wave feminists have often defined their feminism by stressing what it is not, articulating the "new" (and "young") feminism in generational terms by contrasting it with the "old" (in both senses of the word) feminism of the second wave.[5] In so doing, some third wave feminists have relied upon the language of the mother–daughter relationship to describe the conflicts in contemporary feminism. For example, in an essay in *To Be Real*, contributor Elizabeth Mitchell writes: "I was not born into sisterhood: I closed a line of sons. And so my search for a feminist self is most naturally not a communal enterprise but one against, and for, my mother and her generation."[6] Rejecting the metaphor of sisterhood, many young feminists have instead chosen another familial metaphor—the mother–daughter trope—to articulate their feminism, speaking as "daughters" rather than "sisters."[7] Rather than developing their feminism *with* their generational peers, third wavers have instead chosen to argue *against* second wave feminists.

Taking a generational stance against the second wave has given many third wave feminists a way to enter into feminism. Articulating this new wave primarily in generational terms, however, has hindered the development of third wave feminism as a political movement or as a critical perspective, particularly because such a movement or perspective requires solidarity premised on more than just generational location. Although the third wave has coalesced by taking a unified stance as the first post-second-wave generation, it appears to lack the other forms of collectivity that were so central to much second wave feminism. Third wave feminists rarely articulate unified political goals, nor do they often represent the third wave as sharing a critical perspective on the world. Rather, third wave texts are replete with individual definitions of feminism and individualistic narratives of coming to feminist consciousness.

The third wave's "ideology of individualism," to quote Leslie Heywood and Jennifer Drake, has found its ideal form in the autobiographical essay, the preferred writing genre of third wavers and one that shares little with the group manifestos of a previous generation.[8] The majority of third wave anthologies published since the mid-1990s have been structured around such personal essays and, correspondingly, personal definitions of feminism. As Baumgardner notes, "the personal frontier is where my generation is doing most of its work."[9] Such essays can be seen as the first step in the consciousness-raising process developed from the earlier women's liberation movement.[10] That is, they provide a means by which to express individual experiences and to analyze those experiences in larger social and political terms. Where the third wave has often appeared stuck, however, is in moving beyond self-expression to developing a larger analysis of the relationship between individual and collective experience, culminating in theory and political action.[11] As Gina Dent has warned, "where there is no process through which legitimate self-exploration is translated into collective benefit, the feminism drops out of Feminism and the personal fails to become political."[12]

Third wave feminists' preference for defining feminism in their own terms—that is, for each individual feminist to define feminism for herself as an individual—can be seen in the original declaration of the third wave, Rebecca Walker's "Becoming the Third Wave," written in response to the Clarence Thomas hearings and published in *Ms. Magazine* in January 1992. Her essay, devoted to explaining why feminism is still needed and why a new generation of feminists must begin to mobilize, ends with the following words: "I am not a postfeminism feminist. *I am* the Third Wave."[13] In calling for a new wave, Walker does not speak in a collective voice. There is no "we" in this statement, just an "I." An early expression of what was to become a common theme within third wave discourse, Walker's essay does not attempt to speak in the name of other women. Rather, she writes about her own individual desire to devote her life to feminism.

This approach to feminism has been echoed in many subsequent third wave texts since the mid-1990s, including *The Bust Guide to the New Girl Order* in which *Bust* editor Marcelle Karp proclaims: "We've entered an era of DIY feminism—sistah, do-it-yourself.... Your feminism is what you want it to be and what you make of it. Define your agenda. Claim and reclaim your F-word."[14] Comments such as these are meant to offer an alternative to the perceived dogmatism of second wave feminism in which there is only one right way to be a feminist and to do feminism. Like many third wavers, Karp steers clear of prescribing a particular feminist agenda and instead celebrates the ways in which feminism can be defined by each woman in her own terms. She tries to make feminism an open space, one which is available to all. Naomi Wolf's *Fire with Fire: The New Female Power and How It Will Change the 21st Century* has a similar goal; ultimately, however, Wolf argues for a feminism so devoid of politics that anyone—no matter how homophobic, antichoice, or racist—can claim it for herself, as long as she's for what Wolf terms "power feminism." In the preface to the paperback edition, Wolf responds to criticisms of her project with the following:

> The question arose as to whether I redefine "feminism" so loosely that it's meaningless. One critic attacked my definition because it was one "no one could argue with." To me that is its virtue.... This redefinition is important because all the negative associations attached to the term are now paralyzing women.[15]

On the one hand, this call for redefinition is meant to invite more women and men into feminism, to make the term *feminist* appealing so that more people will want to claim it for themselves. Given the ways in which feminism and feminists are routinely caricaturized within the mainstream media and culture, this rehabilitation of feminism is important work, to be sure. However, when this rehab project represents feminism as nothing more than whatever one wants it to be, feminism loses its critical political perspective. Without its critiques of white supremacy and privilege, heterosexism, and capitalism—not to mention its continued insistence on examining the ways in which sexism and misogyny continue to operate in the world—feminism becomes nothing but a meaningless bumper sticker announcing "girl power."

This individualistic vision of feminism is perfectly suited for the conservative realities of U.S. politics in the early twenty-first century, in which political and social problems are almost exclusively addressed on the individual rather than collective level. The ultimate expression of such conservative feminism can be found in Karen Lehrman's *The Lipstick Proviso: Women, Sex and Power in the Real World*, in which Lehrman argues that "the original ideal of feminism is rooted in the individuality of women... women have ultimate responsibility for their problems, happiness, and lives." Adding, "[t]he personal, in other words, is no longer political."[16] In its worst form, this feminism marks its progress by the status of white, economically privileged women; so

long as this group of women is doing well, there's clearly no longer a
need for a mass movement. In fact, this appears to be the main thesis of
Lehrman's book. As she argues, "discrimination is not as bad as it's
made out to be," adding, "[w]omen are not 'oppressed' in the United
States, and they're no longer (politically at least) even subjugated."[17] In
this narrow view, feminism is exclusively concerned with gender equality and fails to recognize the interconnectedness of race, class, and sexuality, let alone connect feminism to other social and economic justice
movements. If the third wave has been schooled in the lessons of the
second wave, as many third wavers argue it has been, then it must con-
ceive of feminism as more than just a movement to empower white,
economically privileged women.

Some third wave writers have rightly cautioned against these recent
trends toward redefining feminism to make it as appealing as possible
or narrowly envisioning feminism around the needs of the individual.
In their introduction to *Catching a Wave: Reclaiming Feminism for the
21st Century*, Rory Dicker and Alison Piepmeier write:

> [S]ometimes it seems as if everything and anyone can fit within
> the third wave—it doesn't matter what they actually think, do, or
> believe. We call this the "feminist free-for-all": under this rubric,
> feminism doesn't involve a set of core beliefs that one shares or
> goals that one works for.... This is the worst interpretation of bell
> hooks's edict that "feminism is for everybody": it implies that
> anybody can be a feminist, regardless of her or his actions.[18]

In insisting that feminism "must be politically rigorous" if it is to "transform our lives and our world," Dicker and Piepmeier offer an important
alternative to many of the individualistic definitions of feminism currently being offered.[19] Yet, as they themselves acknowledge, insisting that
third wave feminism be grounded in shared political goals and beliefs is
a challenge to those who value the "new" feminism precisely because of
its amorphous quality. As the next generation of U.S. feminists continues
to define itself over the next decade, it is an open question as to which
direction the third wave will take. Will third wave feminism begin to take
a more overtly political and collective stance, or will it continue to
develop as an individual and generational perspective?

The third wave's penchant for individual definitions of feminism is
particularly striking when put against the universal claims and group
manifestos characteristic of the early second wave. Slogans such as "Sisterhood is Powerful," the ubiquitous catchphrase of the late 1960s and early
1970s, stressed a common sisterhood based on the shared oppression of

all women. Much early feminist theory was founded on this vision, such as the "Redstockings Manifesto," from 1969, in which the radical feminist group relies on a shared sisterhood to call women to action: "We identify with all women"; "We repudiate all economic, racial, education, or status privileges that divide us from other women"; "We call on all our sisters to unite with us in struggle."[20] In its best intentions, the feminist argument that women are sisters in a common struggle was an attempt to look beyond divisions among women toward a definition of sisterhood—and feminism—that included all women. As has been widely discussed by feminist scholars however, the rhetoric of universal sisterhood was often not accompanied by a careful analysis of differences between women, whether of race, class, sexuality, or nationality, in both the first and second waves. As the second wave of feminism developed throughout the 1970s, the idealism expressed in the frequent claim of sisterhood would rightly be challenged, and feminists would be forced to address the very real differences that divide women and which complicate any monolithic definition of "woman"—or of feminism itself.

The feminism "in the water" that third wave feminists take for granted is decidedly postsisterhood in its assumption that feminism cannot be founded on a universal definition of women or women's experience. Critiques of second wave feminism's racism, its homophobia, its class bias, and its inattention to other forms of oppression among women have been at the center of what many third wave feminists have learned as feminist theory and the history of the women's movement. As Ednie Kaeh Garrison notes in 2000, "It is clear now that feminist critiques of feminism are part of the very origins of Third Wave feminism rather than trailing behind an already unitary model of the movement."[21] The foundational role of "feminist critiques of feminism" to the third wave can be attributed, in part, to the central role feminists of color have played in shaping this wave's understanding of feminist theory and feminist practice, a point routinely stressed by third wave feminists of all races. In their introduction to *Colonize This! Young Women of Color on Today's Feminism*, editors Daisy Hernández and Bushra Rehman describe having "grown up with a body of literature created by women of color in the last thirty years—Alice Walker's words about womanism, Gloria Anzaldúa's theories about living in the borderlands and Audre Lorde's writings about silences and survival."[22] This point is also echoed by Linda Garber who writes:

> I am of a generation of lesbian scholars whose "higher education," both inside and outside the academy, includes Lorde, Anzaldúa,

This Bridge Called My Back, Home Girls, and a variety of other works by women of color in the 1980s. It was not something added on later.... [these writers] were the leading voices of feminist and lesbian theory.... Their critiques of racism within feminism were widely accepted as true by the time I heard about them.... What remained for my generation, then, was a choice of what to do with this work.[23]

In stressing that the work of women of color was "not something added on later" to her generation's education in feminist theory, Garber, like Garrison, points to the fact that for many third wavers feminism can never be separated from its internal critiques. That is, many young feminists enter into feminism with the assumption that differences and conflict are inherent to feminism—that there can never be a singular feminist subject presumed to speak for all women, that feminism is, by definition, made up of diverse interests and constituencies. As JeeYeun Lee, a contributor to *Listen Up,* writes:

These days, whenever someone says the word "women" to me, my mind goes blank. What "women"? What is the "women" thing you're talking about? Does that mean me?... I ask people to specify and specify, until I can figure out exactly what they're talking about, and I try to remember to apply the same standards to myself, to deny myself the slightest possibility of romanticization. Sisterhood may be global, but who is in that sisterhood?[24]

Lee's comments illuminate the ways in which feminist critiques of feminism shape third wave thinking. Demanding that feminism speak for and about *specific* women rather than for and about the monolithic "woman" of earlier eras, Lee is wary of universal claims and sees them as a form of "romanticization" which feminists are better off avoiding. Questioning the sisterhood put forward by feminists, Lee instead argues for particularity and for attention to the individuals who make up the larger category "women."

In their insistence that neither "women" nor "sisterhood" can provide the natural alliance these terms once were presumed to convey, third wave feminists critique the concept of identity politics that an earlier generation saw as instrumental to political mobilization. As it was conceived by second wave feminists, as well as other civil rights groups, identity politics posits a relationship between one's gender, racial, or class experience and one's political interests, as in the Redstockings' "[w]e identify with all women." In contrast, third wave writers rarely use identity categories to make claims for an entire group, whether women or otherwise; there is little sense in these contemporary texts that identity categories can provide a coalescing structure to bring people together toward a collective political agenda. This is not to say, however, that identity categories are absent from third wave discourse; in fact, such categories are routinely stressed, but almost always to further individual expression. A good example of this phenomenon can be found in Barbara Findlen's introduction to *Listen Up: Voices from the Next Feminist Generation* where she describes the essays in her collection:

> Women in this book call themselves, among other things, articulate, white, middle-class, college kid; wild and unruly; single mother; Asian bisexual; punk; politically astute, active woman; middle-class black woman; young mother; slacker; member of the Muscogee (Creek) Nation; well-adjusted; student; teacher; writer; an individual; a young lady; a person with a visible disability; androgynous; lapsed Jew; child of professional feminists; lesbian daughter; activist; zine writer; a Libra; an educated, married, monogamous, feminist, Christian African American mother.[25]

In *Listen Up*'s attention to speaking from an embodied and particular position—one that is always inflected by race, socioeconomic class, sexuality, religion, and educational status—the influence of second wave feminism is clear. Yet, rarely does the third wave move beyond these individual assertions of identity to a larger, collective political identity. The Asian bisexual can only speak for herself, not for other Asians nor other bisexuals, nor even other Asian bisexuals. JeeYeun Lee, the Asian-American bisexual writer referred to in Findlen's introduction, describes a retreat organized by the Asian Pacifica Lesbian Network in which this realization was made perfectly clear:

> This was a retreat where one would suppose everyone had so much in common—after all, we were all queer API women, right? Any such myth was effectively destroyed by the realities of our experiences and issues. We were women of different ethnic backgrounds, with very different issues among [us].... Such tangible differences brought home the fact that no simplistic identity politics is *ever* possible.[26]

Rather than using identity categories—whether of gender, race, sexuality, or class—to speak in a collective voice, the third wave has stressed such identity categories in order to express the individual perspectives of each feminist and to recognize the wide range of differences between women.

In *Fire with Fire*, Naomi Wolf argues that recognition of and insistence on differences between women represents an advancement in feminist thinking. She writes:

> We are maturing into the understanding that women of different classes, races, and sexualities have different, and often competing, agendas. Those conflicts should not be a source of guilt to us. They do not represent the breakdown of sisterhood. In the fullness of diversity, they represent its triumph.[27]

In describing this understanding as "maturation" and "triumph," Wolf suggests that this new feminism is moving us forward, taking us to places beyond where the second wave could take us. Other writers have also discussed the recognition of diversity in generational terms, as when Dicker and Piepmeier write, "Many of the goals of the third wave are similar to those of the second wave, though some, such as its insistence on women's diversity, are new."[28] In describing the "insistence on women's diversity" as "new"—that is, as something original to the third wave—Dicker and Piepmeier point to the ways in which feminism has been shaped by the critical insights of second wave feminists of color. It is these earlier feminists who taught third wavers to insist on this diversity. Dicker and Piepmeier nevertheless describe third wave feminism as "new" in its embrace of these insights; that is, they seem not to recognize that many second wave feminists—feminists of color in particular—also insisted on women's diversity. As I have discussed elsewhere, this third wave claim places feminists of color in a paradoxical position: feminists such as Gloria Anzaldúa, bell hooks, Audre Lorde, and Cherríe Moraga, among others, are credited with providing the foundation for third wave feminism, yet these same feminists must be relegated to the margins of what has come to represent second wave feminism so that the third wave can announce itself as "new" and "mature" in its embrace of racial and other forms of diversity.[29]

In arguing that the recognition of differences among women does "not represent the breakdown of sisterhood" but rather "represents its triumph," Naomi Wolf suggests that true sisterhood can only be achieved by incorporating diversity into feminism. Her use of the word *sisterhood* in this passage is striking given the infrequency with which this term is used positively in third wave texts. For many young feminists, the term *sisterhood* seems anachronistic, as seen in the following types of comments: "While linked through common concerns, notions of sisterhood seldom appeal to women of my generation."[30] "Even among women who call themselves feminists, the notion of an all-embracing sisterhood has lost some of its appeal."[31] "Sisterhood is still possible, and also powerful. But for too many people, the word has become as outdated as other concepts from the Seventies, joining the ranks of disco and the leisure suit."[32] In these examples, "sisterhood" seems a relic of the past, something which the current generation no longer finds necessary or desired. While some younger feminists shun the concept of sisterhood as outdated, others argue that the term is no longer viable based on what it represents. For example, in the Canadian third wave anthology, *Turbo Chicks: Talking Young Feminisms*, the editors offer the following definition of sisterhood in their glossary:

> *Sisterhood*: A term meant to imply a connection among women. Using this word within a feminist context is controversial, as the women's movement has not proven to be an inclusive movement. Women of colour, queer women, disabled women, Aboriginal women and poor women have all been excluded (at different times and in different ways) from the feminist agenda and have therefore challenged the use of the term "sisterhood" within feminism and its implications of equality and connection among all women.[33]

Turbo Chick's critique of the term *sisterhood*—and caution that to use the word could prove "controversial"—seems grounded in the feminist history of exclusion that shapes so many of the other third wave perspectives that I've been discussing here. Viewing the term *sisterhood* as naïve, this definition stresses the ways in which differences become erased—and consequently, exclusion becomes inevitable—when the metaphor is evoked. The recent emergence of a transgender movement within third wave feminism may also point to the ways in which "sisterhood" is a problematic rhetorical device given the implied female subject of this sisterly coming together.[34]

The eschewing of universal claims in the name of sisterhood can also be attributed to the political realities faced by feminists at the beginning of the twenty-first century. As Dicker and Piepmeier note:

> [T]hird wave feminism's political activism on behalf of women's rights is shaped by—and responds to—a world of global capitalism and information technology, postmodernism and postcolonialism, and environmental degradation. We no longer live in the world

that feminists of the second wave faced. Third wavers… are therefore concerned not simply with "women's issues" but with a broad range of interlocking topics.[35]

Dicker and Piepmeier highlight the ways in which new world realities shape new forms of feminist activism, suggesting that third wave feminists will have to tackle multiple and interlocking issues rather than any one singular and clearly definable "women's issue," as could second wave feminists. Ednie Garrison echoes this point when she writes, "In the Third Wave, feminist collective consciousness may not necessarily manifest itself in a nationalized and highly mobilized social movement unified around a single goal or identity. At the moment, this hardly seems imaginable."[36] In fact, in its current manifestation, third wave feminism is more about textual and cultural production, local forms of activism, and a particular form of feminist consciousness than it is a large-scale social justice movement with unified goals.

In much of this contemporary writing, the third wave is celebrated for its more complicated, nuanced, and multifaceted understanding of women's experiences and political action—often in terms which contrast this new wave with the perceived simplistic nature of the monolithic second wave. Yet, at moments in this new writing, the inability to speak in a collective voice and for a unified goal is lamented. As Elizabeth Mitchell writes:

> The women of my mother's generation seemed given to this… communal effort, winning victories for the feminist movement, for their sisters, for their daughters. They had the comfort of knowing that what they fought for was needed by all members of their gender; sexual freedom, equal opportunity in the workplace, access to all the institutions of power. They also had more clear-cut antagonists to act against.[37]

Haunting Mitchell's passage is a sense of loss for what the third wave has missed out on: shared struggle, definable political goals, and targeted enemies. She seems to suggest that her generation lacks the clarity of purpose which was indicative of an earlier era. Other writers have described a similar sense of loss, as in one *Listen Up* contributor who writes, "I have always been upset that I missed the protests of the sixties and seventies. Lots of women in my generation have felt that there was no way to actively fight for our rights."[38] Adds Meg Daly in *Letters of Intent*: "We use our anger at our 'mothers' as an excuse for inertia and lack of focus. We're jealous that they got an exciting revolution and we got ... Bill Clinton?"[39] In this recurring motif, the third wave expresses a longing for a political movement to call its own. As Deborah L. Siegel points out, many third wave narratives "are compelled by nostalgia for an ideal of collectivity, the dream of a common language, which was foundational to certain strains of second wave feminism."[40] This new wave appears to lack any unifying objective, eliciting feelings of loss and disappointment over what our generation has missed out on.

In some of the third wave anthologies, one can see signs that younger feminists are beginning to move beyond their individual self-explorations of feminism toward some form of collectivity—albeit one skeptical of any easy or natural sisterhood between women. Take, for example, Joan Morgan's *When Chickenheads Come Home to Roost: My Life as Hip-Hop Feminist* (1999). As with other third wave writers, Morgan takes issue with what she perceives as dogmatic and overly prescriptive second wave feminism. Yet, like many third wave feminists of color, Morgan doesn't resort to defining feminism in solely individualistic terms, as Lehrman, Katie Roiphe, and other more conservative, and usually white, feminists have tended to do, but rather she tries to forge connections with her fellow African-American feminists, even when to do so is difficult and painful.[41] She closes her book with the following words to her readers:

> I know that ours has never been an easy relationship. Sistahood ain't sainthood. That nonsense about if women had power there would no wars is feminist delusion at best.... That being said, know that when it comes to sistahood, I am deadly serious about my commitment to you.... sistahood is critical to our mutual survival.[42]

Making sisterhood her own by infusing it with black slang, Morgan calls for a "sistahood" for a new generation, one committed to the "mutual survival" of African-American women. Rather than distancing herself from her generational peers, she concludes her book by arguing that some form of sisterhood—no matter how difficult—is essential to the future of feminism.

Morgan's point that sisterhood, or collective action, isn't easy has been repeated by other third wave writers in their call to mobilize a new generation. JeeYeun Lee, for example, writes: "This thing called 'feminism' takes a great deal of hard work, and I think this is one of the primary hallmarks of young feminists' activism today: We realize that coming together and working together are by no means natural or easy."[43] Second wave feminists have taught us the difficulties in working with other women on shared political goals; these are the lessons inherited by the third wave, the feminism that we grow up with "in the water." While a nostalgic longing may continue to exist for that clear and unifying agenda of the past—even if that vision of the past is itself a fiction—some third wave feminists have begun to insist that we need to work toward a communal vision of feminism in the present, one that acknowledges differences among women while simultaneously arguing for a shared political commitment. As Sarah Boonin argues in "Please —Stop Thinking about Tomorrow: Building a Feminist Movement on College Campuses for *Today*":

> While feminism does not need to—and should not—mean sameness, it does imply a certain philosophical and ideological connection. We share a commitment to the pursuit of equality. That common pursuit forms the basis of our community.... Unless we think of ourselves as a "we"—a community of students, activists, scholars, and national leaders—we can never be true partners in change.[44]

Boonin's words echo those of bell hooks twenty years earlier in *Feminist Theory: From Margin to Center* (1984). hooks argues that although feminism must speak for and about a diverse range of women and men, we nevertheless need a shared definition of feminism in order to move forward politically. hooks proposes the following definition: "Feminism is a struggle to end sexist oppression." As she argues, "Defined in this way, it is unlikely that women would join the feminist movement simply because we are biologically the same. A commitment to feminism so defined would demand that each participant acquire a critical political consciousness based on ideas and beliefs."[45] For third wave feminists, a sisterhood based on shared biology is an impossibility, in part because of the feminist theory passed down by hooks and others of her generation. Consequently, many third wavers have retreated from thinking of themselves as part of a "we" and instead have chosen to speak solely for themselves.[46] But if Boonin's call is any indication, perhaps a "we" can still be found in that shared commitment to equality, to ending sexist oppression—and all the interlocking forms of oppression that shape women's and men's experience—in the twenty-first century. Ideally, this "we" can encompass more than just the members of one generation. Built on the shared political goals across generations of feminists, this "we" has the possibility to transform third wave feminism from "merely" a generational stance taken by individuals to a critical political perspective that acknowledges diversity and differences within feminism while simultaneously stressing the need for collective action to affect social change.

NOTES

1. Jennifer Baumgardner and Amy Richards, *Manifesta: Young Women, Feminism, and the Future* (New York: Farrar, Straus and Giroux, 2000), 17.

2. Barbara Findlen, "Introduction," in *Listen Up: Voices from the Next Feminist Generation*, ed. Barbara Findlen (Seattle, WA: Seal Press, 1995), xii; emphasis in original.

3. Rene Denfeld, *The New Victorians: A Young Woman's Challenge to the Old Feminist Order* (New York: Warner Books, 1995), 2.

4. Including Barbara Findlen, ed., *Listen Up: Voices from the Next Feminist Generation* (Seattle, WA: Seal Press, 1995); Rebecca Walker, ed., *To Be Real: Telling the Truth and Changing the Face of Feminism* (New York: Anchor, 1995); Leslie Heywood and Jennifer Drake, eds., *Third Wave Agenda: Being Feminist, Doing Feminism* (Minneapolis: University of Minnesota Press, 1997); Ophira Edut, ed., *Adiós Barbie: Young Women Write About Body Image and Identity* (New York: Seal Press, 1998); Anna Bondoc and Meg Daly, eds., *Letters of Intent: Women Cross the Generations to Talk About Family, Work, Sex, Love and the Future of Feminism* (New York: Simon and Schuster, 1999); Daisy Hernández and Bushra Rehman, eds., *Colonize This! Young Women of Color on Today's Feminism* (New York: Seal Press, 2002); Rory Dicker and Alison Piepmeier, eds., *Catching a Wave: Reclaiming Feminism for the 21st Century* (Boston: Northeastern University Press, 2003).

5. For more on generational relationships between second and third wave feminists, see my *Not My Mother's Sister: Generational Conflict and Third-Wave Feminism* (Bloomington: Indiana University Press, 2004).

6. Elizabeth Mitchell, "An Odd Break with the Human Heart," in *To Be Real: Telling the Truth and Changing the Face of Feminism*, ed. Rebecca Walker (New York: Anchor Books, 1995), 55.

7. Commenting on this point, Katha Pollitt recently asked, "When did sisterhood become mother-daughterhood?" Pollitt in Emily Gordon and Katha Pollitt, "Does Your Generation Resent Up-and-Coming Young Women?" in *Letters of Intent*, 31.

8. Leslie Heywood and Jennifer Drake, "Introduction," in *Third Wave Agenda*, 11.

9. Jennifer Baumgardner in Katha Pollitt and Jennifer Baumgardner, "Afterword: A Correspondence Between Katha Pollitt and Jennifer Baumgardner," in *Catching a Wave*, 316.

10. Jennifer Baumgardner and Amy Richards seem hopeful in this regard when they write that such autobiographical anthologies provide "the foundation of the personal ethics upon which a political women's movement will be built." Baumgardner and Richards, *Manifesta*, 20.

11. An exception can be found in *Catching a Wave*, where editors Rory Dicker and Alison Piepmeier explicitly describe their anthology's format as following the second wave principle of consciousness raising in order to move the reader from personal experience to theory and action. See Dicker and Piepmeier, "Introduction," in *Catching a Wave*, 3–28.

12. Gina Dent, "Missionary Position," in *To Be Real*, 64.

13. Rebecca Walker, "Becoming the Third Wave," *Ms. Magazine*, (January/February 1992): 41; emphasis added.

14. Marcelle Karp, "Herstory: Girl on Girls," in *The Bust Guide to the New Girl Order*, ed. Marcelle Karp and Debbie Stoller (New York: Penguin Books, 1999), 310.

15. Naomi Wolf, *Fire with Fire: The New Female Power and How It Will Change the 21st Century* (New York: Random House, 1993), xix.

16. Karen Lehrman, *The Lipstick Proviso: Women, Sex and Power in the Real World* (New York: Anchor Books, 1997), 14, 5.

17. Ibid., 156, 154.

18. Dicker and Piepmeier, "Introduction," 17.

19. Ibid., 18.

20. Redstockings, "Redstockings Manifesto," in *Sisterhood is Powerful: An Anthology of Writings from the Women's Liberation Movement*, ed. Robin Morgan (New York: Vintage Books, 1970), 535.

21. Ednie Kaeh Garrison, "U.S. Feminism-Grrrl Style! Young (Sub)Cultures and the Technologies of the Third Wave," *Feminist Studies* 26, no. 1 (Spring 2000): 145.

22. Bushra Rehman and Daisy Hernández, "Introduction," in *Colonize This! Young Women of Color on Today's Feminism*, eds. Daisy Hernández and Bushra Rehman (New York: Seal Press, 2002), xxiv. Paula Kamen's landmark 1991 study of Generation X's attitudes about feminism also points to the important role of feminists of color. Writing when the third wave was just in its infancy, Kamen notes, "The authors with the most undeniable influence on my generation … are women of color." Kamen, *Feminist Fatale: Voices from the "Twentysomething" Generation Explore the Future of the "Women's Movement"* (New York: Donald I. Fine, 1991), 17.

23. Linda Garber, *Identity Poetics: Race, Class, and the Lesbian-Feminist Roots of Queer Theory* (New York: Columbia University Press, 2001), 4.

24. JeeYeun Lee, "Beyond Bean Counting," in *Listen Up*, 211.

25. Findlen, "Introduction," xiv.

26. Lee, "Beyond Bean Counting," 210; emphasis in original.

27. Wolf, *Fire with Fire*, 208.

28. Dicker and Piepmeier, "Introduction," 10.

29. For more on the ways in which second wave feminists of color seem unable to represent second wave feminism as a whole in third wave discourse, see my *Not My Mother's Sister*.

30. Denfeld, *The New Victorians*, 263.

31. Lehrman, *The Lipstick Proviso*, 178.

32. Kamen, *Feminist Fatale*, 364.

33. Allyson Mitchell, Lisa Bryn Rundle, and Lara Karaian, eds., *Turbo Chicks: Talking Young Feminisms* (Toronto: Sumach Press, 2001), 352.

34. See Emi Koyama, "The Transfeminist Manifesto," in *Catching a Wave*, 244–59. Interestingly, Koyama's essay is written in the collective "we" voice (speaking as and for trans women) and, as its title suggests, is not an autobiographical essay but a call to arms in the spirit of the earlier second wave manifestos. See also Hines, chapter 3.

35. Dicker and Piepmeier, "Introduction," 10. As Daisy Hernández and Bushra Rehman write in their introduction to *Colonize This!*: "We are living in a world for which old forms of activism are not enough and today's activism is about creating coalitions between communities." Rehman and Hernandez, "Introduction," xxi.

36. Garrison, "U.S. Feminism-Grrrl Style!" 164.

37. Mitchell, "An Odd Break with the Human Heart," 52.

38. Melissa Silverstein, "WAC-ing Operation Rescue," in *Listen Up*, 241.

39. Meg Daly in Anna Bondoc and Meg Daly, "Introduction," in *Letters of Intent*, 3. See also Tayari Jones's letter in *Letters of Intent*: Comparing herself to her parents' involvement in the Civil Rights movement, Jones writes, "I, on the other hand, have risked nothing. I feel as though I am assigned as the keeper of a flame that I have not fanned." Jones in Tayari Jones and Pearl Cleage, "Which Come First, Our Paychecks or Our Principles?" in *Letters of Intent*, 37.

40.   Deborah Siegel, "The Legacy of the Personal: Generating Theory in Feminism's Third Wave," *Hypatia: A Journal of Feminist Philosophy* 12 (Summer 1997): 58–59.

41.   See Lehrman, *The Lipstick Proviso*; Katie Roiphe, *The Morning After: Sex, Fear, and Feminism on Campus* (Boston, MA: Little, Brown, 1993).

42.   Joan Morgan, *When Chickenheads Come Home to Roost: My Life as Hip-Hop Feminist* (New York: Simon and Schuster, 1999), 231–32. For more on black feminist texts, see Springer, chapter 1.

43.   Lee, "Beyond Bean Counting," 211.

44.   Sarah Boonin, "Please—Stop Thinking about Tomorrow: Building a Feminist Movement on College Campuses for *Today*," in *Catching a Wave*, 149.

45.   bell hooks, *Feminist Theory: From Margin to Center* (Boston: South End Press, 1984), 24.

46.   As Sara Evans remarks, third wavers "never experienced feminism as a sisterhood of sameness. Indeed they stumbled over saying 'We.'" Evans, *Tidal Wave: How Women Changed America at Century's End* (New York: Free Press, 2003), 230.

6

BRIDGING THE WAVES:
SEX AND SEXUALITY IN A SECOND WAVE
ORGANIZATION

Stephanie Gilmore

In May 2002, the Veteran Feminists of America—a group composed largely of activists from the second wave—sponsored a conference at Barnard College, New York, to honor second wave feminist fiction and nonfiction authors. This event erupted into a rousing debate over the past and future of feminism—something the organizers had not antici-pated. Several panelists raised questions about women's feminist con-sciousness in the twenty-first century. Suggesting that what "we had back then was earthshaking," Susan Brownmiller opined, "I don't hear strong, clear feminist voices today. I don't see women coming up with new theories," while Marilyn French said she feared that young women did not possess a feminist political consciousness. Letty Cottin Pogre-bin perhaps drew the greatest distinction between second and third wave feminists: "We were action-oriented in a public, political context. We had to challenge laws, change patterns, alter behavior. Being able to bare your midriff ... is fine as an expression, but it doesn't mean things are going to change." Of course, not everyone representing second wave feminism agreed. Erica Jong, author of the sex-positive novel *Fear of Flying*, posited, "because of our books, we changed society. Without

Fear of Flying, there would be no 'Sex in the City.' My daughter wouldn't feel empowered." She added proudly, "we have produced a generation of uppity women who feel entitled."[1]

Taking the stance of "us" versus "them" is not only the province of second wave feminists. For example, some third wave activists have suggested, in direct opposition to Pogrebin, that the younger generation of feminists, unlike its second wave predecessor, is action oriented. In Ellen Neuborne's words, "the theory of equality has been well fought for by our mothers. Now let's talk about how to talk, how to work, how to fight sexism on the ground, in our lives."[2] Some, such as Barbara Findlen, see the generational struggle much like a classic mother–daughter one (see also Henry, chapter 5). However, she suggests that third wave feminists "are not 'daughters' rebelling against the old-style politics of their 'mothers.'… If there is a troublesome legacy from the feminism that comes before, it's the burden of high expectations—of both ourselves and the world."[3]

Feminists who identify with the third wave eschew identity politics that they name as "the" problem with movements, feminist and otherwise, before theirs. In particular, they resist the idea that a single feature of one's identity defines one's political philosophy. In Danzy Senna's words, "it is not my 'half-breed' lipstick-carrying feminist muddle that is too complicated, but identity politics which are too simplistic, stuck in the realm of the body, not the realm of belief and action.… Breaking free of identity politics has not resulted in political apathy, but rather it has given me an awareness of the complexity and ambiguity of the world we have inherited—and the very real power relations we must transform."[4]

So in an all-too-familiar way, feminists drew the lines between "us" and "them" at the Barnard conference. Some young women in the audience answered challenges to whether or not third wave feminists are "feminist enough" by countering that the second wave generation is "so preoccupied with its achievements that it's become blind to the real efforts and strides being made by the third wave of feminist organizers." Jennifer Baumgardner, coauthor of *Manifesta*, stated, "because the work doesn't look the same, they don't want to see it." Kalpana Krishnamurthy, then codirector of the Third Wave Foundation, echoed Baumgardner's sentiment: "I think that the impact of the feminist movement was in helping women to achieve a voice. Now, we are articulating that voice in a multiplicity of ways."[5] This debate illustrates how feminists across generations are focused on articulating the differences between the second and the third waves.

While we make "waves" as a way to separate ourselves from one another, we can also build bridges in an effort to dispel myths and find common ground. In this chapter, I highlight some of the activities among members of one feminist organization—the National Organization for Women (NOW)—to document cooperation and continuities between the second and third waves. Founded in 1966 and still active in the early twenty-first century, NOW was one of the first second wave feminist organizations and has survived into the era of third wave feminism. In the late 1960s and early 1970s, chapters began to form, creating at once a national civil rights organization for women and a local force demanding feminist change in women's day-to-day lives. Its members have always been engaged in coalition building, especially at the local level; they openly sought men in the ranks of the organization's membership; and, especially apparent in some chapters, they have had a diverse membership of feminists in terms of class, sexuality, religion, and race.[6] Members were not always successful in representing "all women" as they sought to do, but they pursued a variety of issues that reflected their diverse interests and membership. Because local chapters often grappled with issues that did not always appear prominently at the national level, I analyze NOW's activism at both the national level and among the organization's local chapters. Although it cannot and does not represent the whole of second wave feminism, NOW's history offers a way to rethink divisions among feminists. I do not propose to dismiss differences between the waves in favor of continuities; I propose, however, that second and third wave feminists have more in common than we all might think.

While third wave feminism addresses a host of issues—and like second wave feminism, is hardly monolithic—sex and sexuality resonate with feminists across the generations and provide a useful place to explore continuities among second and third wave feminists. Scholars and activists alike often assume that NOW was concerned only with equality under the law; that issues of sex and sexuality—abortion rights, sexual autonomy, and prostitutes' rights—were the province of radical feminists. But as NOW chapter members and national leaders led the feminist fight for reproductive freedom, struggled with lesbian rights, sought to protect prostitutes on the job, and advertised the fact that they "did it" without shame or fear, they fomented sexual—and feminist—revolution.

REPRODUCTIVE FREEDOM

Reproductive rights have become a symbol of women's freedom and equality in the United States, but most directly and tangibly affect women of childbearing age. Access to abortion and birth control—two ways in which women gain control of individual sexuality—was on many feminists' political agendas, where it firmly remains a third wave feminist issue. As Rebecca Farmer, a self-identified young feminist from Washington, D.C., wrote, "As post-*Roe* kids, we have our activist foremothers to thank for paving the path toward reproductive freedom…. From here on, we're going to protect what we've got and we're going to keep fighting for more."[7] To keep up the fight, third wave feminists descended upon Washington, D.C., in April 2004 for the March for Women's Lives, arriving from cities across the country by bus, plane, and car to demonstrate how reproductive rights is a meaningful issue for young women.

Women and men still fight for control over their sexual selves—a feminist fight that began as early as 1967 with the National Organization for Women. At its first national conference in 1967, NOW members outlined the group's national agenda in an eight-point "Bill of Rights." In addition to equal employment and educational opportunities, issues for which NOW is best known, the group advocated "the right of women to control their own reproductive lives." Such a stance, along with a national focus on equity in rape laws and civil protection for lesbians, cost the group both members and support, revealing early on the diverse opinions among second wave feminists. For example, Elizabeth Boyer, a founding member of NOW, agreed with many feminists who felt that reproductive freedom was too radical an issue and left the group in 1968 to found Women's Equity Action League (WEAL), a group that defined itself as the "conservative NOW."[8] However, by 1972, WEAL leaders also advocated reproductive choice as a woman's fundamental right after they realized that their moderate stance yielded them little respect and influence.[9]

NOW members continued to call for complete repeal of abortion laws in the United States and unlimited access to birth control information and devices. On this issue, second wave feminists joined a preexisting movement calling for the repeal of abortion laws, one that originated in the early 1960s among doctors and lawyers who wanted to allow abortions for such specific reasons as a threat to a woman's health or a severely damaged fetus. But feminists quickly took up the cause, and NOW was one of the first second wave feminist groups to assert the primacy of reproductive freedom, insisting on total repeal of abortion laws so that women could control their reproductive lives and, in a larger context, their sexuality. At a time when there was little consensus on what "reproductive rights" meant, NOW was at the forefront of demanding complete access to abortion and birth control for all women.[10]

Although NOW adopted reproductive freedom as a platform within its first year, many scholars credit short-lived radical feminist groups almost exclusively with bringing attention to such sexual politics.[11] To many observers, NOW seemingly followed the lead of radical feminists on sex-related issues.[12] However, NOW members, both at the national level and in its chapters, had been working diligently for years to repeal state laws controlling women's access to abortion or birth control. In 1969, the New York NOW chapter formed New Yorkers for Abortion Law Repeal with the goal of mobilizing public opinion and lobbying the legislature.[13] In 1972, the Columbus, Ohio, chapter of NOW convened women and men from across the state to discuss the state's abortion laws. After a morning of workshops on the medical, legal, and personal aspects of abortion, attendees debated the values of attempting reform or repeal. Ultimately deciding on repeal, the group, which became a coalition called the Ohio Abortion Alliance, argued for the creation of a "realistic law that will protect the female's right to make her own decision with medical guidelines to protect her health and safety, and legal guidelines to protect her financially."[14]

In Memphis, for example, NOW members teamed up with feminists from Planned Parenthood to insure women's access to clinics. From 1973, when women could obtain abortions legally, feminists often escorted women into buildings while subjecting themselves to verbal and physical assault, demonstrating the extent to which these feminists acted with little regard to themselves in order to insure the safety and security of others. Working in concert with medical doctors, lawyers, and concerned citizens, NOW members in cities across the country pursued a woman's right to choose, one of the rallying cries of the then-emerging rhetoric of reproductive rights and women's power to determine their own sexuality.

That NOW embraced reproductive rights as a feminist issue is hardly surprising. Nor is the fact that its members and leadership were enmeshed in legal battles to ensure women's control over their sexuality through reproductive freedom. After the 1973 Supreme Court decision *Roe v. Wade*, which decriminalized first-trimester abortions and specified conditions under which second- and third-trimester abortions could be legally obtained, NOW feminists fought emerging, so-called prolife organizations that sought to dismantle *Roe*. Opponents to abortion mobilized effectively to whittle away at the *Roe* decision—both in the courts and in public protests and demonstrations—where NOW confronted them.

Since the mid-1970s, NOW feminists have been able to build upon a legacy of liberal activism, lobbying legislators and building coalitions with such national prochoice and pro-birth-control groups as NARAL. Juxtaposing symbols of benevolence and legal behavior against those of terrorism and zealotry (how NOW defined antiabortion activists), NOW leaders and spokespersons framed the debate around abortion as one of women's legal rights.[15] National NOW, with its separate Legal Defense and Education Fund and Political Action Committee, has been a consistent and powerful force in the courts. In addition to writing amicus curiae briefs in the cases of *Webster v. Reproductive Health Services* (1989) and *Planned Parenthood of Southeastern Pennsylvania v. Casey* (1992), the organization sued for and won the right to use federal antiracketeering laws against persons who organized others to shut down clinics through force and violence, which gave feminists greater opportunities to protect themselves and women seeking abortions.[16]

Third wave feminists may debate what sort of abortion women should demand—Inga Muscio, for example, argues from her personal experience with aspiration abortion that we should "let the fundamentalist dickheads burn all those vacuum cleaners to the ground" in favor of natural abortifacients and emmenagogues.[17] But abortion, birth control, and reproductive freedom remain high on many third wave feminists' agendas. As Jennifer Baumgardner and Amy Richards argue in *Manifesta*, "it is not feminism's goal to control any woman's fertility, only to free each woman to control her own."[18] Third wave feminists continue the fight for reproductive freedoms, a struggle that second wave feminists embraced—and inherited from many of their first wave predecessors.[19]

SEXUAL AUTONOMY

Reproductive freedom is one facet of the sexual politics that defined the second wave and are integral to the third wave. Young feminists are redefining sexual liberation—continuing the fight for access to birth control, abortion, and sex education is but one example. Many are also claiming "queer" as a socially constructed sexual identity rather than an identity seemingly fixed in nature or defined by sexual object choice ("lesbian," "heterosexual"). Rather than identify with a singular sexual identity, many third wave feminists embrace many at the same time, such as Anastasia Higginbotham, who identifies herself as a "bisexual lesbian" because "it just works for me."[20] This complicated individual identification, along with such terms as *queer,* suggests how third wave feminists are reclaiming the inherent dignity of such terminology, in part, as Baumgardner and Richards suggest, to challenge homophobia and heterosexism in feminism.[21] It is also a meaningful way that third wave feminists reclaim sexual autonomy.

Second wave feminists, such as those on the panel at the Barnard conference (who *were* young feminists in the 1960s and 1970s), also grappled with how to understand and define sexual autonomy. Some second wave feminists articulated such liberation as freedom from sex. As Robin Morgan wrote, "I claim that rape exists any time sexual intercourse occurs when it has not been initiated by the woman, out of her own genuine affection and desire." New York NOW founder and first president Ti-Grace Atkinson went further, declaring "all sex is reactionary" and suggested that women were obliged to "learn to repress their sexuality."[22] Of course, not all feminists agreed with Morgan and Atkinson; others argued that women could, should, and did pursue ways to be sexually active outside of the context of oppression. Some, such as Ann Koedt, dismantled "the myth of the vaginal orgasm," while others, including Radicalesbians, who issued their manifesto, "The Woman-Identified Woman," argued that women should forego sex with men for the more politically charged sex with women.[23] Women involved in NOW were also engaged in the debates about women's sexuality, particularly over who was an appropriate sexual partner and what was feminist sex.

A survey of NOW's history with lesbians and same-sex sexuality, for example, goes far beyond the scope of this piece, but the "lavender menace" episode reveals the extent to which sex and sexuality were vital, and contentious, issues for NOW members (and feminists in general). In 1969, NOW president Betty Friedan claimed that lesbians in NOW represented a "lavender menace" because their presence threatened the political efficacy of the organization. When, in 1970, some NOW members took the stage at the second Congress to Unite Women in New York City wearing lavender T-shirts bearing Betty Friedan's scornful words, the organization was thrust into a feminist spotlight for being hostile to lesbians. Rita Mae Brown and other women left the organization of their own volition; other lesbian officers of the New York chapter of NOW were not reelected to their positions, which some referred to as the "purges." However, at the same time, the Los Angeles chapter of NOW debated a resolution acknowledging lesbian rights as women's rights. Following the federated structure and the formalized rules of the organization, members moved the successful resolution to the state level, and then to the western regional level, where it was passed at each stage. It was then introduced at the 1971 national meeting, where the membership acknowledged by an overwhelming majority that lesbians' rights were women's rights.[24] By most scholarly accounts, NOW's debate about lesbianism was over—after the passage of this resolution, "at least within NOW, the issue ceased to be a source of extreme division...."[25]

Of course, implementing inclusivity was much more complicated, and lesbians did face many struggles in the organization. In some places, lesbians' issues were not on the organization's agenda—chapters initiated task forces to work on issues of particular interest to members in the local group; as interest faded, so did the task force. So, in Columbus, Ohio, for example, the chapter did not have a lesbian rights task force until 1985 because many lesbians in the city found feminist community in other places, such as the Women's Action Collective or Women's Studies at Ohio State University.[26]

In other places, such as Memphis, Tennessee, members broadened the chapter's agenda to include public and political activism of and for lesbians. Some members challenged the chapter's near-exclusive focus on issues of rape and employment discrimination. In response to Johnette Shane, who wrote a letter to the newsletter editor expressing feelings of alienation because the chapter seemed narrowly focused on these two issues, chapter president Carole Hensen offered that while time, commitment, and money forced the chapter to focus on "the greatest good for the greatest number, ... this does NOT mean that any endeavor, interest, or need will ever be deliberately discouraged.... This is your organization—it exists to do what you or any other member wants it to do."[27] Shaping NOW to fit their needs, Shane and the women who joined the Sexuality and Lesbianism Task Force publicly merged the identities of "lesbian" and "feminist" quite successfully. The task force hosted dances and picnics during the city's Gay Pride weeks throughout the 1970s and offered consciousness-raising groups for women. In 1976, the task force opened the first gay switchboard in Memphis, Tennessee, a telephone hotline that offered both crisis intervention and information on lesbian and gay community activities. It supported the switchboard for three years, when it turned management of the phone line to the Memphis Gay Coalition.[28] By the end of the 1970s, Memphis NOW, through the work of the task force, had secured its public identity, at least in part, as part of the gay and lesbian community by building coalitions and finding common cause across differences of sexuality.[29] Much like third wave feminists of the twenty-first century, who do not separate sexual identity and practice from other facets of identity, second wave feminists in NOW connected their activism to local gay and lesbian liberation, actively grappling with complexity and multiple identities. The face-to-face context of chapter members' actions provides a different and more complicated perspective on second wave feminists' interactions with one another—one that cannot be reduced to particular moments in NOW's history.

Lesbianism, then, did not tear apart NOW and second wave feminism. NOW feminists debated issues of sex and sexuality openly; while some members did leave, others stayed, and still more joined the group. In places such as Memphis, Tennessee in the heyday of the second wave from 1971 to 1982, NOW was the only feminist organization in town. Many women joined NOW to find a feminist community; to them, it represented much of the diversity the city had to offer.[30] In other places, the NOW chapter was less "out" in terms of supporting and embracing lesbian issues as feminist ones. In Columbus, for example, there were organizational options for feminists seeking lesbian community and activism. Although NOW was often as "radical" as the Women's Action Collective, they were perceived as "straight" to WAC's more "lesbian" identity.[31] In contrast to both of these locations, women of color, lesbians, and their allies left San Francisco NOW in 1974 because the chapter's leadership was "racist and homophobic."[32] Rather than join the myriad feminist groups the city had to offer, the women formed the Golden Gate chapter of NOW, a chapter that was in existence from 1974 into the early 1980s. (As an alternative, the women might have surrendered NOW membership in favor of concurrent membership in the other feminist groups in the city. Membership overlap was not uncommon and was one of the ways that women forged a strong and diverse feminist community.) Such examples highlight differences among chapters with regard to sexuality and sexual orientation. Throughout the 1970s, women in NOW expressed their sexual selves in a variety of formats. In speak-outs, they talked about being raped and how they felt powerless both at the time of the attack and in dealing with a legal system that further victimized women. As one might expect, they worked to strengthen rape legislation, lobbying Congress and state legislatures, and building common cause with other feminist groups. In Memphis, they "took back the night" in a march commemorating the fifty-fifth anniversary of women's suffrage—another example that mirrors the experience of feminists across the country, both in and beyond the organizational boundaries of NOW. But they also worked within the political system, creating in the space of five years (1973–78) a Comprehensive Rape Crisis Program that orchestrated police, hospitals, and the legal system in ways that would treat women who had been raped with dignity and respect instead of shame. What began as a grassroots issue became "an integral part of the city government."[33] This example illustrates how NOW members worked both within and beyond the political system to create safe spaces for women in their particular cities. Far more than just rhetoric, the actions of this one chapter are but one example of how NOW fought sexism at the grassroots level, indicating how second wave feminists merged theory and practice.

While members of NOW across the country did challenge the power that accompanied rape, pornography, and sexual relations between women and men, they did not eschew sex altogether. In chapters across the country, feminists in NOW spoke openly about the pleasures of "doing it." In April 1973, for example, Columbus NOW chapter secretary Sandra Stout published a short poem in the chapter newsletter:

Man, oh, Man—I do not need your name
Fame I have in my own name
With my name yours it would be lost—
And at such cost:
So I can do your laundry
your dishes,
your kinky sex wishes.
Man, oh, Man—I do not need your name,
your laundry,
your dishes—
But once in a while I'll do your kinky sex wishes.[34]

As the poem suggests, women such as Stout felt free from housework and the obligation of taking a man's name, presumably in marriage—a sentiment many feminists echoed. At the same time, she also felt free enough to want kinky sex with him.

While we cannot know what Stout meant by "kinky sex," she was clearly interested in sex and sexuality, a theme that runs throughout NOW's history, especially at the local and state levels. In 1973, California NOW held its second annual convention in San Diego. Alongside lists of events, task forces, and photos of NOW members in action were advertisements for *Playgirl* and *Venus* magazines. The *Playgirl* ad was the magazine's November 1973 cover, which featured a naked man and woman smiling at one another while in a close embrace. In addition to a "four-page foldout" of "our Man for November," the cover promised that its pages would feature an article entitled "Nursing—Modeling: Myth vs. Reality." The *Venus* advertisement was also its magazine's November 1973 cover. The young, heterosexual couple are clothed, but are about to engage in a romantic kiss. In addition to "November's Centerfold," *Venus* featured an article on "Erotic Films—Produced By Women, Defended by Linda Lovelace, Viewed by the Hip Elitist." Superimposed on the cover (but not covering the couple or the promised contents of the issue) was a salute to California NOW, which lists the *Venus* editorial board—all women and all NOW members.

NOW members clearly solicited such sponsorship, likely with the goal of embracing sex and sexuality as feminist issues. Indeed, the California NOW task force on sexuality and lesbianism stated that its goal was to "expand the understanding and awareness of society to the wide range of female sexual expressions and lifestyles."[35] NOW members were having open and frank sex-positive discussions about sex and sexuality and did not necessarily fear repercussions for doing so—the types of conversations in which third wave feminists engage and encourage. One important cultural task third wave feminists have undertaken is reclaiming the derisive terms that accompany women's sexuality. "Cunt," "slut," and "bitch" take on different and positive meanings in the hands of such authors as Inga Muscio, Leora Tanenbaum, Elizabeth Wurtzel, and the editors of *Bitch* magazine.[36] Baumgardner and Richards also redefine such words in their "*Manifesta's* Lexicon," which they penned after some readers challenged their seemingly casual usage of such words that some second wave feminists found sexist. By their definition, "a slut is a woman whose sexuality belongs to no man."[37] Feminists across the waves continue to debate issues of power in pornography and express outrage and speak out against the perpetuation of rape and abuse against women in American society, and make meaningful and dignified the variety of sexual practices and debate the terms with which to describe them.

PROSTITUTES' RIGHTS

In addition to proclaiming their own sexual identities, needs, and desires, many third wave feminists have also joined the prostitutes' rights movement. Some third wave feminists' perspectives on prostitution contend that a woman's sexuality, even in the context of sex work, ultimately belongs to herself. As Emi Koyama wrote in *Instigations from the Whore Revolution: A Third-Wave Feminist Response to the Sex Work "Controversy,"* feminism and prostitutes' rights are integrated movements that share the philosophy that all people should enjoy rights to dignity, respect, and job safety—issues feminists have fought for in a variety of contexts. Rather than chastise prostitutes for getting paid for sex, Koyama and other feminists in the contemporary prostitutes' rights movement recognize and criticize the economic and cultural forces that shape people's labors, including sex work, and constrain individual's choices.[38]

Linkages between prostitutes and feminists are not exclusive to the third wave. In the 1970s, NOW members also debated, and ultimately advocated, prostitutes' rights. Such rhetoric and activism indicates the extent to which NOW feminists were concerned with complexities and multiplicity in women's lives and articulating a feminist voice that would attend to the overlapping facets of women's lives. This awareness of and attention to prostitution indicates that, for NOW members, sex was not only a matter of pleasure or danger, but also an issue of women's material reality and economic well-being. They first raised challenges about the ways in which female prostitutes and male johns were treated differently both legally and culturally. When city leaders in San Francisco proposed to curb what seemed to be rampant prostitution by arresting whores, San Francisco NOW member Del Martin (who later became a member of the national board) demanded full equality under the law, recommending to city mayor Joseph Alioto that "no woman will be prosecuted under the law without the same sentence being given to the male partner."[39]

Beyond legal equality, however, NOW members in a variety of places debated the issue of prostitution as work. Couching her argument in the rhetoric of physical exploitation, Tish Sommers of the Berkeley chapter of NOW urged the organization to go on the record in opposition to "both present discriminatory treatment of prostitutes under law, and so-called 'legalized prostitution,' which is only a mask for greater exploitation of women's bodies." She also insisted that the group end all laws "aimed at government (male) control of women's sexual life" and "fight for real job alternatives for women, which will make prostitution a less desirable economic solution."[40] Her argument suggests that prostitution is only about men's sexual satisfaction and that women only choose it because they have no other alternatives. But if not a sex-positive perspective, Sommers, like many others in the group, discussed prostitution in the context of gender dynamics, labor, and sexuality, recognizing these as interrelated facets in women's lives.

The national organization adopted a different perspective—in February 1973, NOW went on record as being in favor of removing "all laws relating to the act of prostitution per se, and as an interim measure, favors the decriminalization of prostitution." [41] Rather than condemn female prostitutes, NOW worked with groups such as Call Off Your Old Tired Ethics, a prostitution-rights organization (COYOTE), to create feminist solutions to the problems that accompanied prostitution rather than to work to eradicate it altogether, in part because some NOW members approached prostitution as an occupation as well as a sexual identity.[42] One particularly vile issue in the eyes of NOW feminists was the legal requirement that prostitutes must be tested and treated for venereal disease (VD). On "Mayday 1973," COYOTE chairmadam Margo St. James issued a press statement in which she lambasted the current San Francisco city administrators for "coercing prostitutes into unnecessary treatment for VD" because the seemingly sole purpose of this move was "to protect the innocent wives." If female prostitutes were going to be quarantined, St. James intimated that "the husbands should also be deemed promiscuous and at least examined and quarantined as the women are." Furthermore, "VD [should] be regarded, not as a crime but rather as a 'mechanical defect,' much like the highway patrol regards defective autos, needing only to be signed off by the proper authority upon presentation of repair."[43] Venereal disease was certainly a dangerous aspect of sex and likely affected prostitutes disproportionately by virtue of potential exposure to higher numbers of men who might be infected. Such feminists as St. James focused less on the danger of sex and more on the realities of the ways in which such diseases are spread.

Situating prostitution firmly in the context of women's labor and connecting it to the safety and protection of women's bodies, the Nevada chapter of NOW undertook a study of prostitution in their home state, the only one to license prostitution. While some lawmakers argued that licensing "resolved [the state's] prostitution 'problem,'" the NOW chapter argued that it did not protect the women as workers: "to wit: no limitation on the 'house cut' of their salaries, no restriction on the length of their working hours; even no assurance that they can collect their earnings." Moreover, the licensing law "effectively relegates the prostitute to the position of slave to the owner and opens the situation to oppressive extra-legal restrictions which may demoralize the women ... a strictly controlled and confined environment [and] denial of the women's right to refuse or accept clients or to perform any requested services." Echoing Margo St. James's concerns about testing whores for venereal diseases, the chapter also noted that, under the state law, "health restrictions require examination and treatment for venereal disease of only the prostitutes and not of their customers," making the elimination of sexually transmitted diseases impossible and subjecting women to further physical risk.[44]

Beyond working together to raise challenges about the ways in which female prostitutes and johns are treated differently, NOW feminists also analyzed prostitution in the context of structural economic and political forces. In September 1973, the Western Regional Conference of NOW issued the first call for a national "task force or committee on laws affecting prostitution to develop information and action programs concerning prostitution."[45] Underscoring the intricacy of this issue, NOW members debated how to think about and understand prostitution, forcing the membership, and society at large, to think about the interconnectedness of race, gender, class, and sexuality. Seattle-King County NOW chapter copresident Jean Withers indicated that "formation of a National Task Force on Prostitution will also indicate NOW's deep and continuing concern for the poor and the minority women who are prostitutes. It is these women, too poor to enter the less overt forms of prostitution (such as call girls), who become street-walkers. As such, they are most often the victims of customer brutality and repeated police harassment and arrest."[46] For Withers and like-minded NOW members, race, sexuality, class, and gender were inter-locking social systems that operated simultaneously to create different living situations for prostitutes—and all women. Prostitution, then, was another important battlefront in the "sex wars" that raged in the 1970s and early 1980s.[47]

Sommers clearly believed that prostitution led to the sexual objecti-fication of women; others in NOW argued that prostitutes must be protected as on-the-job workers. This debate illustrates that prostitu-tion was, and is, a complicated issue on which there will likely never be feminist consensus. However, NOW members pursued a feminist per-spective on prostitution, one that illustrates the complexity of the issue and the realities of women's lived experiences. Such activism indicates the breadth of NOW's reach, especially at the local level, and highlights how its membership, along with other feminists in the second wave, wrangled with the "nexus of work and sex"[48] in women's lives.

CONCLUSION

Turning attention to activism around sex and sexuality among NOW members during the heyday of second wave feminism highlights one of what may be many threads of continuity between second and third wave feminists. The historical episodes sketched here reveal that NOW and so-called liberal feminism was not monolithic. Indeed, it was, and is, perhaps more compatible with the third wave than we might think. As Rory Dicker and Alison Piepmeier state in their introduction to *Catching a Wave*: "Although there are conflicts between the genera-tions—second wavers may see third wavers as more concerned with image than with material realities, and younger feminists may see older feminists as essentializing gender and unconcerned with diversity — there is far more continuity than discord between the two waves."[49] And much of third wave feminists' activism resembles, in practice and theory, that of the second wave. On college campuses across the nation, young feminists continue to "take back the night." They work at rape crisis centers (in many cases, the same ones second wave feminists founded), escort women seeking abortions into clinics, and criticize the still-rampant sexism in the media. They still grapple with the politics of—and the acts that define—women's sexuality, delineating it not along the lines of heterosexual and lesbian, but straight, queer, and trans. They enroll in the women's studies programs that second wave feminists fought so hard to establish—in fact, they are demanding more classes on college campuses and some are earning doctorates in women's studies. Guerilla Girls, Riot Grrrls, and feminist rap music may be a face and sound of feminism that does not resonate with some second wave feminists, but they build upon a history of merging creativity and feminist protest. Their second wave predecessors are the women who orchestrated the Miss America protest in 1968, who founded Olivia Records, and produced such artists as Meg Christensen, Tret Fure, and Alix Dobkin, and who joined the Chicago Women's Liberation Rock Band.[50]

Rather than rescue second wave feminists in the eyes of their third wave counterparts, I suggest instead that we have to recognize how complex and diverse this movement both is and was. Continuities do not supplant differences, to be sure, but they do provide a sense of commonality and a history that has been ignored. When we focus only on the differences, we risk losing potential and vital allies in the feminist fight for equality. We certainly will still see differences and delineations—feminists across the ages have fought for the ability to articulate one's self-identity and "feminisms" will remain the more accurate way to talk about the variety of collective efforts to improve the status of women. However, we can also enjoy the strength that comes from diversity and multiplicity, adding age to the mix.

Such a thesis is not to ignore third wave feminists' laments that second wave feminists are not listening. As Rebecca Walker poignantly stated, "constantly measuring up to some cohesive, fully down-for-the-feminist-cause identity without contradictions and messiness and lusts for power and luxury items is not a fun and easy task."[51] The comments at the Barnard conference which open this chapter suggest that Walker is right and it is difficult to live up to what may be an unattainable standard that some second wave feminists set for the term *feminist*. Calling attention to the many battles second wave feminists in NOW fought, however, underscores the idea that the differences between "us" and "them" are, in some ways, only as sharp as we want them to be.

Writing feminist history of the second wave also has greater implications. In *Manifesta*, Jennifer Baumgardner and Amy Richards wrote that "because of schools' failure to teach even recent women's history and because of generational tension, many young women are more likely to know the media's image of the movement than the women who actually lived it."[52] This failure of the schools and the apparent success of generational tensions have led to misunderstandings and oversimplifications of the second wave. These misunderstandings undermine progress by neglecting analysis of how we continue to build a movement, in part, upon the activism that has come before us. Scholars have emphasized division and conflict in social movements to point to their demise—but feminism is not dead and we must continue to examine how activists have worked and continue to work together.

Third wave feminists rightly point out that they do not inhabit the same world as second wave feminists did—as a result, their feminism is different. But by continuing to explore continuities—the ongoing struggle for women's sexual freedom is but one—we can avoid such oversimplifications about the movement of which we are all a part. More to the point, we can illuminate ways in which we can find common ground and work together in spite of, and because of, differences in age, perspectives on sexual freedom, lipstick color, and midriff exposure.

ACKNOWLEDGMENTS

I wish to thank Leila J. Rupp, Anne Collinson, Cynthia Harrison, Sheila Tobias, Susan K. Freeman, and Elizabeth Kaminski for reading several drafts of this chapter and participating in fruitful and fun conversations about second and third wave feminism. I also thank Jo Reger for her ongoing commitment to feminist activism and scholarship, of which this volume is but one example.

NOTES

1. Jennifer Friedlin, "A Clash of Waves: Second and Third Wave Feminists Clash over the Future," *Women's ENews*, May 26, 2002, http://www.vfa.us/Clash.htm (accessed August 9, 2004). Although I attended this conference, I rely on this account of it.
2. Ellen Neuborne, "Imagine My Surprise," in *Listen Up: Voices from the Next Generation*, ed. Barbara Findlen (New York: Seal Books, 1995), 29–35.
3. Findlen, *Listen Up*, xv.
4. Danzy Senna, "To Be Real," in *To Be Real: Telling the Truth and Changing the Face of Feminism*, ed. Rebecca Walker (New York: Anchor Books), 5–20.
5. Friedlin, 3.
6. In NOW's statement of purpose, founders addressed all of these points. However, in the scholarship, NOW is very rarely discussed beyond the national level. Scholars have been turning their attention to local feminist activism recently, with scholars giving attention to Columbus, Ohio; Dayton, Ohio; Minneapolis; Washington, D.C.; and Memphis, Tennessee; however, with the exception of Memphis, these works focus on "radical feminism," to which NOW, as a liberal feminist organization, is considered in direct opposition. However, NOW members did pursue coalitions with

other feminists; have worked consistently with men, understanding feminist issues to be gender issues; and did have a diverse agenda that focused on all women across race, class, gender, sexuality, and religious lines. Studies on NOW include Stephanie Gilmore, "The Dynamics of Second-Wave Feminism in Memphis, Tennessee: Rethinking the Liberal/ Radical Divide," *NWSA Journal* 15 (Spring 2003): 84–117; Jo Reger, "Organizational Dynamics and the Construction of Multiple Feminist Identities in the National Organization for Women," *Gender & Society* 16, no. 5 (2002): 710–27; Maryann Barakso, "Mobilizing and Sustaining Grassroots Activism in the National Organization for Women, 1966–2000" (Ph.D. diss., MIT, 2001); Jo Reger and Suzanne Staggenborg, "Grassroots Organizing in a Federated Structure: NOW Chapters in Four Local Fields," in *U.S. Women's Movement in a Dynamic and Global Perspective*, ed. Lee Ann Banaszak (New York: Rowman and Littlefield, forthcoming); and Jo Reger and Suzanne Staggenborg, "Cycles of Activism in Local Movement Organizations: Organizational Strategies in Four National Organization for Women Chapters," unpublished paper.

7. Rebecca Farmer, "I Was a Post-*Roe* Baby," January 22, 2002, NOW website, http://www.now.org/issues/young/postroe.html (accessed August 9, 2004).

8. Ferree and Hess, *Controversy and Coalition*, 66.

9. Ibid.

10. For more on the early years of reproductive rights activism and, in particular, how feminists gave shape to the debates over reproductive rights, see Anne Valk, *Separatism and Sisterhood* (unpublished book manuscript in author's possession). The debate over reproductive rights was one venue in which some feminists clashed over charges of racism and classism in the women's movement. See Rickie Solinger, *Wake Up Little Susie: Single Pregnancy and Race before Roe v. Wade* (New York: Routledge, 1992); and Jessie M. Rodrique, "The Black Community and the Birth Control Movement," in *We Specialize in the Wholly Impossible: A Reader in Black Women's History*, ed. Darlene Clark Hine, Wilma King, and Linda Reed (Brooklyn, NY: Carlson, 1995): 505–21.

11. See Sara M. Evans, *Tidal Wave: How Women Changed America at Century's End* (New York: Free Press, 2003); Ferree and Hess; Nancy Whittier, *Feminist Generations: The Persistence of the Radical Women's Movement* (Philadelphia, PA: Temple University Press, 1999), 15; Alice Echols, *Daring to Be Bad: Radical Feminism in America, 1967–1995* (Minneapolis: University of Minnesota Press, 1989); Judith Ezekiel, *Feminism in the Heartland* (Columbus, Ohio: Ohio State University Press, 2002).

12. As one scholar wrote, "the radical ideas and cooperative forms of the women's movement were reshaping the more conservative, tightly structured 'women's rights' branch of the movement. [By the mid-1970s] NOW had strengthened its position on issues like abortion and lesbianism and had considerably changed its style." Sara Evans, *Personal Politics: The Roots of Women's Liberation in the Civil Rights Movement and the New Left* (New York: Random House, 1979), 215.

13. Susan M. Hartmann, *From Margin to Mainstream: American Women and Politics Since 1960* (Philadelphia, PA: Temple University Press, 1989), 119.

14. *Right NOW*, Columbus NOW newsletter, April 1972, Columbus NOW Papers, Ohio Historical Society, Columbus, Ohio.

15. Dawn McCaffrey and Jennifer Keys, "Competitive Framing Processes in the Abortion Debate: Polarization-Vilification, Frame Saving, and Frame Debunking," *Sociological Quarterly* 41 (2000): 41–61.

16. The *Webster* case upheld a Missouri law prohibiting the use of public employees and public facilities for the purpose of performing abortions that were not medically necessary. The *Casey* decision upheld many restrictions to accessing abortion services, including requiring parental consent, antiabortion counseling, and a mandatory waiting period. The Court did invalidate spousal notification for abortion, but many

prochoice advocates view *Casey* as a near-evisceration of the *Roe v. Wade* decision. Beginning in the late 1970s, though, the Court issued two other challenges to *Roe*: *Maher v. Roe* (1977) upheld a Connecticut ban on abortions that were funded with public monies; *Harris v. McRae* (1980) upheld the Hyde Amendment, legislation that prohibited use of federal Medicaid money for elective abortions.

17.   Inga Muscio, "Abortion, Vacuum Cleaners, and the Power Within," in *Listen Up*, 160–66.

18.   Jennifer Baumgardner and Amy Richards, *Manifesta: Young Women, Feminism, and the Future* (New York: Farrar, Straus, and Giroux, 2000): 32–33.

19.   For a history of feminism in the context of sexuality, see Stephanie Gilmore, "Feminism," in *Encyclopedia of Lesbian, Gay, Bisexual, and Transgender History and Culture*, ed. Marc Stein (New York: Charles Scribner's, 2003), 1: 381–88.

20.   Anastasia Higginbotham, "Chicks Goin' At It," in *Listen Up*, 3–11.

21.   Baumgardner and Richards, 64–65.

22.   Cited in David Allyn, *Make Love, Not War: The Sexual Revolution—An Unfettered History* (Boston: Little, Brown, 2000): 105–6.

23.   Ann Koedt's and Radicalesbians' pieces are reprinted in Miriam Schneir, ed., *Feminism in Our Time: The Essential Writings, World War II to the Present* (New York: Vintage Books, 1994). For an excellent introduction to the complex and contentious relationship between sexual politics and feminism, see Ann Snitow, Christine Stansell, and Sharon Thompson, eds., *Powers of Desire: The Politics of Sexuality* (New York: Monthly Review Press, 1983), esp. "Introduction," 9–49.

24.   More intricate and detailed versions of this story are recounted in Evans, *Tidal Wave*; Ferree and Hess; Susan Brownmiller, *In Our Time: Memoirs of a Revolution* (New York: Dial Press, 2000); Ruth Rosen, *The World Split Open* (New York: Viking Press, 2000); and Karla Jay, *Tales of the Lavender Menace: A Memoir of Liberation* (New York: Basic Books, 1999).

25.   Evans, *Tidal Wave*, 51.

26.   See Whittier.

27.   *Memphis NOW Newsletter*, April 1974 and May 1974, Memphis NOW Papers, Special Collections, Ned R. McWherter Library, University of Memphis, quotation from May 1974.

28.   See Daneel Buring, *Lesbian and Gay Memphis: Building Community Behind the Magnolia Curtain* (New York: Garland, 1997).

29.   Stephanie Gilmore, "Beyond the Lavender Menace: The Struggle for Lesbians' Rights in NOW after 1971," paper presented at the Organization of American Historians' conference, Memphis, Tennessee, April 4, 2003; Elizabeth Kaminski and Stephanie Gilmore, "A Part and Apart: Implementing Inclusivity in a Social Movement Organization," unpublished paper.

30.   Memphis NOW did grapple with charges of racism and, indeed, race was a difficult issue in the city. See Stephanie Gilmore, "The Dynamics of Second-Wave Feminism in Memphis, Tennessee, 1971–1982: Rethinking the Liberal/Radical Divide," *NWSA Journal* 15 (Spring 2003): 94–117. In the aftermath of King's assassination, already pronounced black-white divisions were further exacerbated. See Joan Beifuss, *At the River I Stand: Memphis, the 1968 Strike, and Martin Luther King* (New York: Carlson Publishers, 1989.)

31.   Whittier; Verta Taylor and Leila J. Rupp, "Women's Culture and Lesbian Feminist Activism: A Reconsideration of Cultural Feminism," *Signs: A Journal of Women in Culture and Society* 19 (1993): 32–61.

32.   Interview with Del Martin and Phyllis Lyon, March 21, 2002. Interviewed by Stephanie Gilmore.

33. "The Wheel," July 1978, MVC Periodicals, Special Collections, Ned R. McWherter Library, University of Memphis.

34. Sandra Stout, *Right NOW*, Columbus NOW Newsletter, April 1973.

35. Box 55, folder 20, San Francisco NOW Papers, Lyon and Martin Papers, International Library of Gay, Lesbian, Bisexual and Transgender History, San Francisco, CA.

36. Inga Muscio, *Cunt: A Declaration of Independence* (Seal Press: 1998); Leora Tanenbaum, *Slut: Growing Up Female with a Bad Reputation* (New York: Seven Stories Press, 1999); Elizabeth Wurtzel, *Bitch: In Praise of Difficult Women* (New York: Anchor Books, 1999). The magazine *Bitch: Feminist Response to Pop Culture* has been in print since 1998.

37. Baumgardner and Richards, *Manifesta*, 399–402.

38. Emi Koyama, *Instigations from the Whore Revolution: A Third-Wave Feminist Response to the Sex Work "Controversy,"* (Portland, OR: Confluere, 2002).

39. Del Martin to Mayor Alioto, SF NOW Papers, Lyon and Martin Papers, Box 55, folder 9, International Library of Gay, Lesbian, Bisexual and Transgender History, San Francisco, CA.

40. Trish Sommers, SF NOW Papers, Lyon and Martin Papers, Box 55, folder 9, International Library of Gay, Lesbian, Bisexual and Transgender History, San Francisco, CA.

41. "Prostitution Resolution, Passed as Amended by the 6th Annual Conference of the National Organization for Women in Washington DC, February, 1973," SF NOW Papers, Lyon and Martin Papers, Box 58, folder 21, International Library of Gay, Lesbian, Bisexual and Transgender History, San Francisco, CA.

42. Heather Lee Miller, "Trick Identities: The Nexus of Sex and Work," *Journal of Women's History* 15 (Winter 2004): 144–51. This piece introduces ways to understand prostitution as women's labor as well as a sexual identity.

43. Margo St. James, open letter, SF NOW Papers, Lyon and Martin Papers, Box 55, folder 9, International Library of Gay, Lesbian, Bisexual and Transgender History, San Francisco, CA.

44. Nevada NOW, "Prostitution," SF NOW Papers, Lyon and Martin Papers, Box 55, folder 9, International Library of Gay, Lesbian, Bisexual and Transgender History, San Francisco, CA.

45. "Prostitution Resolution, Passed as Amended by the Western Regional Conference of the National Organization for Women Meeting in Las Vegas, Nevada, September 1973," SF NOW Papers, Lyon and Martin Papers, Box 58, folder 21, International Library of Gay, Lesbian, Bisexual and Transgender History, San Francisco, CA.

46. "Proposal for a NOW National Task Force on Prostitution."

47. For more on prostitution and sex work as labor in the United States, see Miller, 144–51; and Siobhan Brooks, "Exotic Dancing and Unionizing: The Challenges of Feminist and Antiracist Organizing at the Lusty Lady Theater," in *Feminism and Antiracism: International Struggles for Justice*, ed. Kathleen Blee and France Winddance Twine (New York: New York University Press, 2001), 59–70. On COYOTE's efforts to organize prostitutes, see Valerie Jenness, "From Sex as Sin to Sex as Work: COYOTE and the Reorganization of Prostitution as a Social Problem," *Social Problems* 37 (August 1990): 403–20. Stephanie Gilmore explores further NOW's efforts in the 1970s to work with prostitutes on decriminalization, unionization, and redefinitions of sexuality legally and culturally in "Strange Bedfellows: 'Liberal' Feminists, Prostitutes, and Sex Workers' Rights in the 1970s," paper presented at Berkshire Conference of Women Historians, Claremont, CA, June 2005.

48. Miller, 141.

49. Rory Dicker and Alison Piepmeier, eds., *Catching a Wave: Reclaiming Feminism for the 21st Century* (Boston: Northeastern University Press, 2003), 16.

50. In 1968, feminists launched a protest on the Miss America pageant, criticizing the event as objectifying women and perpetuating a culture for women in which women's beauty was most highly valued. The protestors also set up a "freedom trash can" into which they threw objects of "women's oppression": bras, girdles, copies of popular women's magazines, and high-heeled shoes. From this event, the media labeled the protestors, and feminists, as "bra-burners" in spite of the fact that nothing was set aflame. In 1972, Jennifer Woodul and Ginny Berson founded Olivia Records. A pioneering women's recording label, Olivia Records was a prominent institution for promoting, distributing, and recording feminist- and lesbian-themed music. Recorders for Olivia Records included Meg Christensen, Tret Fure, and Alix Dobkin, all of whom had, and retain, a loyal following. For more on Olivia Records, see Gillian Gaar, *She's a Rebel: The History of Women in Rock and Roll* (Seattle, WA: Seal Press, 1992), esp. 124–26, and 142. On women's liberation rock music, see Jennifer Baumgardner, "Aural History," *Bitch* 23 (Winter 2004): 75–80.
51. Walker, xxxi.
52. Baumgardner and Richards, 220.

7

WHEN FEMINISM IS YOUR JOB: AGE AND POWER IN WOMEN'S POLICY ORGANIZATIONS[1]

Susanne Beechey

Being able to say I'm a professional feminist and this is the work I do … it's amazing! (Laura)

The prospect of being a professional feminist is a relatively new phenomenon, made possible by the feminist institution building of the second wave. After majoring in women's studies or perhaps participating in a summer internship program at a women's organization, some young feminists are embarking on careers in women's organizations. Yet the experiences of young women in national women's organizations remain relatively uninvestigated in the literature on third wave feminism. In her preface to *Manifesta*, Jennifer Baumgardner writes of walking out on her job at *Ms. Magazine* at age twenty-six, in the face of declining working conditions, long hours, and low pay.[2] In *Catching a Wave*, Sarah Boonin describes in a positive light her experiences working for the Feminist Majority Foundation, highlighting the substantive responsibility with which she was entrusted and the mentoring she received.[3] These brief and differing glimpses raise a question that the third wave feminist literature has yet to fully investigate: How are young feminists faring in national women's organizations?

Third wave feminists are generally defined as twenty-something; indeed, the Third Wave Foundation, the first self-styled third wave organization, is dedicated to feminists between the ages of fifteen and thirty.[4] Second wave feminists are more generally seen as coming of age in the 1960s and 1970s.[5] Relationships between the second and third waves of feminists are often characterized as confrontational, uncooperative, and even hostile, yet upon closer inspection, we may find greater continuity between second and third waves than first expected.[6] For example, it remains somewhat unclear the extent to which agendas and strategies are sites of divergence between feminist generations. Beginning with the title, the anthology *Third Wave Agenda* infers there are such differences, positioning third wave feminists as primarily focused on cultural production and critique. *Manifesta* also lists a thirteen-point agenda for the third wave; however, many of the items and strategies show a strong connection to concerns of feminism's second wave.[7]

Today the National Council of Women's Organizations lists almost two hundred member organizations, which include mass membership organizations, single issue groups, electoral campaign sector organizations, coalitions of direct service providers, and expert-driven policy organizations.[8] This study focuses on the latter type of national women's organization, women's policy organizations,[9] which provide specialized technical and legal expertise for policy advocacy in state and national policy arenas. These organizations publish research, mobilize constituencies, draft model legislation, provide expert testimony, and lobby members of Congress and other government officials. Several emerged from once largely voluntary organizations, while others were women-focused off-shoots from existing nonfeminist advocacy organizations.

Despite their diverse roots, women's policy organizations today have developed professionalized forms, characterized by hierarchical and bureaucratic organizational structures.[10] For tactical reasons these organizations have mastered Washington-insider politics, although this has created tensions between preserving feminist ideals and maintaining legitimacy within dominant policy circles.[11] These conflicts emerge not only across the broader social movement of feminism, but also within the confines of individual women's policy organizations. This study seeks to investigate the internal sites of tension within women's policy organizations, from the perspectives of young feminist staff members. By investigating the match between personal ideology and organizational constraints, I find that what first appear to be generational ideological differences are instead based in positions of power and hierarchy within organizations.

Women's policy organizations are apt locations for interrogating understandings of third wave feminism and apparent generational differences within feminism. Policy organizations grew directly out of the second wave of feminism, emerging primarily during the 1970s and 1980s and evolving into active interest groups. While these organizations claim to advocate on behalf of all women, they have been criticized for being too white, middle class, and heterosexual in focus.[12] Beginning in the 1980s, most organizational leaders attempted to responded to these criticisms, with varying degrees of success, by recruiting more diverse staff and constituencies, and defining their agendas more broadly.[13] The current third wave discourse at times continues to cast national women's organizations as pejoratively second wave and irrelevant to the concerns and politics of third wave feminists. Yet young feminists continue to work in these organizations and choose careers as professional feminists.

Covering a broad set of important national issues, these organizations tend to be financially strapped, with more work to be done than resources with which to do it. The salaries are lower than those paid by the government or private sector.[14] Ideology, commitment to the issues, and personal relationships often motivate initial recruitment to this workforce and inspire willingness to remain. Access to power and the media are also seen as nonmonetary forms of compensation to justify long hours and low pay.[15] Staffs are composed of well-educated, generally middle-class women, and student interns are often used to augment the permanent staff. Even after an individual leaves a given organization, she often remains part of an extensive network of contacts and social ties.[16]

The analysis that follows is based in a series of interviews conducted in 2003 with feminists in their twenties who were currently or in the past year had been employed by a women's policy organization in Washington, D.C.[17] Seven organizations were chosen including both research and advocacy organizations, working in both the federal and state arenas. The participants from those organizations were chosen based on purposive sampling, emphasizing information rich cases. The primary criterion was age, with racial and ethnic diversity incorporated to the extent represented by the organization's staff. The seven young women who participated range in age from twenty-two to twenty-eight years old, five identify as white, one as Asian, and one as Asian-American. All self-identify as feminists and all have at least one college degree. Few of the women self-identify as third wave feminists and only about half were familiar with the term. At the time of the interviews they had worked at a women's policy organization for periods ranging between nine months and over four years. Some had worked at multiple women's organizations. Two of the women had since left the community of women's organizations and were employed in allied advocacy and research organizations in Washington. Drawing from the experiences of these young women, I now examine the tensions that arise for young feminists working in women's policy organizations.

PRACTICING WHAT YOU PREACH

The internal policies of women's policy organizations have a great effect on the experiences of young feminists. While young feminists recognize the financial constraints organizations face, they remain critical of the ways in which these constraints are negotiated through formal and informal organizational policies. The low pay for long hours combined with the failure of some organizations to provide adequate health care coverage or formalized family and medical leave policies seem to young feminists like a failure of women's organizations to practice what they are preaching to policymakers and corporations. Allison gave an illustration of the disconnect between feminist ideology and personnel policies within women's policy organizations. She said:

> Then there is also the issue of practicing what you preach. You can say that we believe that all women should get a living wage and get maternity benefits, you preach this. But then at the same time, being a small nonprofit, you don't have the money to pay people basically a living wage. So it's kind of —I don't want to say it's hypocritical because it's not intentional—but at the same time, there are issues there.

Laura agreed, critiquing the differential pay scale in her organization, "A disconnect that I've found is the way that they'll definitely say that you're like an integral part of the movement, but when it comes to compensation, they don't pay anyone what they're worth, except for the top people." Bette concurred:

> None of us are getting paid what we are worth, and those of us who are younger, come in with a pretty strong critique questioning why should I work for less than I am worth. This is not a volunteer society, we can all do that in our spare time, but right now I'm giving all that I've got so I should get paid fairly.

Laura gave an example of inadequate compensation from her past, "At one point with the two internships I was working about twenty-six hours per week and I think I was making about $100." AJ also expressed dissatisfaction over her low pay; a frustration complicated by the fact that her boss is in a position in her life to be able to volunteer her time, in stark contrast to her younger employees. AJ said:

> My boss doesn't get paid. She's a volunteer. So I think that some-times, since she doesn't ever have to worry about money—she's pretty set—that she doesn't think about me and how broke I am. I live pretty well pay check to pay check, just try to keep current with all my stuff, and if something comes up like with my car.... So a lot of times I think that they will forget what it's like not to have money.... But they pay my health insurance, which is good. So there's give and take.

Bette too connected these issues of compensation to age and genera-tional differences in the ability or willingness to work for little pay and no health benefits. She said:

> The younger group of us had issues with some of the health care policies....When the organization was founded in the early 1980s the women who staffed it were wives of middle- and upper-class husbands who were out working, so they could do this for very little pay. The culture has continued that you do this work because you love it, but it's going to pay you dirt. So I think our organization was very late to get benefits on board because these women had benefits through their husbands....Things like that, we younger staff really had trouble with, because we needed health coverage.

Laura echoed the feelings of many young women when she tried to put these frustrations in some perspective, yet in the process highlighted that these policies serve to limit the types of women who can afford to seek employment in these organizations. She said:

> I am really lucky that I get to do what I want to do. I'm so lucky to have a job!... I mean I have health benefits, which so many people don't and I get paid a decent wage hourly.... If I had kids this would be a little different, but there are so many people out there who survive on so much less.

Lola also pointed out that low pay in women's organizations is not only an issue of fairly compensating women's work, but also an issue of limiting the staff of women's organizations to those who can afford to work for little pay.

> I think that is a huge problem and I think that is what closes the pool of applicants. It is very, very small the number of people who can afford to live on those salaries. I think also it is part of making people feel appreciated, just having less things to worry about financially, and being able to put more focus and more energies into the cause.

Issues of benefits and compensation become all the more troubling when questions of family and medical leave are introduced, as Laura pointed out. "I knew this woman who worked for another women's organization. She was younger and she found out she was pregnant and they did not want to give her maternity leave." Indeed many young women reported that they were not aware of any formalized leave policies within their organization. Bette gave an example of how her organization has recently struggled through the application of an informal maternity leave policy while navigating generational, age, and power differentials across the staff. She said:

> We are a small organization and we have limited resources, so I think that means we can't support mothers or new mothers in the way that we should. One of the younger staff was pregnant and didn't tell anyone for the longest, longest time. I think she was legitimately concerned about what would happen if she asked to take maternity leave. The personnel manual says it is on a case by case basis, you have to go before the board, they aren't required by law [to grant maternity leave], and they just can't afford to. So a woman with very little power in the organization had to go to the higher ups and say, "Here's my situation, I need this much time off at the very least, I can't afford to do this, I don't know what to do, I really want to work here." They worked it all out, she took leave and then came back. I think she probably had to come back sooner than she wanted to. But I sense also resentment from some people about it, that, "Oh, she got maternity leave and she's coming back." I think a lot of the older staff, when they were at that time in their life they just took time out of the workforce entirely and came back whenever was convenient for them. I know that if we really thought about it we would like to be able to do more than that. We know that it's inconsistent with feminist principles, and unfortunately that is just the way it is right now.

It's really frustrating to some of us—some of us more than others—some of us who could see ourselves in that position.

Lola relayed a similar encounter with informal leave policies when she sought short-term medical leave from the president of her organization, with whom she had an otherwise strained relationship.

When I had some health problems I had to miss work and I was worried about having to take too much leave, and so when I told the president that I would have to go through this, she was very understanding and told me that I could take as much time as was needed. Which I thought was great and really supportive.

In both of these situations, organizational structures required young, relatively powerless women to go to the seat of power in the organization to explain their personal circumstances in detail in order to get special dispensation for the kind of family and medical leave for which women's organizations have advocated for decades.

Christina also pointed to maternity leave issues as an example of "things that we've done that are not in line with my ideal of what a woman's organization would do." Christina highlighted her own conflicted views on balancing the needs of employees and the needs of the organization when over half the staff in her organization were pregnant at the same time. She said:

It was really hard for me to both feel for them and understand and want to fight for a better package deal for them, and at the same time think about what was best for the organization.... I think a lot of people can't decide whether or not to be more on the side of the workers and what's best for them or to be on the side of what's best for our organization. In a small nonprofit, if over half the staff is on leave and doesn't come back for months or ever, it can kill an organization.... For me it has been a struggle trying to decide, if I was in that position as a director what would I do.... I don't know, that's a tough call to make. You can sort of empathize with both sides of it, I think. As I stay there longer I think I start to become more in the director perspective of it.... That's been really difficult for me because a lot of our [women's studies] classes talk about what we can do—giving women more maternity leave, giving women more child care options, and better health insurance—and then I go back to the organization and say, okay, we need to make sure everybody has a salary.

If somebody gets free child care that means somebody else's salary is lost, and that's a struggle.

Bette also tried to keep the financial realities in mind, "I try to be aware of that. I really do, and try not to be too harsh. But on the other hand, your bottom line is also your staff and if you can't take care of them you've got no business being in business."

Young feminists recognize the financial constraints organizations face, even as they remain critical of the ways in which these constraints are managed. They recognize that the low pay and inadequate benefits serve to close out feminists who otherwise would like to work for women's policy organizations but cannot afford to do so, reinforcing the middle-class status quo within women's organizations. While young feminists may be disproportionately affected by these organizational policies, because they are less likely to have health coverage through a partner, and more likely to envision the prospect of needing some form of maternity leave in their future, they indeed influence staff members of all ages. However, young feminists are generally not in positions of power within these organizations from which to negotiate the application of informal policies or the redress of inadequate formal policies. Thus if the occasion arises when a young woman must seek special dispensation from her older, more powerful boss for the kinds of family and medical leave that women's policy organizations externally advocate, these organizational failings can appear to be generational tensions. Relationships with bosses and supervisors can also be a source of tension for young feminists.

MENTORING A NEW GENERATION

Young feminists reported a broad spectrum of interactions and relationships with their bosses and supervisors at women's policy organizations. By and large the bosses were women in their fifties and sixties, although a few were in their thirties or forties. All but one was white; most held advanced degrees. The young feminists' relationships with their bosses ranged from beneficial mentoring to "nonboss" status.

The positive relationships young feminist reported with their bosses where characterized by mutual respect and deliberate mentorship. AJ's comments about her relationship with her boss exemplify this sense of mutual respect and highlight the value of good mentorship to young feminists.

My boss is an awesome writer, so I like working together with her, and I know that she respects me too. When she writes something she'll say, "Why don't you look this over," and most of the time when I get my red pen and make my corrections she'll say, "Oh yah," and that makes me feel good. I'm like, this famous, well-respected feminist just said my suggestion was good!... I think we work really well together. We don't have too many disagreements.... She is one of the smartest people I know, ever. So I like to be around her and to learn from her. The experience really is priceless to me.... But I know that other people haven't had the best experiences as far as getting to do things. My boss rarely says, "No, you can't do that." If I want to work on something and if I want to take something on, then she is really receptive to that. She like never condescends [to] me or anything. She really wants me to succeed, and wants me to move on one day.

Christina described her relationship with her boss as characterized by mutual respect. However, this relationship did not come naturally, and is something they have had to establish over the years. She said:

Our relationship is very close. It definitely has changed over the years. I am the first and only original intern who has really stayed on.... It's been a struggle for me to get her to see me as something other than someone really young, to get her to take me seriously. She's always taken me seriously in that she knows the quality of my work, but to take me seriously in the way of being able to do what my other colleagues are doing, or being capable of, that has been a struggle for me, I think. But you know, through that she and I have become really close. I have a lot of respect for her. The fact that she is the founder and executive director who's been able to keep this thing going.... I have over the years learned a lot about her background, she was a real pioneer.

Laura has had more than six supervisors at various women's organizations, where she has worked either as an intern or full-time staff member. Her experiences offer a picture of the breadth of interactions and relationships with bosses, and highlight the importance of mentorship and mutual respect. Laura, speaking of three exemplary bosses she has encountered in her career, commented about one of them:

My boss there was really committed to making sure there's another generation of feminists; because she knows, what I think some other people don't know, which is that someday they're going to have to retire and there's going to have to be someone there to take

over. And if you treat people like shit, there's not going to be anyone there…. She also spoke to me and asked me about my
opinions, which definitely didn't happen at my first employer.

She continued, speaking of another boss:

> My first supervisor there, she's the best all-time boss and feminist
> ever, I think, or one of the best…. She knows how to treat every-
> one like a person…. She did a really good job of just checking in
> with people and saying, "How are you doing? How are you really
> doing?" And my boss now does that too. Like she'll say, "I know
> last week was kind of crazy. How are you doing? Is everything
> okay?" Which no one else has done. And also my boss now and
> the other senior staff member, they say, "Thank you, thanks for
> doing that." Which even though it's only two words, it makes you
> feel like your work is appreciated.

Like Christina, Laura also had a boss with whom it took time to
develop a positive relationship, but she has found that effort paid off.
Laura said:

> One of my bosses—it was hard for me to understand how she
> looked at things and her methodology for getting things done in
> the beginning…. But she would always talk to me like a person.
> I had to do the same kinds of administrative tasks for her, but she
> would definitely invite me to things and give me little lessons, and
> I valued that. Even though at other times she did things that I
> found, really, you know. Like one day she told me the shirt I was
> wearing to work, that I wasn't respecting myself by the way I was
> dressed. I definitely probably shouldn't have worn the shirt to
> work. It was based on my previous experience at a grassroots
> organization and another women's organization where my
> coworker would wear whatever she wanted to wear. If she had a
> problem that's okay, but to couch it like, "You're not respecting
> yourself"? That's like not very feminist! So, but overall she was
> definitely concerned about being a mentor…. I talked to her
> about the problems I was facing at work and she was really help-
> ful about giving me advice…. After she'd moved on, she actually
> helped me get my next job.

These relationships, characterized by mutual respect and deliberate
mentorship, reveal that generational tensions need not exist between a

young feminist and her older boss. Indeed these bosses appear genuinely interested in mentoring a new generation of feminists and the young women are appreciative of the guidance and support. Even in cases where tensions at first occur, they can be overcome if both parties are willing to work on developing a foundation of respect and communication.

Judging from other experiences of young feminists with their bosses, interest in mentoring future generations of feminists is not a universal belief. Even basic respect is not always valued or practiced by both parties. In addition to the bosses that were supportive of Laura and became important mentors for her, she also has encountered less supportive bosses. The first she called "the nonboss."

> She was kind of like a nonboss. She would just kind of like ask me to do crazy things and not really talk to me. I was always busy and then she'd talk to me occasionally and be like, "Hey can you research the phone bill situation, why is this so much?" It was like, okay I'll just drop everything and answer your stupid questions for you, even though you don't care about that, I know you don't.... I was asked to work on a project for another division of the organization that just sort of landed in my lap. My boss kind of like refused to get involved, but if something had gone wrong no one had my back and my boss would have totally blamed me for the whole thing.

For Laura, however, the absent, nonboss was clearly preferable to her encounters with the type of boss that she termed "the crazy feminist leader."

> My first experience with a crazy feminist leader was when I interned at this organization. The executive director there, she's crazy. While I was there she was verbally abusive to the staff. Everyone on the staff had changed over since she took over. Something would go wrong and she would just start yelling at people, to the point where you thought she might start swinging. I just couldn't believe it.... Two of the younger members of the staff actually quit while I was there.... She never really yelled at me. She would say things to me like, "Don't you know how to think your way out of a paper bag?"

For Laura this kind of treatment was all the more frustrating when it happened to her as a full-time staff member at another organization.

I've been treated like a nonperson a lot. As an intern you can kind of understand that because sure it's learning experience. But as an admin person, as a full-time professional staff person? That was just, you know, I couldn't handle it. Like, one of my favorite stories was when another boss of mine, who never really talked to me at all, asked me to buy her tampons. Actually told me to buy her tampons.

Laura continued to describe how she might have anticipated this sort of behavior in a large corporation, but for her it was unbelievable that this kind of behavior was happening in women's organizations. Yet in conversations with her peers she found her experiences were not isolated instances.

I've talked to other young women and complained and it seems like across the board—and most of their bosses were older than my boss—that there was something about the way that they treated their underlings, workers, that just seems to me very unfeminist. To be a feminist and to have worked for this your whole life and to not treat the people who work under you with respect, I don't understand how that can be. How you can do that?

Madison, Lola, and Allison also described their relationships with their bosses as characterized by daily frustrations and disrespect. In Allison's words, "people were constantly being made to feel like what they are doing isn't valued." These frustrations related to issues of authority and hierarchy established within the organizations. Lola said of her boss:

There is a lack of belief in anybody else but herself. There's really no balance of power it seems, because all authority rests in one person, from signing off on whether or not we can buy batteries for our camera for taking pictures of events, to travel expenses, to signing off on every single letter, to approving the color of a communication's cover, to whether or not I filled out my time sheet correctly.

Madison had similar experiences. She said:

I think I was definitely treated the same way by both supervisors, oftentimes very insulted, very put down, not valued—those are generally my memories. I mean, honestly, if we are talking about my boss, then yes, it was a very difficult working environment.

Allison agreed, "There [are] a lot of daily frustrations and there is some disrespect as you go down the hierarchy. It's a question of practicing what you preach." For Lola, the issue was the way authority was deployed within the organization. She said:

> The authoritarianism is very offensive on a personal level. Not just by the ways it's done, but verbally, comments are made that are offensive, very offensive personally. We are made to feel like, we are expected to do a lot of work and be autonomous and not have to be told every single thing, yet we're constantly being criticized for what we do.

These relationships between young feminists and their bosses could serve as models, and warnings, for other cross-generation encounters in feminism. The lessons here indicate that there need not be generational tensions when both parties can relate from a position of mutual respect. Many young feminists are hungry for mentorship and many older feminists are keen to play such a role, if both groups can find the means to communicate and work together toward these ends. In situations not characterized by such respect or mentorship, generational tensions can indeed appear. In such cases more is at stake than one young woman's enjoyment of her job. These kinds of negative interactions between young feminists and their older bosses lend support to the strand of third wave feminism that depicts second wave feminists pejoratively and serves to intensify generational discord. Furthermore, these work experiences can turn off young women to working within the feminist movement. Indeed some of these young women have since left the women's movement to work in liberal organizations. During her interview, one even vowed never to work for a women's organization again.

Yet while these appear to be generational tensions, some of these bad experiences could be related to the low power, entry level administrative assistant type positions that young feminists often hold in women's organizations. As Allison commented, "When things would go wrong, things would blow up, and when things blow up, the administrative assistant is the first person who gets a call. You're in the line of fire." Lola made clear that the disrespect poisoned her entire office, regardless of position or age.

> It got to a point where my supervisor, a person who I respect so much who has done a lot of amazing work in her life … was so nervous because she was so continuously criticized that she could

not write an e-mail without checking it ten times. And the exact same thing with another senior colleague. These were women who were in their forties and fifties, who have been in the movement for so long, and they were such a mess that it was affecting them physically, that they would come into work with stomachaches, throwing up, and getting sick all the time.... Another thing that I thought was terrible was that in the meetings I would see my supervisors being berated in front of everybody by the president. I thought that was really disrespectful for them and really awkward for us who had to sit there and listen to it. Also the way that I was complimented for doing something, I felt that it was done to kind of snub my supervisor.... Whenever she would come up with a product or create a report or something, you know, the president would go and find a thousand mistakes and then give me a compliment almost as if to say, "Hey, look this younger person is doing a better job than you," as opposed to it being a real compliment for me. Saying I'd done a good job is something I think is really important in a women's organization, but the way it was done for me was done in a way that—like I would get stars, literally gold star stickers ... other times "good job" written like that—like a teacher was giving back a paper or exam I had written, and I don't remember getting that since I was in primary school.

Lola's story illustrates an important lesson in these stories. While age or generational differences may be a factor in a relationship between a young feminist and her boss, age does not always work in a straightforward manner. In her story, Lola's age functioned to justify her boss treating her like a child in primary school, yet also served to shame older and more senior staff members. Indeed these may not be issues of generation or age at all, but rather relative position in a hierarchy of power.

GENERATIONS WITHIN ORGANIZATIONS

These tensions that young feminists encounter within women's policy organizations are not always satisfactorily captured by an emphasis on generational differences. By investigating the relationships between young women and other feminists connected to their organizations, the generational model is further interrogated. Bette offered an example of generational tensions not being restricted to interactions between boss and staff, but also affecting interactions with an older woman served by her organization. She said:

I was talking with an older woman our organization serves the other day just about trends in the nation, changes in foreign policy, and you know the whole John Ashcroft thing. She said, "When this happened to my generation, we were out in the streets, and I would just hope that your generation will also take up the charge if you need to." We had a pleasant conversation, but afterwards I thought, well, you know, "Screw you." We were out in the streets a year ago. I looked around and there were so many young people....When I go out to the [pro] choice rallies I see young girls and young women out there. We aren't really different than previous generations. I think it takes a galvanizing event—like a preemptive war against Iraq, like the legitimate threat that the court might take away Roe vs. Wade—to get people energized.

Bette's is a classic example of generational tensions in feminism from the perspective of a younger woman: an older woman she respects, using a yardstick of the 1960s and explicit generational language, dismisses or ignores the activism of today's youth and holds an individual young feminist accountable for the actions (or lack thereof) of her generation. It was exactly these tensions that Laura feared when she started her job in an office where the other women were significantly older than her.

I thought I would get a lot of this, "You won't understand this because you're like twelve years old." But that hasn't happened at all. People have been really welcoming and so happy that someone so young would want to be involved with these issues. So it's been a very affirming move for me.

Generational tensions, such as those Bette described do exist, as do concerns about disrespect on the basis of age, as Laura illustrated. Emerging from these stories is the realization that there is no single formula for generational divides within women's organizations. Sometimes they appear where least expected and other times are absent where we might predict they would be most prevalent. Indeed the very concepts of age and generation are problematic. Is the issue that Bette's generation doesn't live up to a previous generation's model of activism or that Laura is too young?

The concepts of age and generation are further complicated by the experiences of Christina, Allison, and Madison. Age is a continuous rather than dichotomous idea, and perceptions of age are influenced by other factors, including position within an organization, as Christina's experience demonstrates.

Obviously my boss is sort of the most important to prove my
worthiness to, because she's the boss, but I've had to do that to
the other older people too. Some of them don't care. Some of
them have worked with young people before.... But you know,
sometimes people have issues with it. I think especially when I
have to directly hand over orders to someone, it can be challenging. I think the funniest part of all of it is when the interns find
out how old I am, because they always think I am like ten years
older than I am. Last year I was like six months older than one of
them, you know, and nobody had any idea. So I always think
that's funny when people find out.

Christina is not only seen as older by some of the staff and younger by
others, but she is also in the position of giving direction and supervision to women who are older as well as those who are younger than
herself. Her experience highlights the fact that these are relative terms.
Age can be read in multiple ways and can take on a different meaning
when one holds a position in the organization that does not track with
one's age. Both Allison and Madison described tense relationships with
their bosses or the leaders of their organizations, which they described
in generational terms, but both made a point of describing the more
positive relationships they had with midlevel management and other
coworkers of various ages. Allison said:

My relationship with the midlevel management, the in-between
generation, is more just like, they're really great, funny, nice people who encourage you to do what you want to do. It was more of
like a good mentoring relationship.

Madison related similar experiences, she said:

With my coworkers, it was so different! You know, there were just
some people in the office who understood what it's like to go
though that sort of event, to be in that position, to have a boss
sort of looking over you and maybe not treating you as well as
you deserved to be treated.... That to me was such a source of
comfort and support. To know that I wasn't overreacting, being
picky, or whatever, petty. And that helped. That really helped.

The midlevel management to whom Allison refers were women
between her and the president of her organization, both in terms of age
and position in the organization. Similarly, the coworkers Madison

describes were both older and younger than her, some of whom though not directly supervising her, held middle management positions in the organization. The existence of these women in the middle—the middle management between the entry level staff and the president, the middle generation between what we refer to as second and third waves—complicate the dichotomous thinking of younger versus older, worker versus boss, third wave versus second wave.

As evidenced by their stories above, Allison, AJ, Bette, Christina, Laura, Lola, and Madison gave mixed accounts of their experiences working in women's policy organizations. From their stories emerges a picture of loyalty and connection to issues and colleagues, along with a strong critique of individual supervisory practices and organizational structures that run counter to feminist ideals. Many of the conflicts within women's policy organizations that they expose could be interpreted as the kinds of generational or age-based tensions that might be described by appealing to the notion of third wave feminism. Yet third wave is not a term utilized by these young women.

When Allison and her colleagues would talk about generational differences in the office, "no terminology was used, just our director's generation and our generation." Christina and Bette seemed to have similar experiences in their offices. Christina said:

It's really just two. It's her traditional ways of doing things and the new way of doing things—so things are just referred to as before and after. I don't really know what the defining moment is for that, but I've noticed other people in the organization talk about that too, like the old way of doing it and the new way of doing it.

Bette's perceptions were similar, she said:

We didn't talk about generational, it was more junior and senior staff. And that is like official language: It was more the five of us would think this way and the twelve of them would think that way. And it wasn't even stated that we were the younger generation and they were the older, it was just kind of known that there were two camps and it broke down by ages.

While this dichotomous thinking seems to resonate with notions of second wave and third wave, it seems important that these young feminists do not choose this terminology. Bette commented that "the term third wave has never come up in discussions. It seems to be more of an academic term." Laura agreed, "I definitely don't really use the term *third wave* to classify myself or people that I know … it's not something that really resonates with me." Indeed for Lola the disconnect was not only with the term *third wave*, but with the very notion of common experience based in generation or age. She said:

> Young women in the women's movement events, organizations, concepts scare me. I feel alienated by it. I guess because when mainstream women's organizations have young women events and things, I feel very much that I don't belong there. I guess I never feel legitimate…. Identifying as an Asian, and not as an Asian American but as someone who has recently immigrated to this country, I feel even a further step back, and constantly feel questioned about my legitimacy in the movement.

Within the third wave feminist literature, it sometimes seems that if a horror story transpires between a young feminist and an older feminist, it must be a generational thing; but in their own usage and interpretations, Allison, AJ, Bette, Christina, Laura, Lola, and Madison complicate this understanding of third wave. They have each, to varying degrees, experienced some form of tension or conflict with an older feminist in their professional lives. Yet none of them use the idea of third wave to understand these moments.

If the tensions in women's policy organizations that on the surface appear to be generational can be alternatively understood as issues of relative positions of power within a hierarchy, this may raise useful questions for the general usage and understanding of third wave feminism. How much of the rhetoric of third wave feminism is in practice a mechanism for creating a space of power from which those at the bottom of the feminist hierarchy can speak? To what degree does the term *third wave* conflate age with generation and both with relative positions of power in what are increasingly professionalized, hierarchically structured feminist institutions? Is the "trump card" of generation played by young feminists, students, and entry level workers—whether administrative assistants in women's policy organizations or junior faculty in women's studies programs—an attempt to garner legitimacy, a site of power in an unexpectedly hierarchical space?

This is not to argue that the term third wave should be abandoned. Indeed it should be used to the extent it assists in conceptualizing differences and tensions within feminism, and to the degree that it helps bring voice to otherwise silenced groups. Nevertheless, we must resist the urge to reify this generational model. Third wave or generational difference should not become the sole model for understanding what on the surface appear to be differences between younger and older feminists. To do so supposes stable, fundamental differences that may in fact be temporary, relative positions of power. If the tensions within feminism are illustrated by generational lines, problems get located within relative ages or generations of individuals rather than within systems, organizations, institutions, or feminism as a whole. Under a generational model each side gets to blame the other, as tensions across generations become a reified fact rather than a conceptual model; and the logical solution becomes waiting for second wavers to retire. If today's young feminists locate the tensions they face as residing in the older generation, how can we expect things to be any different when today's young feminists become tomorrow's leaders of women's organizations? Furthermore, a generational model serves to hide the responsibility of relatively powerful feminists to address the negative experiences of younger and other less powerful feminists, and to use their positions of power to ensure that women's policy organizations strive toward feminist ideals not only through external advocacy but also within the organization itself. We all need to think about ways that women's organizations can continue to do the vital work of national policy advocacy, while better fulfilling the promise of feminism within those walls, and nothing, including tensions between feminists and the models that construct them as generational, should get in our way.

NOTES

1. I gratefully acknowledge Jo Reger for her useful comments and my young feminist colleagues for their insights and encouragement. A special thanks to the young women who agreed to be interviewed and share their experiences.

2. Jennifer Baumgardner and Amy Richards, *Manifesta: Young Women, Feminism, and the Future* (New York: Farrar, Straus and Giroux, 2000), xvii.

3. Sarah Boonin, "Please—Stop Thinking about Tomorrow: Building a Feminist Movement on College Campuses for Today," in *Catching a Wave: Reclaiming Feminism for the 21st Century*, eds. Rory Dicker and Alison Piepmeier (Boston: Northeastern University Press, 2003), 138–56.

4. Yet age and generation often are conflated, as those who write of a third wave generation have typically done so around their twenties. For example,"the 'generation' addressed in *Third Wave Agenda*, whose birth dates fall between 1963 and 1974" would have been between the ages of twenty-three and thirty-four when the book was published. See Leslie Heywood and Jennifer Drake, eds., *Third Wave Agenda: Being Feminist, Doing Feminism* (Minneapolis: University of Minnesota Press, 1997), 4.

5. Heywood and Drake; Rebecca Walker, ed., *To Be Real: Telling the Truth and Changing the Face of Feminism* (New York: Anchor Books, 1995); Dicker and Piepmeier, 10.

6. Dicker and Piepmeier, 15.

7. Baumgardner and Richards, 278–81. See also Gilmore, chapter 6.

8. National Council of Women's Organizations, www.womensorganizations.org (accessed February 7, 2004); Joyce Gelb and Marian Lief Palley, *Women and Public Policies: Reassessing Gender Politics* (Charlottesville, VA: University Press of Virginia,

1996), 24–25; Roberta Spalter-Roth and Ronnee Schreiber, "Outsider Issues and Insider Tactics: Strategic Tensions in the Women's Policy Network during the 1980s," in *Feminist Organizations: Harvest of the New Women's Movement*, eds. Myra Marx Ferree and Patricia Yancey Martin (Philadelphia: Temple University Press, 1995): 105–27.

9. Although all of the organizations work to produce feminist outcomes and have feminist guiding values or goals, I use the term *women's organization* as opposed to *feminist organization*. Neither the organizations nor the women interviewed used the term *feminist* to describe the organization, and indeed most emphasized the fact that the organizations had made specific decisions to eschew a feminist label for pragmatic political and fundraising reasons.

10. Gelb and Palley, 22–26.

11. Spalter-Roth and Schreiber.

12. Paula Giddings, *When and Where I Enter: The Impact of Black Women on Race and Sex in America* (New York: William Morrow, 1984); bell hooks, *Ain't I a Woman: Black Women and Feminism* (Boston: South End Press, 1981).

13. Spalter-Roth and Schreiber, 121.

14. Gelb and Palley, 45.

15. Ibid., 39.

16. Ibid., 38.

17. A semistructured interview format was used, posing open-ended questions to elicit in-depth description of the personal experiences. Each woman was offered the opportunity to choose the pseudonym used to represent her in this discussion and was given the opportunity to review and amend her comments based on the interview transcript.

Part III

What Brings Change?
Tactics of the Third Wave

8

TALKING ABOUT MY VAGINA: TWO COLLEGE CAMPUSES AND *THE VAGINA MONOLOGUES*

Jo Reger and Lacey Story

My vagina's angry. It is. It is pissed off. My vagina's furious and it needs to talk. It needs to talk about all this shit. It needs to talk to you. I mean, what's the deal? An army of people out there thinking up ways to torture my poor-ass, gentle, loving vagina.... Spending their days constructing psycho products and nasty ideas to undermine my pussy. Vagina Mother-fuckers.

"My Angry Vagina," The Vagina Monologues[1]

Shocking, angry, poignant, joyful, in the last several years Eve Ensler's *The Vagina Monologues* has changed the cultural landscape. A series of monologues based on interviews with more than two hundred women, *The Vagina Monologues* have grown from a one-actress production by the author to star-studded assemblies performed across the nation. In the monologues, Ensler explores issues such as rape as a war crime, body image, menstruation, Native American genocide, along with celebrating women's sexual lives and the female anatomy. Gloria Steinem describes the monologues as offering a "personal, grounded-in-the-body way of moving towards the future" where the audience will emerge "with alternatives to the old patriarchal dualism of feminine/ masculine, body/mind and sexual/spiritual."[2] As the productions of the monologues have multiplied, so has the response. Overwhelmed with audience members' personal "vagina" stories, Ensler, with the help of activists from Feminist.com, created the V-Day organization in 1997.[3] The mission of V-Day is to end violence against women by increasing awareness and raising funds to support organizations working to ensure women's safety.

In 1999 the V-Day organization established the college initiative, which gave permission for universities and colleges to perform *The Vagina Monologues* and use the proceeds to stop violence against women and children in their communities as long as they followed organizational guidelines.[4] Within five years, *The Vagina Monologues* has gone from being performed at sixty-five colleges and universities to 602.[5] The college campaign for 2002 raised almost $2 million and more than $14 million has been raised worldwide since it was started.[6] In sum, *The Vagina Monologues* has sparked grassroots, national, and global activism.

The Vagina Monologues has spread on university campuses at a time when there is some ambiguity over the state of contemporary feminism. In the media, "post"-feminism has been declared and young women and men are portrayed as rejecting feminist ideas. Scholars and activists argue that feminism is not dead but has reemerged in a third wave different from previous feminist generations. To explore the state of contemporary feminism, we examine how two college campuses react to the women-centered *Vagina Monologues*, constructing case studies over a four-year period. On one campus, we find the monologues serve as an awakening for individuals through the reclamation of language and sexuality and by fostering a sense of feminist community. On the other campus, the reaction is mixed, with some students embracing the monologues and others dismissing them as exclusionary and one-dimensional. Based on these different reactions, we argue that *The Vagina Monologues* serves as a cultural "thermometer" for contemporary feminism, illustrating how different communities of feminists respond to the production's women-centered message. Depending on community context, response to the monologues runs from hot (serving as a political experience and sparking feminist community) to cool (bringing forth contemporary feminist and gender-related issues and controversies). In sum, this analysis, although limited to two contexts, allows us to gain a more nuanced view of contemporary feminism set in community contexts.

Our findings are based on two case studies of college campuses, one in the Midwest and one on the East Coast. We also draw upon our experiences as an organizer of (Lacey) and participants (Jo and Lacey) in 2002 and 2003 *Vagina Monologues* productions. To construct the case studies, we interviewed twenty-four young feminists,[7] did participant observation, and collected relevant documents.[8] To provide anonymity, we created pseudonyms for the colleges, interviewees, and campus organizations. At the Midwest site (Woodview State University), the fourteen interviews drew participants from the only visible feminist organization. This group served as the center of a feminist community and produced the monologues each year. At the East Coast site (Evers College), the ten interviewees were from a more diverse mix of progressive and feminist organizations and included women who had attended, worked on, and performed in the monologues. Our sampling strategy was to identify and interview self-identified feminists on both college campuses. Our goal was to examine their experiences with *The Vagina Monologues*. At the time of the interviews, all the women considered themselves to be feminists and shared a basic definition of feminism and its goals.[9] The definition included the belief in equality, and the embracing of a variety of human rights, including freedom of choice, freedom from gender stereotypes, and freedom for all oppressed individuals. Before examining reactions to the monologues on these campuses, we first briefly describe each case study site.

THE CASE STUDIES

In many ways the two campuses are a study in contrasts. The Midwest case study is in an environment largely ambivalent about feminism and politically conservative. The other case study is in an East Coast community known for its progressive and liberal politics. Because of its progressiveness, the women-only college attracts faculty, staff, and students who are open to the ideas of feminism and feminist politics.

Woodview

The university is largely a commuter campus and lacks the sense of community formed around residential campuses. The university (i.e., students, faculty, and administrators) is also rather conservative in its political and educational stances. For example, when the first director of the women's studies program brought to campus Inga Muscio, the author of *Cunt*, she had a difficult time advertising the event when some of the staff and faculty objected to the word *cunt* being used on flyers. While there are groups on campus sympathetic to feminist causes, such as a gay/lesbian/bisexual student group and the Green party, these groups have little campus visibility.[10]

Feminist activism emerges mostly from the student organization, Forum for Women (FFW), which was founded in 2001 largely as a result of the efforts of one dynamic undergraduate student, who had worked for two years to establish the group, and an incoming director of women's studies. The founding of the group was spurred by the creation of a women's studies program, which developed after existing several years as a concentration of study. According to Laura, former president of the FFW, the goal of the group is "to educate the people on campus" about the issues facing women and also about feminism. Being feminists, she said, "is a part of who we are and who we associate ourselves with." Over the past years, the group has organized several educationally focused events including a white ribbon campaign where men pledge to stop violence against women, breast cancer information distribution, and a Love Your Body Day. The group also organized the 2002 through 2004 performances of *The Vagina Monologues.*

FFW is a central meeting place for feminist activists with weekly meetings that have an attendance of anywhere from ten to twenty-two women. While men are present at the meetings, women make up the majority of members. The ages of the members range from nineteen to twenty-five. While not all the women know each other, many are connected through friendship networks and the meetings often start with women greeting each other with hugs and introductions to those who are new faces in the group. The women's studies program plays a role in the group's recruitment, with several of the members coming to the group after taking a women's studies course. The group is mixed in terms of sexuality, with women identifying as straight, bisexual, and lesbian and is predominately white with few women of color attending.

Evers College

Students, faculty, and the administration at Evers College are generally liberal in their politics and the college has traditionally fostered a feminist environment. A variety of student organizations exist that address issues of gender and other forms of inequality. Those organizations include Feminist Alliance; Feminists United; the Lesbian, Bisexual, Transgendered Alliance; Council for Students of Color; Prism (a support group for lesbian, bisexual, and questioning women of color); Native American Women of Evers; and the Women's World Affairs Committee. *The Vagina Monologues* has been performed yearly since 2000 and productions have been directed and performed by students. It should be noted that for the 2000 through 2003 performances, the events were organized by an Evers staff member. It was not until 2004 that a student organized the event, hiring directors, and coordinating the production.

The most visible, overtly feminist group is Feminists United, which held several well-attended programs related to reproductive rights and abortion in 2002. The organization's visibility is largely the result of one student who is interested in issues of reproductive choice, and only a few women attend the planning meetings. Group members in 2002 did not play a role in producing the monologues on campus. Students credit the lack of interest in Feminists United (and feminist organizing overall) to a sense that they are in a nonsexist "bubble," at an all-women's college, which is nestled in a progressive community. Many note, however, that their interest in feminism will probably increase once they graduate and enter the working world.

At Evers, women's studies is not the same conduit to feminism that it is at Woodview. Many of the women interviewed had not taken women's studies courses at college. Several of the women explained that most of the courses offered at Evers were "women's studies" classes because of the focus on women's issues and feminist ideas, although the courses were not specifically designated as a part of the college's actual women's studies program.

As a result of this environment, Evers women engage in issues not addressed at Woodview. The focus on female empowerment and multiple courses on gender and sexuality led many of the students to move away from critiquing traditional sex, sexuality, and gender norms and the resulting oppression, and instead to focus on creating new systems of gender and sexuality. As a result, six of the ten students interviewed identify as "queer," a gender and sexuality beyond the dichotomy of heterosexual and homosexual, and several students on the campus identify as transgender. Vanessa Edwards-Foster has defined the term *transgender* as "an umbrella term used to describe anyone who is gender different: someone born of one gender, but having either a casual affinity for clothing, and/or affectations of the opposite gender; or someone with an innate identification as the opposite gender."[11] As a result of the profeminist environment and presence of transgendered men (female to male)[12] on campus, many of the Evers students focus on transgender and queer activism versus feminist issues. For example, a major initiative of several student groups is to lobby the administration to incorporate transgender language into the school's policies and to acknowledge transgendered students' rights.

In sum, Woodview and Evers are campuses that diverge in many ways, yet both sponsored student-directed and organized productions of *The Vagina Monologues*. We next discuss the concept of political generations and the influence of the monologues in these two different settings.

POLITICAL GENERATIONS AND COMMUNITY

One of the ways scholars have conceptualized how people become politically active is through the concept of a political generation. According to Karl Mannheim, a political generation occurs when, "common and historical experiences during one's youth produce a common frame of reference from which individuals of similar ages would view their later political experiences."[13] Political generations are then the result of experiences that bring together a group of people and politically "awaken" them at the same time, influencing their future beliefs, values, and political involvements.[14] For example, Faye Ginsburg argued in the 1980s that the women more likely to join the abortion protests of the time did so because of their experiences in the earlier women's movement.[15] Scholars believe late adolescence is often a time for political generation formation.[16] As young adults interact, they reflect on the ideas that they have internalized through interaction with their families, peers, and communities and develop a sense of their own place in society. Braungart and Braungart argue that young adults are most likely to be critical of the political legacies of the generations before them in the formation of their worldviews.[17] Henry labels this process "disidentification," a time when political generations engage in a particular idea or ideology as a result of generational conflict or distancing.[18]

In the past, scholars critiqued the use of political generations arguing that it treats all groups the same, particularly in terms of age. One's sex and gender (in a society with gender inequality) can prompt a political experience and promote the development of a political generation. Schneider argues that without the recognition of gender, the practices and meanings of political generations are not fully understood. "When women are put at the center of inquiry, it raises questions that have not been raised about who, how, and when social groups come to experience similar perceptions and understandings."[19]

Along with sex and gender, community context can also shape the formation of a political community. Whittier argues that political generations are not the result of age or life stage but are the result of experiences set in a particular community context. These experiences forge multiple groups, or "micro-cohorts" of people who enter a movement at different times in diverse locations and who have unique political experiences.[20] We draw upon the political generation literature and argue that *The Vagina Monologues* is a politicizing feminist experience based on identification with gendered narratives, fostering different political generations depending upon the community context.

WOODVIEW'S FEMINIST GENERATION

At Woodview, we argue that the production of the monologues directly influences the fostering of a feminist microcohort, and identify two ways in which women experience this political awakening. The first is by reclaiming and revaluing of words traditionally considered taboo or derogatory by society through the production and the fostering of a voice. The second (and related way) is through the fostering of a feminist community on campus.

Reclaiming Language and Sexuality

One of the ways that people experience being a part of a political generation is through gaining a political voice that can articulate politicizing events. Feminist theorist bell hooks describes voice as the embodiment of the individual and the "moving from silence into speech as a revolutionary gesture."[21] Gaining voice means more that sharing a common language; hooks conceptualizes voice as an act of resistance:

> Speaking becomes both a way to engage in active self-transformation and a rite of passage where one moves from being object to being subject. Only as subjects can we speak. As objects, we remain voiceless—our beings defined and interpreted by others.[22]

Becoming subjects (i.e., active) rather than objects (i.e., passive) can entail reclaiming language that has objectified and denigrated women. In her book *Cunt*, Inga Muscio reclaims words such as *cunt, whore,* and *bitch* and argues that in the past these words had positive associations.[23] However, the process of reclaiming words and moving from object to subject as the women of Woodview staged the monologues was not always an easy process.

In order to be able to be comfortable on stage saying words such as *vagina* and *cunt* or even moaning (as called for in one monologue), students had to come to terms with the monologues' language in a less public way. It should be noted that the word *vagina* is spoken approximately 130 times in each performance. In 2002, while planning the event, group members often discussed the production with visible discomfort. They were often hesitant to say the word *vagina*, or talk about anything that was related to vaginas. Ensler acknowledges the negative connotations in much of the language when she wrote, "Vagina: it sounds like an infection at best."[24]

Over the span of eight months of planning, the women reported becoming comfortable with using these words and even began to have an affinity for them. As the meetings continued words such as *vagina*, *cunt*, and *orgasm* became a part of the talk even when the script was not being discussed. During these meetings it became common for the women to share amusing or disturbing stories about gynecological visits. Some women also began to talk openly about sexual experiences. One woman who observed this change said she could tell that women were becoming "increasingly comfortable with the idea of sharing their own real life experiences."

This newfound sense of liberation was evident in the last week before the 2002 performances. A group of the women decided to go into the busy student center during the lunch hour and chant *vagina* and *cunt*. They also yelled from one side of the student common to the other, "*The Vagina Monologues* are coming!" "The what?" "*The Vagina Monologues!* Are you going?" "To what?" "*The Vagina Monologues!*"

By reclaiming the language and learning to express it publicly, group members began to resist the words' negative connotations, reclaiming their voices and a vision of themselves and their sexuality. Jane, who participated in the 2002 and 2003 productions, said:

> *The Vagina Monologues* allows women to be empowered by their own bodies and existence. They make you question why you feel the way you do about a particular word or phrase. You begin to question why you believe what they, society, have constructed you to believe, that many times language is pulling women down and we so often allow this to happen. *The Vagina Monologues* tells women to grab onto what they deserve, [not to] let language make you feel ashamed, but instead let it empower you.

The process of gaining voice was also aided by a "vagina workshop" attended by many of the women in the production. During the workshop they performed "vagina" exercises in which they used their bodies and voices to express emotions of their vaginas through movement, sound, voice, or even silence. After each individual articulated an emotion, the group would echo it. The women also had a chance to share their personal experiences with other women who were at the workshop, creating a sense of closeness amongst the participants.

As *The Vagina Monologues* allowed the women involved to reclaim their voices and revalue words, it also enabled them to talk about body image and sexuality in a more personal way. Openly discussing sexuality and female anatomy with other women has often been seen as a taboo.[25] For one woman, Sally, the play brought back memories of her own experiences growing up. She said one of her favorite parts was a line where the speaker is talking about menstruation and how drops of blood look like paint in the toilet. She said, "I remember when I was younger I was so fascinated by that. When I first read it I was like 'Oh my God that's what I thought when I was like 15 years old.'" The monologues provided her with an opportunity to reclaim her past experiences as positive. She continued:

> I was so like "Wow, that's soooo cool" and [the monologues are] women reclaiming sexuality, talking about birth, and talking about female genital mutilation and talking about rape and all these different issues and kind of saying "You're normal, you're ok, vaginas are beautiful. ..." It's kind of reclaiming your right to be sexual. Your right to, I don't know, all these things. [It is] kind of normalizing a lot of things too [such as] menstruation.

Other women had the same experience, using the monologues as a way of coming to understand their lives or bodies differently. Maria said:

> In a way it gave a reason to be able to talk about women's bodies ... my body ... in a more open way, to be able to embrace positive feelings about my body and sexuality. It wasn't such a hush, hush thing to talk about anymore.

Another cast member, Naomi, said, "I felt that this experience gave me the opportunity to become comfortable and confident with the language of my own sexuality." This sense of awakening and gaining a voice politicized the women and helped them to forge a common bond with each other.

This coming to voice was not limited to words but included other expressions of sexuality. One particular monologue, "The Woman Who Loved to Make Vaginas Happy," consisting of many different types of moans that women make during orgasms, played a role in many of the performers' coming to voice. One woman, Andrea, noted that this monologue gave her permission to have a sexual voice. She said:

> [The performer's] moans were just such a universal release. Everyone laughed because guaranteed everyone had made at least one of those sounds at one time or another. I hadn't realized how

sexy moans actually were, that it was okay to enjoy yourself and be loud and aggressive. I had always been afraid to be loud [during sex], even with women, because I don't know, I had been quiet for years and did not know why. I just was.

In sum, *The Vagina Monologues* serve as a mechanism for women to move from object to subject in language and expression, and establish a voice that resists negative definitions of what it means to be a woman and a valued sexual being. An important aspect is the public nature of performances. At Woodview, the audience consisted primarily of other students, faculty, family members, and some community members. The relations between the audience and cast removed any sense of anonymity from the performers and intensified their sense of "speaking out."

Fostering Community

The second way the women experienced a political awakening was through the fostering of a feminist community on their campus. Buechler argues that through the participation in social movements, women can come to create a free space in which to explore their lives and participate in the creation of a social movement community.[26] When women experience this coming together and free space facilitated by a political event, the result is a social movement community fused around a political generation.[27] Evidence of this community is an expressed sense of belonging to the group and a feeling of connection. Several of the women interviewed discussed how a sense of sisterhood was created among those who were involved in the monologues. For some, this was slow to develop. According to Sally:

> I don't think I really was too involved [in the group] until we got going on *The Vagina Monologues* and then I decided to ... spend all my time doing stuff with the [group].... Before, I noticed the membership was kind of shaky. People would come and go and then once we were like focused on something it was like, people came more steadily, and since *The Vagina Monologues* there's at least a steady group of ten. People come and go, but there's like a base group that always comes, which is really good for a student organization.

For many of the women, the process of doing the monologues drew the group together. Kyra, who had felt alienated by some of the group dynamics, said:

I don't know, but once, once we actually started getting into the monologues it was cool because … I really got to be like pretty good friends with [group members] and stuff.

As the group focused on the monologues, they began to know each other in a more personal way. This led to the creation of a community. Emily said:

I know for a fact that being a part of the [group] on campus and performing *The Vagina Monologues* I was able to meet so many people that I would have never had the opportunity to talk to. It was extremely refreshing to be around women from so many walks of life. It was as if the only thing that mattered was that we were all women who wanted to see change and to create some of that change. From the time we first announced *The Vagina Monologues*, to the first time we read the script, to the first time we flyered, to the first night's performance, the positive growth that we had as a group could only be called a sisterhood in my opinion.

For Kyra the experience was unlike any other in her education and made her realize the importance of women in her life. She said:

You know I felt so good after we did the monologues, I felt like I was part of something and I haven't done anything extracurricular at [Woodview]. I never really even did anything like that in high school. But it's sad, like I mean all my friends are guys.…

The process of working together also brought the women a sense of empowerment. Andrea said:

To be part of a woman-based team was extremely liberating in the sense that we were creating change. We were part of a huge worldwide movement, which is the V-Day organization, in performing the monologues. It was especially liberating to talk to other women who had performed the monologues at one time or another and to share ways to get the word out.

While the majority of the FFW women did not know each other when they became involved in this production, through attending group meetings and preparing for the monologues they developed relationships based on common feminist beliefs. Although the members have diverse interests in education, music, and pop culture, they created a community where they share similar feminist beliefs. The monologues' focus on violence and reclaiming sexuality was reflected in the group's projects on campus such as The Clothesline Project (i.e., a project where shirts made by survivors of violence are hung out for display) and Take Back the Night (an antiviolence march to reclaim women's safety).

Along with creating a community for those involved, some of the women suggested that *The Vagina Monologues* creates a type of sisterhood and community for women in the audience as well. Paulina said, "It allowed women in the audience to identify with other women and realize that there is a community out there of people who go through the same things and to be able to talk about it gives a sense of freedom." Although all of the women in the audience may not be of the same age, or hold the same feminist belief system, *The Vagina Monologues* provides a forum for women who are concerned about these issues. In doing so, it has the potential to draw generations of feminists together. Because of the impact of these performances, some women from the audiences joined the group the following school year.

Being involved in these activities, along with the actual performance, created a series of experiences affecting the women's political beliefs. The women interviewed felt stronger about their feminist beliefs and many made a commitment to a feminist lifestyle. Felicia said she makes it a point to keep up with feminist issues and to "jump into" participating in any events that are related to those issues. She graduated right after the 2002 performances and sought jobs and internships as a feminist activist. Others expressed a stronger commitment to feminist activism than had previously been the case. As Maria, a graduating senior, said:

> I think my feeling for the feminist movement and activism are much stronger after *The Vagina Monologues*. First of all, it was the biggest activist project I've ever been involved in, one that took planning and work over months and months. So it was the first time I had the experience of working with other women and feminists toward a specific goal over an extended period of time … this made me feel my commitment to feminism and my desire to be active more than ever. Also, our results were amazing. I actually got to see and hear people being affected by our work and opening their minds. Being immersed in it so long made me want to never stop working for feminism.

Many of the women who did not graduate stayed active in the group and continued to plan performances in 2003 and 2004.

In sum, on the campus of Woodview State University, *The Vagina Monologues* is a powerful influence in establishing a feminist community and affecting the lives of individual women. Because of the public productions, feminism and feminists are made visible on campus. Through the production of the monologues, women participate in a politicizing experience that revolves around issues of gender. This experience forges a political generation on the campus, invigorated by the monologues. This political generation accepts the monologues as feminist in content, and fosters a sense of community and activism on related issues such as sexual assault, domestic violence, breast cancer awareness, and eating disorders. In other words, the women and men of Woodview's feminist community take the issues of the monologues and make them their own. However, the staging of the monologues on college campuses is not without controversy and not all campuses react in the same manner.

EVERS COLLEGE'S POLITICIZATION IN A "FEMINIST BUBBLE"

The criticism of *The Vagina Monologues* in the nationwide discourse takes two general directions. Some find the content of the monologues and the use of words such as *cunt, pussy,* and *vagina* offensive. A festival related to the monologues was called a "classless act of debauchery" by one political leader and another media pundit warned that the monologues were killing heterosexual romance on campuses.[28] Several student groups across the country interested in putting on the monologues have faced barriers from administrators, community, and political leaders.[29] While some feel the monologues have gone too far (linguistically and romantically), others have criticized the play for not going far enough. In 2003, participants on a women's studies listserv engaged in a long critical conversation about the play's view of women, its too Western orientation, and the invisibility of transgendered people in the play. The latter concerns are evident in the Evers students' approach.[30]

While the women of Woodview enthusiastically embrace *The Vagina Monologues* as a form of feminist empowerment, Evers students were much more ambivalent. Some of the Evers College students echoed the critique that the monologues do not go far enough in dismantling cultural norms. Others find the monologues a welcome, but not terribly empowering addition to the feminist culture on the campus. We argue that these different reactions are the result of the feminist-friendly Evers community. We first discuss Evers College's "feminist bubble" culture and how the play is viewed as positive by some and harmful by others. We then examine how criticisms of the play illustrate the issues that do mobilize the Evers community.

Adding to the Culture

Students noted that in a feminist-friendly environment, the fostering of an active feminist community is difficult. All of the students interviewed discussed the idea of a campus "bubble" that insulates students from "real life" including acts of sexism and discrimination. Within this bubble, mobilizing feminists can be difficult. For example, the most visible and overtly feminist group is Feminists United, which held a few well-attended programs in the 2002 to 2003 school year but overall was not a very visible campus organization.[31] Therefore events that can bring out large numbers of women and contain feminist issues are seen as beneficial to feminists on campus. Terri summed up this perspective. She said:

> I think it is [a feminist event.] Practically every school I know has that [the monologues]which I think is really good and I think it is an interesting thing to do, and especially since it is around Valentine's Day. It's a nice little reminder, like "Hey we're here," and I think it reaffirms women's right to be outspoken, especially about matters of sexuality, and to sort of claim the spotlight, you know. There's no one talking about penises up there.

For Abby, who had organized the 2004 *Vagina Monologues* on campus, the play was important because of the V-Day fund-raising and not so much the content. She said, "As I get older I think parts of it are kind of, you know, cheesy and not typical, but I like *The Vagina Monologues* because of the [V-Day] campaign now. I like what it is trying to do." In addition, Abby noted there is some ambivalence on campus to the play. She continued:

Jo: So what do you think *The Vagina Monologues* means to a place like [Evers]?

Abby: (Sigh) For a lot of people it's you know this rahh rahh feminist third wave empowerment thing. For a lot of people it's cute, and it's funny, and it's touching. I mean there are monologues that I think are absolutely amazing and there are some that absolutely everyone I've ever met hates. It's out there more for what it's used for, what it's supposed to be doing. It is for women and girls to stop sexual violence. So of course that's really why I'm there because I care so much about [this issue]. And there are some people that are there purely for the theater. It just goes all across the board and I don't know if I'm really qualified to tell you how everyone reacts to it. You know my friends range from, "Oh that's cheesy and awful but I'll come see it 'cuz it's your thing." For some people it's like, "Oh I love Vagina Monologues. It's so great. It's so funny. It's so sexy" and whatever and everything in between.

Sabrina, who has been involved in performing the play for two years, said that being at an all-women's college gave the monologues special meaning. She said:

It's kind of like a solidarity thing and here at [Evers] I think it's a combination of that and also this is a place where we are young women—we just want to do everything we can that might be considered outrageous, you know? And if it means twenty of us getting up on a stage and ranting about vaginas—that's great. That's good for us and it's a campus that is extremely willing to embrace that kind of effort.

However, that need to be outrageous and the overtly sexual nature of some of the monologues did dilute some of the messages in her opinion. Sabrina continued:

Unfortunately sometimes I think here at [Evers] *The Vagina Monologues* is more about the sex part than anything else. And it's just another excuse to just belligerently talk about sex. That's the way that I kind of say that [Evers] women talk about sex sometimes because we are so liberated or whatever and we're in this environment where anything goes almost … to me it's just violent the way that we overuse sex in our conversations. You know? Like everything is about flirtation. Like people create drama around it because it's something fun to do and *The Vagina Monologues* is like Valentine's Day and people get to go with their significant others…. It turns into some kind of creepy foreplay thing …

For some, the content was not what was important but the fact that the monologues offer an opportunity to advance their own political issues. Skye, a student somewhat ambivalent about claiming a feminist identity, sees the monologues as mobilizing the campus. However, she used the event as an opportunity to advance her own political issues. She said:

> We did *The Vagina Monologues* at [Evers] a few weeks ago and I had Amnesty [International] put out a letter about some lesbians in Ecuador who had been beaten up. So I guess I've tried to personally emphasize my activism on human rights and sort of incorporated [it] into a feminist agenda on the campus.

In sum, while the play is seen as an appropriate cultural addition to Evers, the production does not foster a feminist community. Instead, students enjoy the sexual nature of some of the monologues and support the cause of ending violence against women.

Spreading the "Wrong" Message

So, while three students did not see the monologues as significant on campus and did not mention them while talking about feminism at Evers, three students did list a variety of concerns ranging from the play being essentialist to the lack of gay/lesbian/transgender people represented. For Becca, the concern with the monologues was not its political content but the fact that it has become a political fad. She said:

> Well, I feel like people like it because it is so outrageous. They still see it as outrageous you know.... They get to say that they saw it and everything.... Obviously it's a product of a global movement but I don't know [if] it's in line with their politics [or if] they would just like to say they were there and everything. I went for my first time just a few weeks ago. It was the first time I ever saw the monologues and I was unimpressed honestly.

Along with it being a political fad, Becca echoed some of the criticism leveled by other Evers feminists that with the focus on the vagina, the play views women in essentialist terms and does not address forces such as socialization and culture that shape women's lives. Becca continued:

> I almost found it offensive like the skits "you are your clitoris" and I was like "No, you are not. You are something beyond that." And isn't this something you are trying to get into people's heads? ... I almost felt like it was a step back. Some of the skits were "We are—we are vaginas." No we are human beings. We have parts other than that.

Essentialism is the belief that women's biology and psychology are inherently different from men's. As an ideology, essentialism has been blamed for conceptualizing all women as a universal group and ignoring the differences between women's experiences with class, race, ethnicity, sexuality, and power. The criticism that the play focuses on women as a universal category was elaborated on by Sandra. She viewed the monologues as focusing too much on the lives of Western women and ignoring the situations of women in the non-Western world. She said, "What would happen if you threw in somebody who was a Hindu female woman…, what would they say about it?"

While Sandra was troubled that the monologues largely ignored the lives of non-Western women,[32] she was also concerned by the lack of lesbians in the production. Only two longer monologues specifically deal with a lesbian relationship.[33] One is between an older more experienced woman and a younger woman ("The Little Coochi Snorcher that Could") and the other is a lesbian who has multiple sexual partners ("The Woman who Loved to Make Vaginas Happy"). Sandra explained:

> The fact is *The Vagina Monologues* is very straight oriented. I watched it for the first time, I hadn't seen them until this year and I was kind of let down because I had them up on this [pedestal]. [I thought] I'm gonna really love this, it's really gonna say a lot because you know women being proud of their anatomy, and I went there and I was like, [this] doesn't work for me, doesn't fit me in there.

In her view, the monologues reflect second wave feminism by focusing predominantly on heterosexual women. Some feminists in the 1970s and 1980s were criticized for not addressing their homophobia and for purging lesbians from feminist organizations.[34] Sandra listed those whose sexual experiences are not included in the monologues. She said:

> First of all I mean anyone who's not heterosexual, people who are not comfortable in their gender identity, and also, people who are asexual who really don't think that their anatomy and their sexual orientation has anything to do with their life [are left out].

Her comments reflect the concern many groups have expressed about the lack of attention to transgender and intersexual people's experiences in the monologues. Intersexuals are "people born with sex chromosomes, external genitalia, or internal reproductive systems that are not considered 'standard' for either male or female."[35] Activists from the Intersex Society of North America have attended productions of the monologues, passing out informational flyers. One of the pieces in the monologues that has drawn the most fire from intersex activists is the one in which a father promises his daughter, born without a vagina, that "we're gonna get you the best homemade pussy in America." According to activist Emi Koyama, the laughter following that segment is hurtful and offensive to intersex people, making genital surgeries a joke.[36] The Intersex Society has organized events at a variety of college campuses, and has persuaded some college organizers to donate money to intersex organizations. In addition, Ensler has been pressured to add a transgender monologue. The author defended the lack of transgendered stories:

> Vagina stories found me, as did the people who wanted to produce the play or bring it to their town. Whenever I have tried to write monologues to serve a politically correct agenda, for example, it fails. Note the lack of monologues about menopause or transgendered women. I tried. *The Vagina Monologues* is about attraction not promotion.[37]

The debates about transgendered and intersex people affected the 2004 Evers production. Abby said of the relationship between transgender and the play:

> I guess it's complicated because of the particular identity that [Evers] has. We're all biological women but there is a growing transgender population on this campus so the reaction of trans men and boys to *The Vagina Monologues* is interesting sometimes. I had someone who was going to be helping me with this show who is male identified ... and then decided he didn't want to be involved here because that was getting really complicated for him.

The presence of the "feminist bubble" along with controversies on the content of the play means that *The Vagina Monologues* draws a mixed response from Evers students. Some expect the monologues will be performed, "a given" on a campus like Evers. Others find the monologues essentialist, colonialist for "othering" non-Western women, and ignoring the diversity of women, particularly in terms of gender and sexuality. These issues led Becca to express concern that many schools, in the process of producing the monologues, are not engaging in any other forms of feminist activism that would start dialogues about the situations of non-Western women, transgender, or lesbian/gay/queer people.

DISCUSSION AND CONCLUSION

Ferree and Hess suggest that each feminist generation offers its own unique opinions, values, and ideas that shape and mold an ever-changing movement.[38] Recent work on contemporary feminism supports their contention. Although there is still much debate about the idea of a third wave, definitions of a third wave of feminism include the idea that it is a form of political generation resulting from individuals' experiences in a society that saw a surge of feminist activism in the 1970s and the cultural and political backlash in the 1980s and 1990s. We view *The Vagina Monologues* as an event experienced by women that has the potential to foster a political generation in particular contexts. However, as our research illustrates, third wave feminism emerges in microcohorts, which differ from each other depending on the community.

At Woodview, *The Vagina Monologues* mobilizes feminism through the reclaiming of language and by providing a vehicle to establish a feminist community on campus in which young feminists can bond and share experiences, creating a political generation. At Evers though, the play has less of a direct effect on campus feminism. While some Evers students find the monologues important and interesting, others log serious criticisms of their content and ideology. We can conclude that the monologues are an empowering experience in environments suffering from a dearth of visible feminists or an overt hostility to feminism, such as at Woodview. In environments such as Evers, the monologues play a less important role because feminism is not absent in this environment and the culture encourages questioning and critique of sexuality and gender norms.

Drawing on Whittier's notion of generational microcohorts, we predict that as more women enter the Woodview and Evers campus communities, the type of political generation, and consequentially the feminist activism, will change as *The Vagina Monologues* becomes a more culturally embedded, familiar phenomenon. At Woodview, many of the performers and audience members are seeing the monologues and hearing their vagina-centered messages for the first time. This creates an atmosphere of empowerment and excitement not seen in a context such as Evers where the monologues are an accepted and expected part of the cultural landscape. In addition, discussions of transgender and intersexuality are just starting at Woodview, whereas Evers students are engaged in a more in-depth dialogue.

Whether or not the monologues are a problematic vehicle of feminism, as evidenced by Evers students' critiques, or are responsible for sustaining feminism, as illustrated at Woodview, remains to be decided. This study does indicate that contemporary feminism is alive and complex, varying greatly by community context. Young women (and men) are doing feminism, but not in exactly the same manner in every locale. Instead, the environment, community, and culture provide a context that shapes the experiences which in turn create new political generations.

For scholars of the women's movement, this study reveals the difficulty of describing any of the "waves" of feminism in absolute terms. Separated by miles, politics, and culture, two groups of young women, similar in age, race, and class, create different understandings of the social world. As argued by Mannheim, these experiences shape a political understanding that can continue throughout an individual's life.[39] Whittier argues that social movements change as new groups of people enter, bringing with them different experiences, and creating new understandings.[40] Contemporary feminism is full of microcohorts entering at different times at different places, creating a complex type of feminism, not easily categorized. *The Vagina Monologues*, both positively and negatively, are a part of that creation.

NOTES

1. Eve Ensler, "My Angry Vagina," in *The Vagina Monologues* (New York: Villard, 2001) 69–73.
2. Gloria Steinem, "Foreward," *The Vagina Monologues* (New York: Villard, 2001), xvi.
3. Ensler, xxxii–xxxiii.
4. The guidelines are: 1. Only one person at each school can be the official campaign organizer. 2. There must be an active e-mail address. 3. Students must be involved in all aspects of the production to the greatest extent possible. College campaign productions must be primarily student-run, student-acted, and student-directed. 4. Men are invited to participate in College campaign productions but not as actors. 5. Schools should strive for diversity. 6. College campaign performances must be done in on-campus venues. 7. Schools must use the V-Day version of the script of *The Vagina Monologues* and the new script must be followed. Organizers may not edit any introductions or monologues or exclude or change the order of any of the monologues. Music, dance, and/or testimonials can be added. 8. If your college campaign production is performed in a language other than English, you must get the translated script from V-Day and you must acknowledge the translator in the program. 9. In promoting and publicizing, schools must adhere to the "identity guidelines" and other publicity guidelines. 10. Organizers must fill out an online follow-up report within 30 days of completion of the V-Day Campaign production. "Guidelines for Joining," http:// www.vday.org (accessed December 12, 2003) College Campaign.
5. "Participating Schools," http://www.vday.org (accessed August 9, 2004).
6. http://www.vday.org/contents/vcampagins/indiancountry/join (accessed December 12, 2003).
7. The women interviewed were between the ages of nineteen and twenty-six. Twenty women (83%) identified as European-American; one woman identified as Pakistani, two as biracial and one as African American. The social class of the women ranged from poor to upper middle class, with most (75%) identifying as lower to upper middle class. Almost 70 percent of the women identified as queer/lesbian/bisexual.

The interviews were open-ended, structured, and lasted between forty-five minutes and two hours. The interviews at Evers were gathered through a snowball method and the Woodview interviews consisted of a selection of participants in the feminist group on campus.

8.   The case studies were selected to examine regional variations in feminist activism and identities. The participant observations are ongoing for each site. Documents collected included flyers, notices of events, and e-mails sent to group participants.

9.   One woman was ambivalent about claiming a feminist identity but did, however, consider her activism to be feminist.

10. It should be noted that the gay/lesbian/bisexual group reorganized after 2003 and was beginning to gain more of a campus presence.

11. Vanessa Edwards-Foster, "Frequently Asked Questions," (1999) http://www.ntac.org/resources/faq.html, National Transgender Advocacy Coalition (May 12, 2003).

12. At the time of the interviews, most of the transgender men or boys on campus were transitioning or had chosen not to have surgery and were still considered biologically female. Therefore, they were allowed to enroll in an all-women's college.

13. Karl Mannheim, "The Problem of Generations," in *Essays on the Sociology of Knowledge*, ed. Paul Keckemeti (London: Routledge and Kegan Paul, 1952), 276–320.

14. Richard G. Braungart and Margaret M. Braungart, "Life Course and Generational Politics," *Annual Review of Sociology* 12 (1986): 205–31; Mannheim; Beth Schneider, "Political Generations in the Contemporary Women's Movement," *Sociological Inquiry* 58 (1988): 4–21.

15. Faye Ginsburg, *Contested Lives: The Abortion Debate in an American Community* (Berkeley: University of California Press, 1989).

16. Mannheim, 303–304.

17. Braungart and Braungart, 210.

18. Astrid Henry, "Feminism's Family Problem," in *Catching a Wave: Reclaiming Feminism for the 21st Centruy*, eds. Rory Dicker and Alison Piepmeir (Boston: Northeastern University Press, 2003), 209–231.

19. Schneider, 5–6, see also Margaret Braungart, "Aging and Politics," *Journal of Political and Military Sociology* 12 (1984): 79–98.

20. Nancy Whittier, "Political Generations, Micro-Cohorts, and the Transformation of Social Movements," *American Sociological Review* 62 (1997): 760–78.

21. bell hooks, *Talking Back: Thinking Feminist, Thinking Black* (Boston: South End Press, 1989), 12.

22. Ibid., 12.

23. Inga Muscio, *Cunt: A Declaration of Independence* (Seattle, WA: Seal Press, 1998).

24. Ensler, 5.

25. See Ensler; Muscio; Barbara Stern, "Advertising to the Other Culture: Women's Use of Language and Language's Use of Women," *National Forum* 77 (1997), 35–39; Leona Tanenbaum, *Slut: Growing Up Female with a Bad Reputation* (New York: Seven Stories Press, 1999).

26. Steven M. Buechler, *Women's Movements in the United States: Woman Suffrage, Equal Rights and Beyond* (New Brunswick, NJ: Rutgers University Press, 1990).

27. See also Nancy Whittier, *Feminist Generations: The Persistence of the Radical Women's Movement* (Philadelphia: Temple University Press, 1995).

28. Jennifer Yachnin, "Making a 4-letter Word Respectable (to Some)," *The Chronicle of Higher Education*, January 5, 2001, 8; Laura Vanderkam, "Cupid Combat Rages on Campus," *USA Today*, February 14, 2002, 17A.

29. Ensler, 134.

30. It should be noted that Ensler added a trans gender-themed monologue as an option in the 2005 script.

31. According to respondents, Feminists United was not visible at all in the 2003–2004 school year.
32. The production includes monologues by a Jewish woman, a Bosnian rape victim, a Southern woman of color, and a lesbian (and later versions a Native American woman). The rest of the monologues do not specify race-ethnicity, class, or sexuality.
33. It should be noted that the monologues are changed from year to year and new monologues are added.
34. See Karla Jay, *Tales of the Lavender Menace: A Memoir of Liberation* (New York: Basic Books, 1999). See also Gilmore, chapter 6.
35. Vanessa Edwards-Foster, "Frequently Asked Questions," (1999) http://www.ntac.org/resources/faq.html (accessed May 12, 2003).
36. "Intersex Advocates Educate Playgoers," *Just Out,* (January 4, 2002), cited on Intersex Society of North America website, http://www.isna.org/events/vday/20020104-justout.html (accessed August 9, 2004).
37. Ensler, xxvi. In 2003, an Evers student wrote a transgender/intersex series of monologues titled "The Naked I: Monologues from Beyond the Binary." However, the Evers respondents were undecided if the play was in opposition to *The Vagina Monologues.*
38. Myra Marx Ferree and Beth Hess, *Controversy and Coalition: The New Feminist Movement across Three Decades of Change* (New York: Twayne, 1994).
39. Mannheim.
40. Whittier, "Political Generations, Micro-Cohorts," 775.

9

SEARCHING FOR A HOME PLACE: ONLINE IN THE THIRD WAVE

Barbara Duncan

As an ideal medium for communications and grassroots activism, the Internet brings about a different sort of interconnectivity and activist engagement than was possible during the second wave of feminism. Online discussion groups and other online feminist organizations are now able to quickly activate through immediate asynchronous networks. Moreover, online feminist discussion groups explore the idea of creating a home, a place where participants can replenish and sustain themselves for their everyday and ongoing activist goals.

Activism in many of these third wave communities is what Jennifer Baumgardner and Amy Richards refer to as an "everyday activism" that has no immediate or directly visible effects or consequences.[1] In this sort of activism, leaders are not as visible, and groups are formed in response to immediate and temporary political actions. Although it may seem vague and ambiguous in its effects, third wave activism has the potential for a slow accretion of results and the ability to make change on a personal everyday level. Activism in third wave communities rarely results in definitive, immediate, or decisive victories; rather, it is molded by small, everyday, niche events or protests, and is driven by temporary leaders who take up for a particular cause at a particular time. While this is also true for second wave feminism, third wave feminism provides, through the medium of technology, a potentially strong voice to every participant, and a mobilized and ever present sense of home and community. Online networking in the third wave provides feminists with a home place, a protected space to return to and build a community after working toward activist goals.

For this discussion of third wave activism I examine the online community that formed out of the production and distribution of *Bust* magazine, which is representative of third wave feminism as Jennifer Baumgardner describes it.[2] At www.Bust.com, a thriving third wave community has come into existence with the initial production of a zine/magazine. *Bust*'s first issue came out in 1993 and spoke to a new generation of feminists who felt that their mothers' feminism was not quite appropriate for their ideals and values. The website was created as a way for feminists to explore issues in an ongoing and safe context, and as a way to bring together young feminists (ages 20–35) all across the globe in a forum where everyone's conversation and participation mattered. As the editors put it, *Bust* is "for women with something to get off their chests," meaning that *Bust* is a space for women to speak freely about various everyday injustices that they might encounter in their lives.[3] So the magazine developed out of a zine, which later became an independently owned magazine, and the website was added as a companion site to the magazine.

The unofficial goal of the *Bust* website is to act in various capacities, including the idea of providing a support group and to help redefine the goals of feminism through the contributions of everyday people doing feminism in a way that makes sense to them. More than 7,500 women post messages (referred to as Busties) to this discussion board and are registered as members of *Bust*. While the demographic tends to be single white women, posters from different ethnicities and nationalities post on the site.

The discussion threads fall into roughly eleven different categories, including the media, feminism, sex, feminine pastimes, dating/mating, the body, work, friends and family, politics, teen issues, and website/magazine issues. Much as *Ms. Magazine* solidified and provided an accessible and potent identity for feminist readers of the second wave, *Bust* does the same for the third wave with the magazine in conjunction with the website. Indeed, *Bust* draws upon what was perceived to be the strength and value of *Ms. Magazine*, its readers, to create a virtual world online. It is in this virtual space where participants are creating a networked community with a unique form of activism.

This chapter draws upon a comparison between *Ms. Magazine* and *Bust* magazine reader communities to highlight the similarities and tensions between these two forms of feminist groups and to illuminate a small part of what is happening in terms of feminist activism. Even though *Ms. Magazine* exists today in a different form, with similar webpages and discussion forums as *Bust,* during the 1970s, *Ms. Magazine* provided an outlet for feminists through the contributions readers submitted via their letters to the editor and the support they brought to the magazine. But *Ms. Magazine* readers were limited to a simplified, one-way dialogue over many issues of the magazine. *Bust* provides not so much a compendium of personal reader experiences, as in a "how to" manual for being a feminist, but rather is more of a coffee shop community, where activists work to reestablish and negotiate their priorities so they can connect with others to sustain their activist goals.

In order to study the *Bust* online community, participant observation, that is to say, what Norman Denzin refers to as the "method of instances," provides a framework through which to make sense of the unorganized and chaotic nature of data collection on the Internet.[4] More specifically, several discussion threads on the www.Bust.com website that pertained to issues having to do with community formation, feminism, and the evaluation and maintenance of the magazine and website were read for about a period of eighteen months (August 1999–March 2001). Another large collection of writings were collected and examined on the subject of *Ms. Magazine,* where community members from both *Bust* and *Ms.* visited each other's websites in an attempt to initiate and encourage discussion. Much debate about the nature of feminism and the distinction between *Bust* feminism and *Ms.* feminism took place during the month of January 2001. A few key members were also interviewed through e-mail in addition to several revelatory postings on community threads as to the nature of the study and to invite feedback. In addition, issues of the magazine dating back to 1995 were read, with particular attention to reader and editor conversations in the letters section. I attempted to remain participatory in a limited sense in that, on occasion, several questions were posed to the website about the magazine, but for the most part I remained more of an observer.[5] For the comparison with *Ms. Magazine,* I read the letters to the editor for *Ms. Magazine* from 1972 to 1987 as compiled in the collection, *Letters to Ms.*[6]

In this chapter I argue that third wave activism is more than just a beginner stage of activism, and has advanced to require new formations of community, ones that sustain and renew rather than just inform. Online communication serves these new purposes well, and creates an activist community that is not so much about doing feminism as it is about being a feminist in a safe and respectful place. These are still activist communities, but they are not always concentrated on doing activism using the venue of the magazine/media form.

HOME AND PLACE IN THE
TECHNOLOGIZED COMMUNITY

What makes a community a community? One of the traditional signifiers of a community is locality, or the idea that it exists in space, as an artifact of some kind of geographical location. In Ferdinand Tonnies's conception of *gemeinschaft*, the ideal form of close-knit community is a town or village where a "spirit of brotherly sharing and cheerful giving lives on to some extent."[7] In his account of the ideal form of human association, Tonnies argues that physical separation is what renders community impossible and the insertion of distance, time, and space leads to the disintegration of an important form of everyday human communion. As Benedict Anderson argues, however, what is commonly understood to be a central feature of community is often an idea, or rather an "imagined community," in that what binds the community together is the collective imagination and desire of a certain group of people, rather than a physical location or place. In his words, "all communities larger than primordial villages of face-to-face contact (and perhaps even these) are imagined. Communities are to be distinguished, not by their falsity/genuineness, but by the style in which they are imagined."[8] Anderson claims, therefore, that imagined communities are based around writing artifacts, such as documents like the U.S. Constitution, that bind a nation or a community together as a whole and allow for a shared vocabulary to develop, thus creating a community around a discourse.

Second wave communities were often tied to writing through consciousness-raising and body awareness groups, in part initiated by a health movement that involved abortion rights and the Boston Women's Health Book Collective which produced the extremely popular feminist health book, *Our Bodies Ourselves.*[9] Indeed, the inspiration for the book began with a small discussion group based out of a woman's conference in Boston in 1969. Other notable women's communities of the second wave involved the formation of the National Organization for Women (NOW) in 1966 with all its chapters. In addition, the publication of *Ms. Magazine,* under the leadership of writer/activist Gloria Steinem, was the basis for a popular magazine-affiliated readership support community.[10] Most of these initial feminist groups were face-to-face, but the publication of *Ms. Magazine,* along with other feminist newspapers and publications, brought about a new sort of "imagined community" that was founded upon the personal and individual voices of readers in relation to a consumer product.

"Imagined communities" have been around in a number of forms that relate to reader communities. In particular feminist or women-oriented readers have typically been associated with writing their lives in the form of letters or book clubs.[11] As Janice Radway's research shows, readers of romance novels have also created a kind of virtual community in a world without the Internet through book clubs and personal communications.[12] Moreover, recently zines (independently published magazines) also have created fan communities and fan fiction, where readers participate in a community constructed around writing about and deconstructing a central narrative in popular culture, often science fiction, as in slash zines.[13]

Similar to book clubs and reader communities, readers from *Ms. Magazine* helped in numerous ways to perpetuate the magazine and to provide a sense of community for the feminism that was being created from the pages of the publication. Readers wrote numerous letters (on average 200 per week) to discuss their personal experiences and to comment on particular aspects of the magazine's direction and editorial perspective. In fact, *Ms. Magazine*'s first issue brought no less than twenty thousand letters of response from readers. Reader letters were invaluable for the continuation and longevity of the magazine; as Gloria Steinem states in the introduction to *Letters* that "those moving thoughtful intimate letters, much more than the statistical fact of the Preview Issue's success, had given us the courage to keep going."[14] *Ms. Magazine* was also referred to as a "portable friend" and created an important and lasting bond between its readers. Indeed, ongoing conversations in the letters to the editor section helped to create a different sort of community that was established by writing, by "imagined" connections.

In contrast to the second wave community of *Ms. Magazine,* the readership community at www.Bust.com has an electronic home or community. The lounge or the discussion space at bust.com provides online participants with a sense that they are not alone, that they have a home due to the fact that Bust.com is always present. Participants can come to this public space at any time of the day or night and find other members with whom they can relate. In the case of virtual space, the geography is much more ambiguous and difficult to identify, but there are some important aspects of virtual communities that provide this essential feeling of place, which in agreement with Anderson is still "imagined," but nevertheless essential for the formation of a coherent and active group. Daysleeper wrote about this feeling of place:

> I've always gotten a comforting sense that I'm not the only one who thinks you can be feminist without being sexless or humorless; from the site, I get a feeling of camaraderie and community with (generally) like-minded people.

Likewise Gaijingirl addresses the importance of this community:

> I've gotten a lot out of BUST: fun, great discussions (and occasionally some not-so-great ones, but that's life! LOL[15]), a community/sense of belonging (absolutely life-saving during my bouts of homesickness in a foreign land), postcards, phone calls, and general information about life/love. I'd have to say that the lounge and the magazine are some of the best things that have happened to me recently.

Indeed, the lounge or discussion forum on Bust.com, is a place that evokes images of home, comfort, and informality. It is a place where people feel welcome and congregate with the intention of enjoying each other's company. Community members who have been absent for a certain amount of time, or who seem to vanish with no communication are, as in any community, missed, and appreciated when they return. It almost seems a part of the life of this community that members will come and go, but that small escapes are considered normal and crucial for rejuvenation. It is this ever present sense of "being there" that provides a sense of community that is long lasting and always available directly via a personal Internet interface.

In some ways Internet communities can be even more vital than communities that are based in a geographical location because the community is accessible through a global network exchange that transcends geography. Due to the nature of Internet discussions, many participants have found a home on web spaces particularly because the Internet adapts to the needs and time constraints of various community members who are able to interact with others regardless of the time of day or location. Furthermore, multifaceted people can more easily find others with whom they might connect if their access is widened to include people all over the globe. Moreover, participants are not judged for their outward physical appearance, but rather their skill with the English language. In this sense, these online communities are more accessible and ever present to those who may need a community.

The online discussion space at Bust.com provides a sense of what Ray Oldenberg refers to as a "great good place" or a "neutral space" where participants are able to interact with others who are not a part of their normal spheres of life, home, or work.[16] The Internet is an important social environment, in the same way as the local coffee shop, the barbershop, the hairdresser, or the local café used to be, and has the same function of these spaces where people gather to exchange their daily lives with one another, although in the lounge, participants can come by at any time to catch up on conversations, and they no longer have the same separation between their public/feminist selves and their personal selves. Participants can engage in a political discussion at any time of the day and do not have to formally convene a meeting to work on a feminist problem. This everyday conversation allows for a more "natural" realization of feminism in a context that is able to address personal and local issues. There does not have to be an official conference on the right to life, or the problems of anorexia/bulimia, in order for these feminists to learn and understand from each other. The conference is ongoing and every day.

Along with a sense of a new or third space, a sense of home is promulgated in the *Bust* web space through the daily contact of members. As Wenger, McDermott, and Snyder assert, "many of the most valuable community activities are the small everyday interactions—informal discussions to solve a problem or one-on-one exchanges."[17] This is a community where daily communication helps to preserve the bonds between community members, particularly if it just involves "checking in" or logging in without any specific purpose, that is to say, making contact with no particular conversational goal other than "being with" the community. This is when the goals of communication and knowledge construction overlap, and even more to the point, are transcended by the life of the community and the exploration and camaraderie that it encourages.

Conversations on Bust.com often revolve around very personal issues and serve to make the community a part of posters' lives from an intimate and long-term perspective, much like a family or home. While some posters come and go, others have remained for numerous years, creating a sense of belonging and familial obligation. For example, in the case of Ravenspirit, a very popular older member of the *Bust* community, Busties were able to follow her daily travails with her pulmonary sickness, offering advice and cheering her up when she was frustrated about being ill for such a long time. The following interchange over two days captured that sense of connection:

raven- how are you feeling? sending lots of love and healthy vibes your way. (Love)

Ravey, I hope you feel better soon! Go to the hospital for sure ... I was thinking something with your meds must be wrong, actually. (Pickle)

Raven, get thee and thy lungs to a doctor. That does not sound good. (Chrissy)

Thank you ladies ... I'm actually feeling worse as time goes by. My cough is trying to hack but it's just dry which also scares me. I should be (warning: gross mucus comment ahead) coughing something up with all this tightness I'm feeling. (Ravenspirit)

Raven: hospital. now. (Hotlips)

Peeve: Just got back from the doc. I have bronchial pneumonia. It sucks. I hate it. She gave me a shot in the butt. I'm on steroids. I can't leave my bed until Monday at least. Patooey. (Ravenspirit)

Getting through tough times with the *Bust* community with everyday sorts of postings helps to solidify the bonds between community members and provides them with a strong social base with which to face their daily struggles as feminists, activists, and human beings. Moreover, participants can act out the roles of mothers or sisters with each other, providing much needed advice and concern, similar to what a home is supposed to provide. Indeed, this electronic space allows even younger members to take on the role of "mother" as the technology hides physical characteristics. As a result, traditional roles of older and younger relationships can be easily reversed. In so doing, the *Bust* online web space can act as a family and an important home where stereotypes and standard roles can be circumvented and turned around. There is no longer a clear distinction between learner and teacher or mother and daughter; both happen simultaneously online and with much more flexibility.

Several of the main threads of conversation have turned into spaces where Busties share aspects of their lives in an ongoing saga of ups and downs. In particular, the thread called "Pet Peeves" has grown into a space where many of the core Busties post every day and keep up with each other's life developments. Other daily threads, such as "Kvetch Up!!," "The Mutual Admiration Society," and "Braggin Rights" also serve as daily contact points for the core group of Busties who write to each other every day. Indeed the community appears to revolve around the daily problems and issues arising not only in real life, but in the online space as well. There appears to be a special kind of enjoyment that is derived from the reading and writing of ordinary and complex lives that are fraught with conflict and uncertainty.

The online space allows readers to gather, share, and experience each other's ordinary lives, and in doing so helps these women to understand their struggles within a context of a small but emotionally important community. In this way, identities within the community are constructed through the continual and daily negotiations of postings on the website. The ideological discussions that take place in these sorts of online communities are as important as the way in which these daily interactions help to frame each person's consciousness in a way that renders it connected, in some significant way, to all the others. Indeed the community feeds on its own moods and emotional highs and lows as members deal with the cycles and challenges of their lives.

This emphasis on sharing daily pleasures, emotions, and struggles is one of the significant ways that the *Bust* online discussions work to create a community that has particular value as an activist home for feminists through the active relationships that are created through the negotiation of the meaning of feminism. As bell hooks suggests, a "home place" is a site of resistance, a place to heal and nurture oneself and to rethink what it means to be black, a feminist, or both.[18] In other words, Bust.com provides some important aspects of home, that is to say it is a place where one returns to find healing, comfort, advice, and ideological compatibility; Internet technology allows this home to be an extended comfort zone that subverts traditional patterns of authority and encourages the blending of home lives and activist lives.

Similarly, the readers formed a virtual home at *Ms. Magazine*; however, it was of a different nature. The central focal point for the home that existed in and around the activities of the magazine was the central office. While *Bust*'s home is to a large degree in the ephemeral writing of space as places to converse and engage in daily relationships, *Ms.* readers view their home place as a physical space within the confines of the *Ms.* editorial staff. Indeed, the home created from the office space was symbolic of the philosophy created and established by the magazine, as a democratic and harassment-free workplace, but it also was a real home where workers brought their children to work, which in essence became a home away from home. Acting as kind of a daycare center, the *Ms.* offices had an atmosphere of casual support, where members of the staff would feel comfortable enough to bring their children to work and let them wander around deriving insights and guidance from the entire office.

The *Ms.* editors also created a sense of home and family by relying heavily on an approach that attempted to communicate and be guided by their readers. As a way to instill this sense of family and commitment, editors included a "Personal Report" depicting the trials and tribulations of *Ms.*, and asking for direction, support, and advice. In *Ms. Magazine*, the office, staff, and magazine were the central artifacts around which the readers' notions of home develop. Thus, for *Ms. Magazine* staffers, home is a mixture of work life and home life—a unique blend of the two life experiences.

At *Bust*, home is much more flexible and underdetermined. The Internet provides a site for the readers to focus on themselves, to explore the virtual home that they create online. The readers at *Bust* have created, established, and maintained the vital home on the Internet through the kinds of daily subnetworks and connections that are now possible through the Internet. This differently focused approach toward a home, a central grounding location for feminism, has led to a much broader definition of feminism, due also to the possibility of multiple subcommunities and home spaces created through the Internet.

READERSHIP AND ONLINE ACTIVISM

The community that was established through the readers of *Ms. Magazine* created a kind of "readerly-writerly" activism that was able to work toward various goals concerned with analyzing messages and spearheading collective actions based on the mailing list. Indeed, one form of activism was analyzing the messages in advertisements and in particular the advertisements in the magazine itself. Cigarette advertisements in the magazine provoked much controversy, as in the example of Philip Morris's advertisement of Virginia Slims. Many readers objected to the slogan "You've Come a Long Way Baby" claiming it infantilized females. Readers wrote in to complain about a small "test" advertisement from Philip Morris that was run in a calendar, and *Ms.* editors took up the cause to try to get Philip Morris to change its perspective. In the end, however, *Ms.* refused to publish the advertisement.[19] In this manner, readers took charge of the magazine and made it theirs by actively working to exclude companies they found offensive or harmful to women.

Similar to this sort of consumer-oriented activism, a popular section titled "No Comment" allowed readers to send in advertising, memos, or newsletters and to participate in a discussion of consumer messages that affected their everyday lives. This also created a new form of activist community where members were able to create a place to share a bond with other females who were experiencing the same sorts of derogatory messages. In the following message, one writer chastises her fellow feminists, and encourages them to engage in the act of consumer activism by actively not purchasing:

Will "ring around the collar" commercials go on year after year *forever?* Am I the only one who feels insulted when the camera zooms in on the face of the *wife* looking guilty and ashamed? For heaven's sake, it's *his* shirt! I'm ashamed that American women continue to buy the product.[20]

The reader community at *Ms. Magazine* also developed a kind of activism around the requests of readers for *Ms. Magazine* to be carried at local bookstores and newsstands, the magazine often being the target of ridicule and fear. Another form of activism that came about through the readers and their connections to the magazine was the reader survey. *Ms. Magazine* did a number of major surveys of their readers on such topics as rape and race, and found that nearly 6,000 readers were eager to respond and tell their stories in a kind of massive national consciousness-raising session.[21] Other avenues of activism occurred through this reader community by the existence of a viable mailing list that could be sent to different organizations, such as the NOW, who used it to help organize local chapters and to work on passing the Equal Rights Amendment.

While many argue that the third wave lacks a sense of strong activism, I suggest that the third wave has developed new forms of technological communities that take advantage of the networks of women in a way that was never before possible. This connection to other women suggests that the third wave is still working with a notion of community, but that these communities are much more fragmented and unstable. Third-wave communities take many forms and activism is now spread out within a whole series of activities and political goals.

Similar to the second wave, a large section of activism in the *Bust* community exists around the reading and writing of consumer messages. The "No Comment" section of *Ms. Magazine* has, in essence, been expanded to multiple discussions on Bust.com, including the analysis of various media forms, such as television, movies, music, magazines, and books. Participants in these discussion forums go beyond a "no comment" section and argue extensively about all forms of popular culture. One particular thread, perhaps closest to the "No Comment" section of *Ms.*, is titled simply, "Annoying Ads." In fact, the new ad campaign for Virginia Slims is the subject of the following message from Jezebel:

Okay, I just saw something today that pissed me off enough to post this. I was bored enough to open my roommate's copy of Ladies Home Journal (he doesn't read it, he has a subscription for his office waiting room). Within the first five pages I found the most irritating Virginia Slims ad yet. The photo is of a beautiful African woman, carrying cloth bundles on her head and smiling, and the copy reads "Kila mtuana uzuri wake" and then the translation: "No single institution owns the copyright for beauty." The new Virginia Slims tagline is "Find Your Voice." Okay, I have enough of a problem with Virginia Slims targeting women to sell cancer sticks, But what is this shit, equating Virginia Slims with A) Finding your voice? B) Beauty C) Indigenous African tribal women??? This just really rubbed me the wrong way. Has anyone else seen it? Any other ads that really irk you?

In most of these sorts of postings, the activism is limited to a kind of consciousness raising, but it is in debate form, which makes it much more open to dialogue and the ongoing exchange of ideas. Most of this sort of feminist activism on Bust.com happens in smaller niche groups that cannot rely on ultimate or decisive victories, but rather works as a kind of political awareness group for a larger body of issues, both political and personal. For instance, one thread titled "Inauguration Protest: Washington, D.C., Jan. 2001!!" attempted to enlist *Bust* participants in a protest of President Bush's inauguration. But rather than just remaining an announcement and a "call to arms," the topic turned into a discussion of the value of protesting versus other forms of activism. One poster brought up the idea that protests do not effect any real change, but, rather, are organized to provide a sense of solidarity and communion. Alligator wrote:

> The primary purpose (indeed, the only purpose) of these "protests" is [to] give the protestors a cheap, easy political-activist vibe. It doesn't change anything, and no one involved expects it to. The point is to socialize, take part in a lot of "2468, you are bad and we are great!" chanting, and then return to college and catch up on any new Napster downloads.

In response, another poster, Tj Pax, writes:

> I do agree that the main work isn't done at the demonstration. I am heartened to hear that y'all are so politically active! Personally I am currently involved with a small fund raiser for a media/educational project to help this city focus on how we use cars and what alternatives are available. But, ya know what? I am going to DC and I don't care if the FBI photographs me, and I don't care if traffic gets tied up, and I don't care if you stay home.

In both these posts, participants in the forum argue that protesting no longer has the same impact, and as Tj Pax suggests, people are now more involved with smaller, local projects that make sense in their lives. This technological conversation helps to bring participants to a new level of awareness of the reasons and goals behind political activism. Often political action is personally motivated and the debates on Bust.com help develop individual ideas about what constitutes a valuable political goal.

While third wave feminist activism may seem to have lost a certain amount of direction and force in the 1990s and beyond, this sort of activism is crucial for understanding the ways in which specific individuals and smaller communities can also make a difference in everyday lives. Many readers write in comments about why they like the website and magazine and argue that it is a place where they can come (as activists) and be accepted in a variety of different forms and guises. In a letter to the editor, one reader wrote:

> I really respect the fact that BUST acknowledges that there are many voices within feminism, and that we all experience a lot of the same (very human) ambivalence and contradictions as women. BUST attests to real women's lives as opposed to some academic construction of our lives, as so many "feminist" publications do.

One of the most powerful aspects of this personal activist community, however, is the speed and rate at which activists from all over the nation (and globe) can participate and quickly organize. The relatively unmonitored medium of the Internet provides an ideal space through which activist communications can convene without fear of reprisal or breach of privacy. In the following conversation, Bust.com participants organize themselves around the April 25, 2004 march in Washington, D.C. and are able to assemble a contingent of *Bust* participants to meet and possibly even share rides together. MCLL 2004 wrote:

> Just a reminder—the March for Women's Lives is rapidly approaching. If you're interested in making an appearance and/or helping out check out the march website at www.marchfor-women.org or our website at www.feminist.org. Hope to see you in Washington DC in 31 days!

Aquagirl responded:

> People that want to meet in DC:
> that would be so great! I am from there and I think we should

meet meet meet!
What do you guys think about meeting at the Stegosaurus outside the Natural History Museum? No, wait, it's a Triceratops. Well, there's only one dinosaur out there, anyway.
We could have a sign there, and meet between 9:30 and 10, or something. Do we start marching at 10 exactly? march march march

Another poster, jilliana, wrote in to make plans:

> I live in central NJ and would like to drive to DC for the march on Sunday (would probably park at a suburban station and take the train/bus into the city). Anyone from NYC/Jersey/Philly want to carpool and march together??

Her request was addressed by Nickclick:

> jilliana, i live in jersey too, but i'm taking a bus from east brunswick, which is $20 and should be fun. plus, we are leaving at 6 A.M. and i can sleep for a couple of hours. go here if you want to find a bus/train to go down: www.nownj.org.

In this immediate and interconnected manner, *Bust* participants are able to organize and redirect their activist selves toward personal and social relationships. Both larger and smaller niche communities of *Bust* participants work together to create an intimate activist climate that helps connect with their own interests and ways of being.

In *Bust*, activism is based more around the immediate emotion of being involved and is motivated through writing, but this writing is of a different nature. It is much more spontaneous and unplanned, leaving those who are not confident in their writing abilities to feel less exposed and analyzed. Writing is more like a conversation on the *Bust* website and less like a formal proposal or statement. *Ms. Magazine* readers had to be fluent enough and confident to write in about their experiences and therefore presumably would be drawn from a less diverse group of feminists.

Much of the reader activism in the *Ms. Magazine* community was in a manner of self-revelation leading to a kind of activism that was a kind of reaching out to inspire other women, but was often somewhat disconnected and individualistic. For example, one reader writes: "I guess the main reason for this letter is to get this all off my chest."[22] For instance, in *Ms.* the common reader activist position was to write in about a personal moment that led to a revelation, a confession of sorts. In other words, readers often wrote about their transformations or "click" experiences concerning feminism through their outrage at a particular personal experience:[23]

> It's the late 1960s, and the empty-nest syndrome may be a cliché, but it's no joke. I'm forty-three, and my job is phasing out. I never finished the M.A. in math; I decided I wanted to write more than I wanted to mathematize. Now my writing is blocked. I have written myself out, and nothing new is coming in.
>
> I read an article about a women's consciousness-raising group. Click.[24]

These forms of self-revelation also were somewhat self-focused in that there was no real conversation or exchange going on between readers. As one reader put it, "For most of us, *Ms.* is our only contact with the feminist movement. We could use a little support from our sisters."[25] The main form of communication with the community was a letter of introduction, and there it ended. Most letters began with a personal statement:

> I am a woman who, almost all my life, believed without question what I was told—women aren't as smart as men, women aren't happy being successful, to get ahead you should be pretty, witty, and secretly wise.[26]
>
> I have been working for six years in a suburban law office in New Jersey, where the staff consists of seven secretaries (female) and four lawyers (male). It has always been the custom in this office for each "girl" to have her turn at "kitchen duty."[27]

The main activist quality of *Ms. Magazine* was its ability to provide a voice and a community to a wider audience in a mainstream popular form, but this community was by necessity limited to one-way sorts of exchanges and a focus on the individual consumer in relation to the magazine. In the third wave, as represented by *Bust*, the activism is immediate and spontaneous, leading to activities that might spring up overnight. Letters to the magazine that created the *Ms.* readership community led to an important form of activism, but one that was more formal in nature and more focused on traditional rules of writing as a form of communication, and individual self-revelations.

CONCLUSION

Online discussion groups highlight the examination of feminism and what it means to be feminist in an environment that itself emphasizes the instability of identity and the various forces that work to construct societal definitions of feminism. While the activism on the Bust.com website is limited to dialogue and calls to act on certain issues, this aspect of activism is vital not only because it provides a virtual place for activists to come together and feel normal, but also because it gives rise to multiple definitions of activism, and shows how participants are all involved in local projects that have meaning in their lives. Bust.com creates a home away from home for activist activity and connects women with other women on a global and immediate scale.

Ms. Magazine worked more as a kind of "how to" manual for feminists who shared their experiences through personal confessions and responses that revealed their feminist transformations—their "click" experiences. While this was not the beginning of the feminist movement, it signaled a stage of early activism where the main goal of the movement was to empower a wide range of everyday women. *Ms. Magazine* served this purpose well and was an ideal introduction to the world of feminist values.

Bust, however, has a slightly different purpose and the activism that is created from readership engagement with the magazine/website is of a different nature. Much of what goes on in this web space devoted to feminist values is not only to inspire other women to become a part of a revolution, but also to provide a home and sustenance for those feminists who are in the constant battle and fighting the cause. The home space created at the website is not so much derived through a working relationship to the magazine, but rather as a site to renew the self amidst the battles of feminism. The website provides a much needed pressure release and break from doing feminism. Here activists can be feminists and take pleasure in their home and community.

As opposed to *Ms. Magazine* where the readership created a community through collective action, but mostly remained individualistic in its approach toward feminist enlightenment, *Bust* demonstrates a stage of activism where the activist community now serves a different sort of purpose—one of relaxation, pleasure, and rejuvenation alongside activist activities. This makes the reason for engaging in the community more about the need for solidarity and connection with other like minded people, and less about the need to organize. Even despite the difficult and unsettling ephemeral nature of communities online, *Bust* is one of those special communities that has maintained itself as a viable network and home place for grassroots feminist activism.

NOTES

1. Jennifer Baumgardner and Amy Richards, *Manifesta: Young Women, Feminism, and the Future* (New York: Farrar, Straus and Giroux, 2000), 282.
2. Ibid.
3. This phrase is on the cover of each issue.
4. Norman Denzin, "Cybertalk and the Method of Instances," in *Doing Internet Research: Critical Issues and Methods for Examining the Net,* ed. Steve Jones (Thousand Oaks, CA: Sage, 1999), 107–26.
5. Since it is difficult to do justice to the vast amounts of conversations and discourse that occur on www.Bust.com every day, I borrow a vision of analysis taken from Denzin's philosophy, where rational empiricism is not the goal, but rather an understanding into a "slice" of the community for its rich potential. To this end, I invited and received extended comments to several versions of my studies. I realize that there may be some important elements that are missing; however, as with any large amount of data, analyzing and understanding only happens in stages, in practical subdivisions of work, and it is to this end that I hope to achieve at least a partial glimpse into the worlds created by the readers of these feminist magazines.
6. Mary Thom, ed., *Letters to Ms. 1972–1987* (New York: Henry Holt, 1987); A larger collection of letters, both published and unpublished, is housed in the Schlesinger Library at Radcliffe College.
7. Ferdinand Tonnies, *Community and Civil Society* (New York: Cambridge University Press, 1887/2001), 42.
8. Benedict Anderson, *Imagined Communities: Reflections on the Spread and Origin of Nationalism* (New York: Verso, 1991), 6.
9. Boston Women's Health Book Collective, *Our Bodies Ourselves* (New York: Simon and Schuster, 1973).
10. Miriam Schneir, ed., *Feminism in Our Time: The Essential Writings, World War II to the Present* (New York: Random House, 1994,) 171; and Mary Thom, *Inside Ms.: 25 Years of the Magazine and the Feminist Movement* (New York: Henry Holt, 1997).
11. For a good discussion of women's reading and book clubs, see Elizabeth Long, *Book Clubs: Women and the Uses of Reading in Everyday Life* (Chicago: University of Chicago Press, 2003).
12. Janice Radway, *Reading the Romance: Women, Patriarchy, and Popular Literature* (Chapel Hill, NC: University of North Carolina Press, 1984).
13. Slash zines are a creative rewriting of the original *Star Trek* series where Kirk and Spock are reconstructed as gay lovers (i.e., K/S zines). See Henry Jenkins, *Textual Poachers: Television Fans and Participatory Culture* (New York: Routledge: 1992); and Constance Penley, "Feminism, Psychoanalysis, and the Study of Popular Culture," in *Cultural Studies*, eds. Lawrence Grossberg, Cary Nelson, and Paula Treichler (New York: Routledge, 1992): 96–97.
14. Thom, *Letters*, xii.
15. Laughing out loud.
16. Ray Oldenberg, *The Great Good Place: Cafes, Coffee Shops, Community Centers, Beauty Parlors, General Stores, Bars, Hangouts, and How They Get You Through the Day* (New York: Paragon House, 1991).
17. Etienne Wenger, Richard McDermott, and William M. Snyder, *Cultivating Communities of Practice: A Guide to Managing Knowledge* (Boston: Harvard Business School Press, 2002), 60.
18. bell hooks, *Yearning: Race, Gender and Cultural Politics* (Boston: MA: South End Press, 1990).
19. Amy E. Farrell, *Yours in Sisterhood: Ms. Magazine and the Promise of Popular Feminism* (Chapel Hill, NC: University of North Carolina Press, 1998), 132.

20. Thom, *Letters*, 165.
21. Robin Warshaw, *I Never Called it Rape: The Ms. Report on Recognizing, Fighting, and Surviving Date and Acquaintance Rape* (New York: Harper and Row, 1988).
22. Thom, *Letters*, 224.
23. Click experiences were inspired by Jane O'Reilly's "Click! The Housewife's Moment of Truth," *Ms. Magazine*, July (Spring 1972): 54–55. In her article she describes her revelations and instant understandings—where she has a "click" of recognition. This term was taken up by readers at large, creating a form of discourse that sustained and motivated the community to share similar experiences.
24. Thom, *Letters*, 211.
25. Ibid., 217.
26. Ibid., 209.
27. Ibid., 104.

10

ZINES: VOICES OF
THIRD WAVE FEMINISTS

Dawn Bates and Maureen C. McHugh

Young women today are often characterized as disinterested in or resistant to feminism. Alternatively, young women are seen as subscribing to a different form of feminism in comparison to their mothers or to previous generations (see Henry, chapter 5). In this chapter, we examine zines as a way in which young women identify and confront sexism and gender oppression. We contrast zines with the tools and strategies of previous generations of feminists and examine the content of zines as voicing the issues and concerns of young feminists.

There are tens of thousands of zines being produced today and they are reaching a total audience in the millions. Zines are do-it-yourself (DIY), self-published magazines that combine elements of personal journals, newsletters, collages, and magazines.[1] The DIY nature of the zine is an important aspect of its appeal. Zines are often photocopied pamphlets or booklets that are given away, traded with friends, or sold through online distribution centers or at independent music and bookstores. Zines can also take the form of webpages, which can be accessed by other girls. They often contain stories about the author's life, essays, poetry, short stories, comics, recipes, lists, and reviews of books, bands, or other zines. According to Green and Taormino, "Among other things, zines are sites for communication, education, community, revolution, celebration, and self- expression."[2] People of varied ages, ethnicities, backgrounds, and orientations are constructing their own zines. Girls are one of the groups that have found a voice in personal zines and zines are an integral part of the girl's empowerment movement. Based on a review of the literature, we describe the nature of the girls' zines and examine zines as third wave feminist activity.

Zines are examined here as a method of feminist empowerment and resistance for young women because they are a self-created and controlled forum in which young women can exercise their voice. Girls' zines contain young women's critiques of underlying cultural systems, especially mainstream media, and represent girls' own created culture. Revealing anger, humor, anguish, and joy, the zines created by girls and young women can help us to understand their lives and perspectives.

We examine zines in relation to the approaches and agenda of third wave feminists as described by Jennifer Baumgardner and Amy Richards.[3] According to Baumgardner and Richards, zines like *Bust, I Heart Amy Carter, Bamboo Girl,* and *Sister Nobody* are influential in the third wave of feminism.[4] Third wave feminists are young women who recognize that their experience of feminism differs from that of their foremothers. As depicted by Baumgardner and Richards, third wavers acknowledge the strides toward gender equality achieved by previous generations of feminists, and view their lives as involving fewer gender restrictions and constraints, with more access and opportunity.[5] Subsequently, third wave feminists focus on how to build on the foundations of earlier feminists, such as working for gender equity from the inside and negotiating new identities and statuses. Not all young women working with or from feminist ideologies identify themselves as third wave, or even as feminists. Another label that some young women adopted for themselves is Riot Grrrl (see Schlit, chapter 3). Jessica Rosenberg and Gitana Garofalo describe the Riot Grrrls as "loud, and through zines, music, and spoken word express themselves honestly and straightforwardly."[6] M. L. Fraser refers to (some) third wave feminists and zinesters as "fringe feminists," those who reside on the fringes of culture and work to create their own culture through independent writing and art with a feminist slant.[7] It is this feminism that we examine in our discourse analysis of zines. To contextualize the importance of zines to third wave feminism, we first offer a brief history.

HISTORY OF ZINES

The growth of the contemporary zine movement is tied to the availability of inexpensive photocopying in the 1970s. The roots of the zine movement, however, may be traced to the fanzines of the 1930s. Initially, fanzines were about science fiction; fans of a particular science fiction series could discuss issues in the series and share articles and science fiction with each other. This phenomenon was quickly followed by comic book fanzines. The shift from fanzine to zine signals a shift in content; zines are not devoted to a particular topic or interest. The label *zine* also identifies a changed relationship between producer and consumer; members of a zine community typically produce and collect and trade zines within a regional, national, or worldwide network. Contemporary zines are also imbued with the spirit of other (historical) independent publishing ventures, like the mail art magazines and underground publications of the 1960s. Fred Wright also points to a parallel between Revolutionary era printers disseminating their politics by pamphlet and contemporary zinesters spreading their opinions through zines.[8]

Most influential to current zines was the punk rock music scene and the punk rock zines associated with it. The punk rock movement began in the 1970s as antiestablishment and anti-institutional attitudes expressed in music, and valued a DIY ethic in both music and zines. At that point, zines were a way to communicate with others within the scene, to spread news about bands, and to review and discuss revolutionary music and attitudes.[9] Girl (grrrl)[10] zines developed out of the punk rock scene. As Riot Grrrl lost its vigor in the late 1990s, girl zines continued, focusing on a wider range of topics and themes.[11]

Feminist zines that address sexism as experienced in everyday life or provide an analysis of gender oppression can also be traced to the self-published tracts of the feminist movement. Self- or collective publishing of essays, speeches, and other tracts was an important aspect of both the first and second waves of feminism. Susan B. Anthony, Elizabeth Cady Stanton, and Margaret Sanger self-published papers and distributed them as part of their work. A notable example from the second wave was KNOW Press. Located in a garage in Pittsburgh, KNOW Press distributed mimeographed copies of the early essays describing women's experiences and analyzing sexism. Printed lists of available articles were circulated and orders were produced, filled, and shipped. The first women's studies classes used these reproduced materials before texts were available. Many of the essays were later included in feminist magazines and anthologies, and some are still read in women's studies classes. Women's newsletters and magazines, including *off our backs, Ms. Magazine,* and *Sojourner,* expanded in the 1970s. These publications laid the foundation for the feminist zines and magazines published today.[12]

AN ANALYSIS OF ZINES

Since 2000, Dawn Bates has been collecting girls' zines. This collection was established through zine distribution centers, the Internet, zine review magazines, and through zine sharing. This collection is the basis for our understanding of the content and meaning of zines. Our understanding of zines is based on a traditional content analysis and also on a discourse analysis, which is concerned with the ways in which language constructs objects, subjects, and experiences,[13] recognizing language as constructive rather than reflective or representative. A discourse analysis involves the reading and rereading of selected passages/articles. In these readings we attend to the messages of the zinesters, considering the functions and impact of the discourse.[14] Fifty-eight zines were selected for analysis from the more than two hundred zines collected. The zines selected emphasized personal experience and were written by women. Bates conducted a survey of young women zinesters and asked them about their motives for and experiences of writing and distributing zines.[15] Of the one hundred zinesters that she contacted, forty responded. The zinesters in the sample were young women with an average age of twenty-three, who wrote their first zines when they were teens (17 was the mean age of first zine), and most of the respondents had been writing zines for a number of years (the mean was 5.4 years). We refer to this survey throughout our analysis of zines and zinesters. Five themes/functions emerge from our analysis: giving women voice; rejection of mainstream media; the personal as political; the healing function of zines; and zines as connection and community. Each of these themes illustrates how zines are a tactic embraced in third wave feminism and we examine each in the following sections.

ZINES AS CREATIVITY AND VOICE

Study participants indicated that creating their own zines was enjoyable and fun, offering a unique way for women to express their creativity and a medium in which their creativity is not censored. For zinesters, the creation of a zine is an intrinsically motivated activity; zines are not constructed to meet anyone else's demands or expectations. Psychologists recognize the importance and meaning of such intrinsically motivated creative activities. Without externally imposed deadlines, criteria, and supervision, creative tasks satisfy the inherent human demands for self-expression and can generate feelings of accomplishment and enjoyment. The respondents contacted by Bates frequently reported these feelings. As one zinester responded, "I do it for fun, to make my voice heard."

The girl creating the zine decides what is art, what is important, and what is creative. She has the opportunity to create without worrying that what she has to say will be changed, deleted, or censored by another. Other authors have similarly described zines as a medium for women to speak authentically about their lives, and as unfiltered, uncensored freedom.[16] V. Vale sees zines as providing inspiration and encouragement to girls to create radical culture and ideas.[17] What girls and young women write in their zines is genuine and accessible. According to one zinester, "Zines come from the heart and are not filtered or censored by editors or advertisers."[18] Another zinester, Pohl-Weary said, "When you are making your own zine, you get to decide every-thing—you get to decide on the message."[19] Thus, through zines we can see young women are "uncensored and free to discuss their realities"[20] as they construct them. Zinesters told Rosenberg and Garafola, "Zines are a way of typing how you feel" and "Zines provide a place where we can create our own meanings … separate from the editor's red pen."[21]

Young women have described their zines as a way of expressing themselves, as finding a voice. According to one young woman, "You have to speak out, allow people to listen to your ideas and what you are saying."[22] Psychologists have suggested that girls in our culture fre-quently find their voices stifled in their adolescent years.[23] Zines can be a way for girls to keep their authentic voice, or to regain parts of the self that were "lost" or silenced. Madhu, a zinester said, "It's about speaking out, not being quiet—Not buying into the whole put up or shut up."[24] Another young zinester agrees, "I feel the insatiable need to express myself and my opinions."[25]

In a society in which there are few mainstream avenues for women to articulate their experiences with injustice, zines are a site where women can describe their struggle to make their way in the world.[26] One of the struggles that zinesters address is the development of self-identity. As one zinester introduces her zine, *Fixing Her Hair*, "Here is me … all laid out, unedited truth.…Years of not knowing how to say what I've always needed to have come out in this zine."[27] Erin McCarley, author of the zine *Glamour Queen*, explains "Its so awesome to be able to revalidate yourself over and over again. To be able to sit and KNOW, even when things are sucking really bad that YEAH I CAN COUNT ON MYSELF."[28] Zines offer a unique opportunity for individuals struggling to define and express themselves. Another zinester writes:

> I understand the power of self publishing—looking at a blank page and knowing it is me who's going to fill it up. We're all here to write and draw and speak. If you are old, rich, poor, serious,

humorous, pissed off, all a giggle, decadent, cute, introverted, extroverted, ambitious, laid back, hetero-homo-ambi-pan or undecidedly sexual, WHATEVER—you can make a zine as an individual and put it out there.[29]

Zines provide girls with inspiration and encourage them to create their/our own radical culture and ideas. As the author of numerous zines explains, "zines have been one way that [I] can get my words & ideas & images out there, & also retain full control of them."[30] One girl writes, "It's an empowering act to create your own culture that has positive messages about you."[31] Labrador sees zines as empowering because they give girls a voice, and that voice is often defiant.[32]

Breaking the silence is a revolutionary act. Feminists from previous generations have similarly seen speaking out, telling women's stories, and expressing one's opinions as political acts that have been denied women. The ways in which previous generations of feminists have "spoken out" were different from zines, however. Early feminists literally used "soapboxes" and any other available speaking platform. Second wave feminists staged demonstrations and rallies to express their collective voices. The materials that feminists self-published or duplicated or struggled to get published through women's presses were essays or stories that conformed to legal, literary, or other accepted disciplinary approaches to expression. Zines represent a unique approach to letting women speak for themselves and break the silence because the voices of zinesters are not censored, filtered, or constrained by any conventions, criteria, or codes. Although zines are individual expressions, they do have a collective voice. As one zinester argues, "Every time we pick up a pen, or an instrument, or communicate with each other, we are creating the revolution."[33]

ZINES AS RESISTANCE

Feminist scholars view zines as providing an alternative to the mainstream press's misrepresentation of our experiences as women.[34] For example, some zinesters refer to themselves as being antigirls; this is explained by alexwrekk in the zine *brainscan 18*:

> I am an anti-girl not because I don't like being a girl, but because I don't like being what society tells me a girl should be … I just don't like being a stereotype. I don't understand the concept of glamour. It seems silly and counter productive not to mention downright wasteful and socially irresponsible … it just buys into ridiculous displays of consumerism." [35]

Commercial and mainstream teen magazines purport to "inform, entertain and give teenage girls all the information they need to make sound choices" according the editor of *Seventeen* magazine.[36] However, numerous feminist critiques have argued that teen magazines emphasize a woman finding her role and her identity in the adult world through consumption of commodities and through relationships with men. Scholars argue that rather than help women find their identity, teen magazines restrict roles for young women and encourage them to subscribe to patriarchal values.[37]

In her study of girls in seventh grade, Finders documents how the "social queens" used the reading and carrying of teen magazines as a cultural practice that defined their group.[38] They perceived the practice of (reading) teen magazines as their own, even though such magazines are produced by adults. Because their mothers, teachers, and other adults did not approve, reading teen magazines became a subversive act. However, Finders points out that reading teen magazines is not subversive; instead it is a way in which girls are acculturated into the normative. She contends that teen magazines are neither benign nor neutral, but a way to get girls hooked into a powerful economic ideology. Other feminist authors have similarly critiqued mainstream media as problematic in the lives of girls and young women.[39] Teen magazines are seen as promoting "a cult of femininity" concerned with appearance and submissiveness.

Zines are a grassroots reaction to this media landscape[40] and subvert mainstream media. According to Labrador, young women use zines to critique, question, resist, and reappropriate the American patriarchal mass culture.[41] For example, one zinester writes:

> Excuse me sirs but do not even try to pass off yer little cultural/ societal dictations as suggestions, to make yer insinuations look like truth; Real womyn who must avoid newspapers & magazines if they don't want to be subjected 2 yer attempts @ making us denigrate ourselves-do not buy into this sort of crap.[42]

Vale views zines as a reaction against "homogenized and corporate produced ads and programs designed to control consumers."[43] Vale continues, "If communication can be viewed as food, then everything the mass media serves has been depleted of nourishment by corporate self-serving agendas."[44] Girls observe that the mass media are male dominated, and zines represent one form of girls' resistance to the cultural construction of femininity and the beauty myth. Women use zines as a forum for reacting to and recreating pop culture.[45] In zines, girls have refused cultural manipulation; zines give the authors space to both critique and to evade mainstream culture. Wray and Steele contend, "Zines allow women to express what they see as the truths about their lives, in contrast to mainstream magazines, which often misrepresent what it is to be a woman."[46] Marie Elia, in the zine *Triplicate and File*, expresses it this way:

> Girls are given magazines to read and movies/tv shows to watch. They're not encouraged to Write about their own lives or Make art about what they experience or who they are. We are being produced rather than given the means of production.[47]

Because zines allow women and others to spread their message, researcher Christine Smith sees them as a form of activism.[48] The creation of alternative media and alternative sources of information are political. Smith, a teacher, encourages her students to create zines that are political, distribute information, or create awareness about violence against women or women's health issues.

In zines, girls observe how patriarchy negatively affects their lives and reflect on gender socialization and women's subordinate social status. Zinesters frequently point out the failure of the dominant culture and attempt to create an alternative. One girl zinester rages:

> You are in congress, the supreme court, the police force, the big important bands, church, school, home. AND IT'S TIME YOU FOUND OUT THAT THE WAY YOU ACT SOMETIMES IS NOT RIGHT, IS NOT ACCEPTABLE TO ME OR MY FRIENDS … and no I won't shut up."[49]

Some zines are explicit about their goal. One zinester states, "We are taught to value make up and diets and fashion models and high heel shoes.… Riot Grrrl is helping to break down all that patriarchy has created."[50] An extended description of the antipatriarchy message of the grrrl revolution is given by the creator of the zine, *Skirt*:

> grrrl is glaring back at the guy who makes catcalls … grrrl is standing up for what you believe in … grrrl is staying up all night with your friends creating a zine … grrrl is refusing to be degraded against and fighting back against the isms … grrrl is coming up with your own definition of style regardless of what abercrombie or j. crew think is cool.…"[51]

About one half of the three hundred zine articles analyzed by Macalister, Perry, Reitsz, and Sperling addressed sexism and the oppression of women.[52] According to researchers, concerns about physical attractiveness, beauty, and fashion are the most frequently represented themes in young women's zines. At least some of the zine writing on beauty and fashion is critical. Amanda, creator of *Soot and Stars*, writes:

> Less time on looks=more time to live yr life. No more expensive painful beauty treatments for me.... Loving your body as a woman in America whatever the circumstances of your appearance, is difficult life long work ... it shouldn't cost us loads of money, pain or our sanity.[53]

And the author of the zine *make me numb 12* explains how fashion images have affected her:

> I had never been very comfortable with my body. My wrists were always too skinny or my hips too curvy, I had too many freckles, nothing was ever right. Day after day I saw magazines and movies and ads, and it all started to sink in, even when I tried to push it away. It was like their sleek thigh and perfect breasts burnt themselves into my subconscious.... Its hard as hell to unlearn it all ... the only way we can change anything else is to change ourselves first...."[54]

Language and prose are seen as the tools for dismantling the patriarchy. Sometimes zinesters expose hidden discourses and make them subversive. They reclaim terms like *pussy, bitch,* and *cunt,* making others uncomfortable with the exposed sexism in the terms. Thus zinesters appropriate the power of mainstream culture by co-opting language. They use language to escape male control and at the same time subvert mainstream (male) culture. In addition to writing about the impact that sexism and oppression has on them personally, zines are a way for young women to share information on everything from vegetarianism to safe hygiene products. Some zines are explicitly political (e.g., *dear mr. bush*[55]) and others advocate for specific forms of activism such as environmental consciousness, reduced consumerism, or peace.

Zinester Noemi Ixchel Martinez reflects poetically on activism:

> ...I've been
> Looking for someone to save me,
> Change things
> But I am the change
> My words and actions

Will move mountains and make
Allies/alley....[56]

ZINES AS HELPFUL AND HEALING

Carlip has been instrumental in introducing zines to girls and girls'
zines to the world, because she herself experienced writing and creative
expression as lifelines during a troubled adolescence.[57] She views self-
expression as an empowering experience. One of the girls she worked
with wrote:

> Riot Grrrl is meant to be empowering for grrrls, having a safe com-
> fortable space to speak openly about anything. It's about standing
> up for our rights and about knowing we have them.... Riot Grrrl is
> showing me that I matter. I count, my opinion has worth.[58]

Psychologists have begun to examine the healing power of telling our
own stories. There are a large number of studies showing the positive
psychological effects of writing. Writing therapies and bibliotherapy
use journaling and poetry writing as therapeutic tools. A therapeutic
approach to psychotherapy, narrative therapy, is based on the telling
and retelling of a client's personal narrative, or life story. Similarly,
Bates finds that writing about one's own experience in zine format
appears to be healing or helpful, according to many zinesters. One survey respondent, Leah Lilith Albrecht-Samarasinka, writes that girl zines
were "more important than I can fucking say in my healing process ...
you can tell the truth about things you were never supposed to live." Liz
Defiance of the zine *Death of a Psyche* writes, "I need to keep writing
about all this because it sparks great dialogues and gets all this shit
away from me. Once I write it, it's released."[59] Xolau reflects on how she
has changed from her earlier zines:

> My needs have changed ... I don't need to photocopy my every
> idea and thought because I feel crazy, or because I have no
> friends, or because I need so desperately for someone to listen to
> me.[60]

The creator of *Satan's Panties*, Allie, writes that her zine "has been
incredibly therapeutic as a creative outlet [during my depression]."[61]
Zines then become a need according to Bianca Biteme of *No, I Don't
Think So*. She writes, "And every time I write a word, I am taking it
back, taking my life back, taking my life back again and again and

again.... But I kept getting restless and I kept knowing that the only thing that kept me sane and grounded was zining."[62] Zinester Lisa of *BITCH DYKE WHORE* reports that zines are more effective than therapy for her, "My zine has helped me sort out my emotions especially about getting raped. I went to a shrink for a while and it never helped, but after I started my zine I felt a million times better."[63]

THE PERSONAL AND THE POLITICAL

Personal zines are a way of expressing oneself about anything or nothing. The unfiltered, unedited description of everyday events, like a conversation with a best friend, creates a sense of intimacy. This focus on the daily experiences of the zinesters, and on everyday activism, can be seen as a form of third wave feminism. Baumgardner and Richards argue that third wave feminism involves living feminism every day.[64] As a part of third wave feminism, zines are young women's constructions of their own lives as lived on a daily basis. In this way zines may serve as a form of catharsis; women release anger and other forms of negative energy as they relay important events in their lives. Most importantly, these zines, like the consciousness-raising sessions of the second wave, recognize that the personal is political. Women's social roles and subordinate status is played out in the mundane aspects of our lived experience. Elia writes:

> Lately I've just been recounting the daily events of my life, which I think is quite valid. I write what I want and anyone can read it and if they don't want to, they don't have to.... My everyday life is somewhat validated....[65]

Older persons, including second wave feminists, may have difficulty listening to and accepting the uncensored thoughts and mundane experiences of young women/third wave feminists presented in zines. For example, at a presentation on zines to the Association for Women in Psychology, audience members expressed their opinion that the material in many of the zines brought for display was not worthwhile, substantive, or well expressed. We argue that this reaction was related to these professional women's internalization of conventional publication standards. The gap in generational expression was exemplified by one attendee's comment that she could not comprehend why anyone would write or want to read the zinester's list of "Ten Boys I Would Like to Fuck." She challenged the value of zinesters' voices in general, and rejected this article in particular. Young feminist students later argued for the value of such a list, seeing it as a proclamation of sexual agency, and recognized that the author was trying to express her sexual desire and assert her (hetero)sexual identity. In *Dilemmas of Desire*, Deborah Tolman argues that we need such a discourse of desire because young women have been taught only negative and repressive messages about sex.[66] The woman in the audience might agree with Tolman in principle, but in reality she serves as a censor for the discourse of desire exchanged in zines.

ZINES AS CREATING COMMUNITY

Young women come to feminism to find a community with like-minded individuals. Zines serve the feminist goal of creating community and sharing common experiences. Zines connect girls who feel isolated. Girls themselves state that it is beneficial to hear the stories of other girls.[67] In Bates's study, the second most often cited reason for doing zines was to connect with others or to form a community. More than a third of her respondents cited the sense of community and connection as the thing they liked most about doing a zine.

Girls who disagree with the cultural majority can find like-minded others in the zine community and scholars see zines as creating networks of feminists across the country.[68] Zines may in fact have the same function as consciousness raising in the second wave. Consciousness raising is a process by which women come together, share personal stories, and connect their individual experiences to larger oppressive structures. Young women who feel alienated and alone in an androcentric world find, through zine production and exchange, that there are others who share their experience and perspective. Zines have connected whole communities of young women, who subsequently prod and affirm each other to higher levels of analysis and consciousness.

Through zines, girls can read about the lives of other girls just like them who are experiencing similar problems. Lisa of Olympia explains "Zines connect them (grrls) to other girls who will listen and believe and care if they say they have been raped or molested or harassed."[69] Since zinesters are often the same age, zines are more realistic and relevant to their lives than traditional teen magazines.[70] Zines often contain pictures of the girls who have written them or their friends, so they do not convey images of perfection and unrealistic beauty standards.

Most of the zinesters are white and from middle- to upper-class backgrounds.[71] This may be related to the resources needed to produce zines, or to the way that individuals are informed and recruited to zines through segregated institutions or networks.[72] Despite the fact that zinesters tend to be predominantly white, zines can provide resources, comparison groups, and social support networks to those who are not reflected within mainstream media or within their schools. Lesbian, bisexual, and questioning girls can find girls like them who do zines and can find acceptance from the community.[73] Girls of color can find zines that address issues of racism and zines done by girls of the same ethnicity.

Survey respondent Albrecht-Samarasinka wrote, "When I started it, I had no idea there were any other girls my age who identified as feminists the way I did—angry slutty rageful girls who took no shit." Some zinesters appreciate the fact that the community with which they are connected is not mainstream or widely known. Describing her discovery of the zine community, Elia said, "Here is this whole other world simmering below the surface, and, like Alice, I've just tumbled down into it."[74]

This feeling of being isolated or of being different from other women is not a new feminist issue. In the second wave, women came together in women's conscious-raising groups and communities of women sprang up, and in doing so, women developed a sense of sisterhood and community with other women locally and nationally.

CONCLUSION

Bates's survey indicates that zinesters experience positive results from creating zines. She argues that her research illustrates that zines offer opportunities for self-expression and creativity; create a feeling of being connected and forming a community; are an enjoyable activity; and bring feelings of accomplishment. She finds that zinesters voice the desire to express their creativity, to share information, and to help themselves and others. However, zines are not only a way to express oneself and to develop one's own voice. When women tell their stories authentically, understandings of reality shift, making it more likely for them to recognize sexism and gender oppression. Many of the young women report experiencing pain and anguish in their zines. Yet, the sharing of that pain is both healing and revealing. While young women's experiences of violence, intolerance, and isolation may not be substantially different from women's experiences in the past, zines afford them a unique form for the unedited, uncensored expression of their experiences, emotions, and ideas. Carlip argues, "Every time we pick up a pen, or an instrument, or communicate with each other, we are creating the revolution." She continues, "Every girl who takes a pen to paper and speaks her word is committing a courageous act of self empowerment."[75] We hope that zines as explorations in self-expression continue to grow and represent an even greater diversity of feminist points of view. We join other feminists of different generations and backgrounds to promote zines as an avenue for self-expression, as a way to establish links in a feminist network, and to work with others to dismantle the patriarchy.

NOTES

1. Francesca Lia Block and Hillary Carlip, *Zine Scene: The Do It Yourself Guide to Zines* (Girl Press, 1998).
2. Karen Green and Tristan Taormino, eds., *A Girl's Guide to Taking Over the World: Writings from the Girl Zine Revolution* (New York: St. Martin's Griffin, 1997), xiii.
3. Jennifer Baumgardner and Amy Richards, *Manifesta: Young Women, Feminism and the Future* (New York: Farrar, Straus and Giroux, 2000).
4. Ibid.
5. Ibid.
6. Jessica Rosenberg and Gitana Garofalo, "Riot Grrrl: Revolutions from Within," *Signs: A Journal of Women in Culture and Society* 23 (Spring 1998): 810.
7. M. L. Fraser, "Zine and Heard: Fringe Feminism and the Zines of the Third Wave," *Feminist Collections: A Quarterly of Women's Studies Resources* 23 (2002): 6–10.
8. Fred Wright, "The History and Characteristics of Zines," *The Zine and E-Zine Resource Guide* (1997) http://www.zinebook.com/resource/wright1.html (accessed October 25, 2003).
9. Stephen Perkins, "Approaching the '80s Zine Scene: A Background Survey and Selected Annotated Bibliography," *The Zine and E-Zine Resource Guide* (1992), http://www.zinebook.com/resource/perkins.html (accessed October 25, 2003); Heath Row, "From Fandom to Feminism: An Analysis of the Zine Press," *The Zine and E-Zine Resource Guide* (1997) http://www.zinebook.com/resource/heath.html (accessed October 25, 2003).
10. Although the Riot Grrrl movement faded, many contemporary zinesters continue to use the term *grrrl* to signifiy empowerment.
11. Colette Labrador, "In Their Own Words: Girl Zines," (2002) http://it.stlawu.edu/~xlclabr/page01.html, Department of Sociology, St. Lawrence University, Student Web Project (accessed October 25, 2003).
12. Baumgardner and Richards.
13. Carla Willig, ed., *Applied Discourse Analysis: Social and Psychological Interventions* (Philadelphia: Open University Press, 1999).
14. Jonathan Potter and Margaret Wetherell, *Discourse and Social Psychology: Beyond Attitudes and Behavior* (Newbury Park, CA: Sage, 1987).
15. Dawn Bates, "You Can't Shut Us Up: Finding Voice in Women's Zines" (poster presented at Association for Women in Psychology meetings, 2002).
16. Wright.
17. V. Vale, ed., *Zines!, vol. 1* (San Francisco:V/Search, 1996).
18. As quoted in Rosenberg and Garofalo, 812.
19. As quoted in Derek Chezzi, "The Counterculture Zine," *Maclean's*, November 20, 2000, 139.
20. Green and Taormino, xxiii.
21. As quoted in Rosenberg and Garofalo, 823.
22. Ibid., 818.

23. Mary Pipher, *Reviving Ophelia: Saving the Selves of Adolescent Girls* (New York: Putnam, 1994); Peggy Orenstein, *SchoolGirls: Young Women, Self-Esteem, and the Confidence Gap* (New York: Doubleday, 1994).
24. Madhu as quoted in Rosenberg and Garofalo, 818.
25. As quoted in Rosenberg and Garofalo, 821.
26. Green and Taormino.
27. Liberte, *quantify 2: part vs whole* (Year unknown), 1.
28. As quoted in Block and Carlip, 117.
29. Ibid., 29.
30. Xolau, *quantify 2: part vs whole* (Fall 2000), 2.
31. Lailah as quoted in Rosenberg and Garafolo, 824.
32. Labrador.
33. Hillary Carlip, *Girl Power: Young Women Speak Out* (New York: Warner Books, 1995), 9.
34. Angela Richardson, "Come on Join the Conversation: Zines as a Medium for Feminist Dialogue and Community Building," *Feminist Collections* 17 (1996): 10–13.
35. Alexwrekk, *brainscan 18* (Year unknown), 10.
36. M. J. Finders, "Queens and Teen Zines: Early Adolescent Females Reading Their Way Toward Adulthood," *Anthropology & Education Quarterly* 27 (1996): 71–89.
37. Pipher; Carol Gilligan, N. P. Lyons, and T. J. Hanmer, eds., *Making Connections: The Relational Worlds of Adolescent Girls at Emma Willard School* (Troy, NY: Emma Willard School, 1989).
38. Finders.
39. Pipher; Jane M. Ussher, *Fantasies of Femininity: Reframing the Boundaries of Sex* (New Brunswick, NJ: Rutgers University Press, 1997); Deborah L. Tolman, *Dilemmas of Desire: Teenage Girls Talk about Sexuality* (Cambridge, MA: Harvard University Press, 2002).
40. Vale.
41. Labrador.
42. As quoted in Block and Carlip, 11. Original grammar and punctuation kept in all quotes to capture style of zine writing.
43. Vale, 4.
44. Ibid., 5.
45. Richardson.
46. J. Wray and J. Steele, "Girls in Print: Figuring Out What It Means to be a Girl," in *Sexual Teens, Sexual Media*, eds. J. Brown, J. Steele, and K. Walsh-Childers (Mahwah, NJ: Lawrence Erlbaum, 2002), 194.
47. Marie Elia, *Triplicate and File* (2001), 23.
48. Christine Smith, "Zines as Activism" (oral presentation, Association of Women in Psychology meetings, 2003).
49. As quoted in Carlip, 40.
50. As quoted in Carlip, 34.
51. Rachel in *ChechelAngel* as quoted in *Skirt* no. 4 (2002): 8.
52. H. Macalister, T. Perry, S. Reitsz, and J. Sperling, "Dominant Themes in Women's zines" (poster presented at the Association for Women in Psychology meetings, 2003).
53. Amanda, *Soot and Stars*. 3 (2002): 8.
54. Author unknown, *Make me numb* no. 12 (Year unknown): 21–23.
55. Anne Nylander, *dear mr. bush* no. 1 (2002).
56. Noemi Ixchel Martinez, *Herman Resist* no. 2 (Year unknown): 29.
57. Carlip.
58. Ibid., 34.

59. Liz Defiance, *Death of a Psyche* no. 16 (2001): 26.
60. Xolau, 1.
61. Allie, *Satan's Panties* no. 5, (2002): 6.
62. Bianca Biteme, *No, I Don't Think So* no. 2, (Year unknown): 5.
63. As quoted in Block and Carlip, 118.
64. Baumgardner and Richards.
65. Elia, 2.
66. Tolman.
67. M. Tiggemann, M. Gardiner, and A. Slater, ""I Would Rather be a Size 10 Than Have Straight A's": A Focus Group Study of Adolescent Girls' Wish to be Thinner," *Journal of Adolescence* 23 (2000): 645–59.
68. Rosenberg and Garofalo; Richardson; Fraser.
69. Lisa as quoted in Rosenberg and Garafolo, 811.
70. Wray and Steele.
71. For a discussion on race and zines, see Schlit, chapter 3.
72. Rosenberg and Garofalo.
73. Wray and Steele.
74. Elia, 7.
75. Carlip, 9.

11

THIRD WAVE FEMINISM AND ECOFEMINISM: REWEAVING THE NATURE/CULTURE DUALITY

Colleen Mack-Canty

In its efforts to reweave the nature/culture duality, ecofeminism works to develop an expanded concept of both human and non-human nature, one that can serve both as a context for social analysis and a connection to our own embodiment and the natural world we have inherited and owe to our children to pass on in at least as good a condition as we received it.[1]

Today many feminists believe we are in a third wave of feminism and much of the literature views it as a generational occurrence. However, considering the theoretical characteristics of third wave feminism allows us to see additional feminisms, removed from issues of age, as third wave breaking down dualistic constructs, and developing explanations from the diverse embodied voices of women themselves, are theoretical characteristics important to third wave feminism. In this chapter, I draw upon women's narratives to explore the relationship between ecofeminism and third wave thought. I discuss how ecofeminism extends the overall feminist analysis of the intersectionality of oppressions such as racism, heterosexism, classism, and sexism to include nonhuman nature. This intersectionality is born out of the understanding that feminism must account for the differing perspectives of actual women. I consider ecofeminism's contribution to the reweaving of the specific duality between culture and nature, a duality that results from the fact that political philosophy in the West is primarily based on abstract, masculinist notions of disembodiment. This philosophy has led to the devaluation of nature, both human embodiment and nonhuman nature. Ecofeminists believe that restoring more balance between the cultural world and the natural world is an especially important endeavor in these environmentally disconcerting times.

THIRD WAVE THEORIES

Third wave feminism can be seen as an uneven evolution in feminist thought from second to third wave feminism. I conceptualize the third wave of feminism as a general theoretical framework influenced by multiple streams of thought. Second wave feminism, in large part, worked to reweave the public/private dualism by addressing the need to include women in public life together with the need to recognize that women's concerns in private life often merited public attention. Later in the second wave, feminists began to work for a general recognition of how classism, racism, and heterosexism intersect with sexism.[2] Third wave feminism responds to additional significant social and political concerns as it continues to expand feminist theory. Among the problems third wave feminists respond to are the fundamentalist Christian backlash to the women's movement, including the so-called postfeminist feminism, traditional sex and gender categorization, a globalizing economy with its accompanying "maldevelopment" projects with their disproportionately adverse effects on third world women and children, and increasingly precarious environmental problems. The higher educational opportunities allowed to women by second wave feminists' policymaking and the subsequent theorizing many of these women undertook, together with the significant contribution of women of color, have contributed greatly to the expansion of feminist theory.

Third wave feminism, having the advantage of a second wave of feminism to build on, is more global in its analysis and focuses on more general notions of oppression. Much of contemporary feminism is able to analyze problems of worldwide magnitude. This ability is also due, in no small part, to the ever increasing knowledge that is being made available by diverse women's voices around the earth.

Primary among third wave feminism's theoretical characteristics is the project to reweave dualistic thinking in general,[3] which divides the world into hierarchical dichotomies with one aspect ranked as superior in contrast to the other, which is regarded as inferior. Additionally, the theoretical perspective of third wave feminism begins with women's points of view, notably the diversity and difference among women.[4] This recognition, and the subsequent awareness of multiple explanations for oppression, begins to break down dualisms. Further, the importance third wave feminists place on the idea that their understandings should emerge from women's various experiential and embodied locations is fundamental. This approach represents a significant break from the traditional practice in Western political theory of developing theories/explanations from disembodied or abstract ideas.

Thus, while third wave feminism generally finds aspects of established Western political theories such as liberalism or socialism useful, the perspective of third wave feminism begins with multiple perspectives among women. Third wave feminism expands on the practice developed in the second wave of adding women's perspectives to established Western political theories or explanations, and working to make women's perspectives, as influenced by their various social locations, *the* explanations. By focusing on the embodied voices of the worlds' women as they describe, discuss, and analyze their lives, third wave feminism is able to expand its explanations for oppression and the solutions that can flow from such explanations.

While not an exhaustive list, important to the current expression of feminism are generational or youth feminism, queer theory, postcolonial feminism, and ecofeminism. Youth or generational feminists refute any notion that feminism is no longer needed. Their experience has shown them that women continue to confront the sexism which unfortunately still exists, albeit often in less obvious forms. In pivotal works such as Rebecca Walker's anthology *To Be Real*,[5] youth or generational feminists use each others' experiences as young women in a gendered society as resources to focus on how young women's lives from a multiplicity of racial, ethnic, marital, and gender combinations interact with feminism today. Queer theorists analyze sexuality from the embodied perspectives of different women. They enlarge on the analysis made by second wave feminists that gender is socially constructed to include the social construction of biological sex, thus further destabilizing a major dualistic category of female and male. Postcolonial feminists regard the continuing ill effects of our colonial/neocolonial history, as expressed by third world women in their various locations around the world, an appropriate focus for contemporary feminism.[6]

All these feminisms broaden the explanatory power of feminist theory. They allow feminists to deal more adequately with the complex myriad of contemporary issues, which were not as evident during much of second wave feminism, such as globalism, multiculturalism, environmentalism, and all the entanglement of isms that must be faced in today's more complicated and interrelated world. The pattern of working to reweave the separation of culture from nature can be seen in each of the feminisms noted here. Rather than working from established and usually abstract foundational theories, they all begin from the situated embodied perspectives of women. These feminisms also engage in the breaking down of dualistic thinking in general, because diversity is the antithesis of the dichotomizing either–or thought constructs upon which dualistic thinking is based. While each of these theories deals with deconstructing dualisms, ecofeminism most directly addresses the duality of culture and nature.

ECOFEMINISM:
CONCEPTS AND PRACTICES IN THE THIRD WAVE

In the United States, ecofeminism began during the second wave of feminism as (mostly) women in the peace movement began to perceive the interrelationships of militarism, sexism, racism, classism, and environmental damage.[7] Ecofeminism contributes a significant additional strand to the project of reweaving the nature–culture duality. In addition to beginning from the situated embodied perspectives of women, it has developed, and continues to develop, a body of complex theory to explain and act upon the interconnected subjugations of women, other humans, and nonhuman nature. It is this inclusion of nonhuman nature that enables ecofeminism to make a more thoroughgoing analysis of the specific dualism between nature-culture. Ecofeminism is a particularly relevant theory for feminism today because of the basic assumption that rejects the assumed inferiority of women, other subjugated people, and nonhuman nature. It extends the analysis of how oppressive isms such as classism, racism, nationalism, and heterosexism interact with sexism, to include the nonhuman world. It offers us a significant focus to consider, restoring more balance in one of the specific dualisms that Western political thought has constructed by deeming nature as inferior when compared to human-made culture.

Culture versus nature, including the human capacity to dominate both our human bodies and nonhuman nature, is one of the conceptual distinctions central to Western ideas.[8] It can be traced back to the Greeks, who developed philosophy and politics largely in a dualistic framework. In the nature–culture dualism, man was seen as representing culture and needing to be unconstrained by and to have domination over natural processes, both nonhuman nature and human embodiment. Men were identified with disembodied characteristics such as order, freedom, light, and reason, which were seen as better than, and in opposition to, women's allegedly more natural or embodied characteristics such as disorder, physical necessity, darkness, and passion.[9]

The importance of reweaving the separation that has been socially constructed between nature and culture is argued by postcolonial ecofeminists Maria Mies and Vandana Shiva:

> [T]oday, the cultural world is expanding at an increasingly alarming rate, by extracting more and more from the natural world. Ecofeminism has been an important force in challenging the assumption of the superiority of culture and its right to denigrate ... nature. In particular, ecofeminists have challenged the relationship between economic growth and exploitation of the natural environment.[10]

The theorizing of how environmental damages related to women's and other people's oppression, together with the perspectives of the women involved, can be seen in works such as those by Irene Diamond and Gloria Feman Orenstein in 1990, Judith Plant in 1987, and Vandana Shiva in 1989.[11] These works began to appear as the larger phenomenon of a third wave of feminism itself was developing in the late eighties and early nineties.[12] While the particular focus of ecofeminism is to mitigate the destruction of nature by culture, ecofeminists also work to reweave dualistic concepts in general. Related to their attempt to understand the ideology that perpetuates the domination of women, other suppressed humans, and nonhuman nature,[13] ecofeminists examine how concepts have been or can be formed. They analyze different frameworks or ways in which our thoughts can be organized to perceive reality in an oppressive manner. Ecofeminist philosopher Val Plumwood, for example, explains how structures of domination are based on hierarchically organized value dualisms such as man/woman, nature/culture, light (skin)/dark (skin), and so on.[14]

Related to its efforts to break down dualistic constructs, ecofeminist theory also works to create equitable and environmentally sound lifestyles.[15] In its use of ecology as a model for human behavior, ecofeminism suggests that we act out of recognition of our interdependency with others, human and nonhuman. In so doing, it builds on Carol Gilligan's "ethic of care" in that the relational caring position (where everyone's needs must be taken into consideration in relation to all others) is extended to other races, nationalities, and to the nonhuman world.[16] The value ecofeminists place on the notion of interdependency is in direct contrast to dualistic thinking which is based on separation and contrast.

NARRATIVES OF ECOFEMINISTS

This analysis draws upon twenty women interviewed in the early 1990s, as third wave feminism was evolving. In exploratory open-ended interviews, the women were asked what motivated their activism and why their work was important to them. In addition, the women were also asked to provide information on their activism, past political activity, and demographics. Most of the women did not self-identify as ecofeminists. Scholars have argued that the women most directly involved in forms of feminist activism often do not label themselves as ecofeminists, feminists, or environmentalists.[17] I also did not ask the women if they thought they were ecofeminists (or feminists or environmentalists) because I was interested in whether or not patterns of ecofeminist action and concerns would emerge from their narratives.

There was considerable demographic diversity within the group of women interviewed. Their ages range from late twenties to late fifties and their educations ranged from high school diplomas to Ph.D. degrees. Most were born in the United States, but two were immigrants. Two were American Indian, one of whom was raised on a reservation, while the other woman was raised off-reservation. The women lived in the western part of the United States in the Rocky Mountain area and the West Coast, specifically the states of California, Idaho, Montana, Oregon, Utah, and Washington.

I have assigned each woman a pseudonym to ensure the confidentiality of the interviews. From the interviews emerged two themes consistent with ecofeminism and third wave thought, the importance of interconnection and a focus on community and global issues. I begin with four of the women's personal histories to illustrate the depth and longevity of their activism.

PERSONAL HISTORIES

For some of the women, ecofeminist concerns originated in their childhood and continue today. This was the case for Sarah Westland Gill and Emma Fromme. A self-identified ecofeminist, Sarah Westland Gill explained that she bonded with the earth as a young child and has had a strong appreciation for the natural environment since that time. She further described how she grew up in a patriarchal household where her mother was unjustly dominated by her father. This experience, together with her cognizance of the degradation of nature, has given her a sense of identification with and awareness of those who are vulnerable. As the mother of two grown sons, she was also concerned about what kind of world we are leaving our children.

Emma Fromme is an at-home mother, married to a long-haul truck driver. She was a grassroots activist with the National Organization for Women (NOW) at the time of our interview. Emma grew up in Cold War-era West Berlin where stories of human suffering experienced by many escapees from East Berlin made a lasting impression on her. Upon moving to San Francisco as a teen, she became involved in the United Farm Workers' cause, antiwar demonstrations, and early recycling efforts. As a young mother, she was active in promoting midwifery, and recently she was involved in a successful grassroots environmental effort to prevent logging in the area that is now her family's home. At the time of the interview, Emma's activism was focused on keeping abortion legal, an issue she sees as connected to other social concerns. She said she believes the abortion issue is being used to keep feminist activists occupied so they will have little time left for other issues such as childcare, pay equity, poverty, and healthcare. She added, "I do, however, think the most serious problem we face today is environmental." Emma speculated that she would soon begin to disengage herself from NOW, to work more on radical environmental issues again. She also thought this would restore more balance to her life by providing her with a chance to work with her husband, who is active in environmental causes. Emma saw women's issues and environmental concerns as interrelated so she did not feel she would be discontinuing her work for feminist issues. She said she would simply be working for women's issues in another setting. In the meantime, she had been writing articles for an alternative press and giving speeches on what she sees as the interrelationship between the control of women's bodies and environmental devastation. She explained:

> Women are used to produce future consumers and soldiers in much the same way the earth is polluted for profit. I see stripmining, logging, etc., as similar to making women produce babies when and how some men want them to do so. In both cases, these men take advantage of their more powerful positions in a society that is organized for their advantage, [and for them to] impose their control.

In addition to early or childhood experiences, heritage was also an impetus for activism, particularly for Native American women. The

Native American women interviewed often expressed a special connection to ecofeminist ideas. According to Native American scholar and Lakota Pueblo/Sioux woman, Paula Gunn Allen:

> Indian people were cognizant of the proper place of woman as creatrix and shaper of existence in the tribe ... before Europeans arrived ... Indian women have been reclaiming their place in the life of their communities that they held before [the conquest]....
> Native women today work in areas such as alcohol treatment, restoring cultural values, serving as spokesperson to non Indian society, organizing against the environmental destruction of tribal lands, forced sterilization, etc.[18]

Grace Longhouse (Oneida) is an American Indian community activist with a strong sense of how the Indian boarding school phenomenon adversely affected the social fabric of most American Indian societies that were closely interwoven with the natural world. Grace remembers her family talking about what they went through in these boarding schools.[19] She said, "Then I started to understand what my grandmother meant when she said, school was so awful and how school should instead be helpful to an Indian child." Her family's experience with boarding schools together with her realization that during the eighteenth and nineteenth centuries a considerable number of American Indian children had been subjected to these experiences, led her to become interested in a career in the field of (re)education. She is currently an education professor at a major regional state university. She develops curricula that enable American Indian students to gain an understanding of their histories, in conjunction with conducting classes for future teachers (who are often Anglo) about Indian cultures. Besides working on these issues, Grace practices "voluntary simplicity," a practice she feels is in direct contrast to the present consumer-driven economy. She said:

> You don't have to have a lot of things to be a wealthy person. We never believed that in the first place, but we were influenced by the Anglo culture. Now we're making a concerted effort to show our young people the value of our former simple way of living that was more in harmony with the natural world.

Like Grace, Jeanne Hill (Northen Ute), a young married grandmother, is active in many American Indian causes. Her career, as a program manager with a Pacifica affiliate radio station, puts her in a pivotal position to facilitate networking through information exchange for her community of intertribal urban Indians. In this work, Jeanne contributes to her people's sense of community while providing them with a public space, and also is able to promote other social concerns through her work at the station. Jeanne has been involved with the antinuclear movement for years and the station publicizes information on demonstrations at the Nevada nuclear test ban site. Jeanne also promotes ethnic diversity through her position at the radio station. She believes that the radio shows must be ethnically authentic. Jeanne said: "I'm adamant that if we don't have a person of that ethnic group available, then we don't have the program. Non-Indians or non-Hispanics aren't likely to understand how to do a show for Indians or for Hispanics as well as Indians or Hispanics would." Jeanne also agrees with Gunn Allen's ideas about the importance of Native American women's activism. She said, "It is important to note that my women friends and I are increasingly aware of how, in the Indian community, it's the women who are doing the work, speaking out, and keeping the community going."

Sarah, Emma, Grace, and Jeanne engage in activities that are ecofeminist. This is illustrated in Sarah's connecting the domination in nature and her own childhood home, Emma's work on women's and environmental issues, Grace and Jeanne's overall effort to restore many Native American values that include Grace's emphasis on education, respect, and diversity, and Jeanne's work with the antinuclear movement and the radio. In addition, Grace's practice of voluntary simplicity and Jeanne's celebration of Solstice (a celebration honoring the sun's seasonal move closer to our hemisphere enabling the perennial new growth of plant life) are examples of indigenous people's valuing of sustainability, which ecofeminists accentuate. As ecofeminists Irene Diamond and Gloria Feman Orenstein explain, a major philosophic strain of ecofeminism emphasizes indigenous people's valuing of sustainability from which "we are led to understand the many ways in which we can walk the fine line between using the Earth as a natural resource ... and respecting the Earth's own cycles."[20] This sentiment of connection and interconnection was repeated in several of the interviews.

INTERCONNECTION

Threaded throughout these women's narratives is an understanding of our need to revalue the notion of interdependency. They work to help others recognize and enact this value. In particular, these activists help others to recognize how our world is made up of diverse interdependent parts, that all these parts are important to the whole, and the separation or destruction of any of the parts is an unhealthy practice.

For example, Jan Kelly, a self-identified ecofeminist, grew up in Appalachia where she worked on mine reclamation projects as a college student. She said:

> As a preteen I made a connection between what was happening to my surrounding physical environment and the subordination of women. I began receiving warnings about getting into cars with men then. At the same time, I started realizing it was certain powerful men who were strip mining, causing the Vietnam War, and who were in politics. It became clear to me where much of the negative power was coming from.

For several years after college, Jan's community was a town in the intermountain West, where she promoted sustainable[21] food production in a feminist organic bakery. During Jan's tenure, the bakery became a thriving institution, inspiring the establishment of similar organizations in surrounding towns. The bakeries use flour grown and milled locally with a focus on educating communities about the value of sustainable food production. Sustainable production is healthy for humans, helpful to the local economy, and increases people's awareness of where their food comes from, and the necessity of allowing nature to replenish herself. Because of her arthritis, Jan was forced to leave her work at the bakery. She had recently obtained a master's degree in landscape architecture. She said:

> I see myself translating ecological concepts I learned at the bakery and pragmatically applying them to my present position as a landscape architect for the U.S. Forest Service. When I think of the earth, of all species and of all life, my current work in public policy regulation translates into biological diversity and its legal protection through the Endangered Species Act, which I now help administer. Another example of how I am presently trying to encourage more awareness of ecological principles is my strip mine reclamation slide show. A couple of months ago, I went back to Virginia to tour reclaimed mine sites. From this tour, I put together a slide show of successful reclamation projects, with images conveying information, and an attitude that we need to start putting our resources into not only changing our environmentally devastating course, but to fixing past problems as well. I presented my show to School of Architecture classes. Students there are now interested in mine reclamation who might never have been.

Like Jan, other ecofeminists combined their ecological and feminist beliefs and took direct action to affect personal and long-term structural change. Sarah discussed the importance of interdependency and connection. She said:

> I believe the food we eat, what we throw away and where, our relationships, our means of livelihood, everything has effects that radiate out from our personal lives into our society and ultimately the whole living planet.

Sarah had recently transformed her own urban residence into an ecologically sound dwelling, an "ecohome," and opened it to the public as a demonstration project. Sarah begins her ecohome tour by discussing sustainable Native American practices, telling her audience:

> Something deep inside of us is attracted to the wisdom that was inherent in most Indian beliefs, that women's influence is necessary for balance in the community and for living in harmony with nature.

Allegorically, Sarah discusses the pictures of Native Americans hanging in her living room, as our spiritual relatives, ones who represent an old ecological wisdom that is now being "discovered" by Western science.

This sense of interdependence is not only between nature and humans but also between women. Carlotta Camberra, a NOW activist, launched and continues to organize a successful International Women's Day (IWD) celebration each year, in conjunction with her position as assistant coordinator of a NOW chapter. She sees the IWD celebration as a way to exhibit this connectedness. IWD is an event where women's shared cultural values (i.e., music, crafts, dancing) are celebrated. This is particularly significant to Carlotta with current global economic policies that harm women and children. Carlotta said:

> I think there is a real lack of acknowledgment or a sense of connection between ourselves and women in other countries, especially third world countries. In a global economy, third world women are too often adversely affected by our actions, especially our consumption patterns. Because this effect is indirect, we often are simply unaware of it. I want to promote the idea that we are all in this world together. We all have our own particular sexist cultures to struggle with, but we also have mutual concerns, whether we live in the U.S. or in Africa. The International Women's Day celebration illuminates our potential for solidarity and our responsibility to each other.

Carlotta's narrative draws attention to the plight of many third world women. Ecofeminism emphasizes local activism, and the narratives I relate are those of women in the United States, but ecofeminism itself also maintains the importance of a global perspective. In ecofeminism, where everything is seen as interconnected or interdependent, there is a serious regard for women whose cultures and soils are being eroded as a result of projects in the third world. Ecofeminists challenge the relationship between economic growth and exploitation of the natural environment[22] and ecofeminist anthologies contain works by and about women resisting development projects in the third world and the West.[23]

LINKING LOCAL AND GLOBAL ISSUES

Ecofeminists do share a broad vision of a society without militarism, hierarchy, and the destruction of nature, but like all forms of feminism, they often have different analyses and strategies for achieving them. Ecofeminist theory does not specifically tell people how they should engage in political activism. Ideally, the relation of ecofeminist theory to political activism is informative, not prescriptive. The activism individuals decide to undertake in these matters results then from their own reflection on the situation or issue they are encountering.

The women interviewed are involved in a variety of local projects. These include endeavors such as reinstating natural spaces in a city neighborhood, restoring traditional values for intertribal urban Indians, educating for racial and sexual tolerance, demonstrating against nuclear tests, and presenting college workshops on Indian Reservations for Anglo teachers to illuminate the notion of a "Two World View" (e.g., indigenous and Western). The women also work with a local economic trading system (LETS), a teenage multicultural awareness/action camp, antihate group action, a program to aid refugee teenagers, an organic food co-op, grassroots prochoice activism, welfare mothers, and a Hiroshima/Nagasaki Remembrance project. These local projects have larger global and theoretical implications. For example, Elaine Nelson and Pati Gibson are two young mothers who work to establish sustainable diverse local economies. They established and now administer a LETS organization that enables people to use their labor and skills in place of cash. Pati said:

> One of the reasons Elaine and I are doing this is to give mothers some support. They can get a break from their constant performance of child care by trading goods or services for baby sitting.

Elaine added:

> However in the long run, the real importance of LETS is that it makes goods available to different people who cannot afford to pay cash or who wish to disengage from the present economic system whenever possible.

The women see LETS as a possible transitional tool, one that might help us move toward a barter economy. Elaine stated, "While I don't think we're getting rid of the federal money system in my lifetime, LETS can help people to begin to consider the possibility of a more barterized economic system." She continued, explaining that while LETS is international, each LETS network trades only within a small geographical area. Keeping resources, labor, and benefits local is central to LETS' philosophy.

Ecofeminist activist Judith Plant sees LETS as keeping with the ecofeminists' bioregionalist notion she calls "Learning to become native to place ... living with the limits of a place."[24] Scholar Irene Diamond, in her vision of a world guided by ecofeminist principles, writes:

> This will entail the repair and creation of democratic self-reliant, frugal, and egalitarian institutions that primarily trade through more barterized and face-to-face modes of exchange. The invention of bioregional[25] ... networks utilizing their own, currencies ... [is an example].

Pati and Elaine, through their activity with LETS, offer people a very real way to begin to visualize an economic system that holds potential for environmental sustainability. In a barterized system, production would occur more on an as-needed basis. Further, a barter system would also work to enhance the value of women's productivity in the home. Women in industrialized societies have performed labor for more immediate consumption, *use value labor* to use Karl Marx's term. Men, on the other hand, have performed labor that has a monetary exchange value or "wage labor," leaving women (and usually children) with less access to money for goods and services. While most women today also work for wages, in the aggregate they earn considerably less than men. Feminist scholars have discussed how the undervaluing of women's work in the home, which occurs in large part with industrialization, contributed to their unequal status.[26]

In addition to revaluing women's labor, a barter system would most likely also reduce useless production as barter systems are based on local economies with goods and services in this system being produced more on an "as needed" basis. Further, it seems that if the barter system concept is seen through to its logical conclusion, it would probably not only eliminate much of the need for wage labor but also the unnecessary control that has been inherent in this sort of production. It could also curtail the economic devastation that occurs when these wage labor jobs migrate to countries with lower wages and no environmental controls. In sum, LETS, along with other forms of activism, link local and global issues and contribute to the prospect of reweaving the nature–culture dualism by revaluing natural resources and human connections.

CONCLUSION

If we look beyond age-defined feminism, we see how other feminists are third wave. The feminisms I mention in this chapter—youth feminism, queer theory, postcolonial feminism, and ecofeminism—are all third wave feminisms. Each constructs explanations/theories from different women's embodied locations and all work to break down dualism. Each of the feminisms, however, does have a different focus or emphasis regarding which oppressions in the intersectionality of isms with sexism should be emphasized. In the case of ecofeminism, it is ecology including nonhuman nature.

We can see how third wave ideas are carried out in the actions of ecofeminists. The women describe their reasons for activism, which, in contrast to dualism, flow from a sense of interconnection/interdependency. Additionally, the women challenge some aspect of the oppressive ways in which dualistic constructs identify women, other marginalized people, and nonhuman nature as inferior. Concepts of interconnection and the linking of local and global issues had their birth in second wave feminism and continue today rearticulated in a unique third wave way. In ecofeminism, these ideas work in multiple ways to reweave the nature–culture dualism.[27] Ecofeminism emphasizes local activism, but it also maintains the importance of a global perspective. Ecofeminists see everything as interdependent. They are concerned for women in the third world, who are suffering from the environmental devastation of their natural resources. While in the developing world itself, "women's struggles … are, of necessity, [most often] also ecological struggles. Because so many women's lives are intimately involved in trying to sustain and conserve water, land, and forests, they understand in an immediate way the costs of [development projects that] … pillage the Earth's natural riches."[28]

Ecofeminism has much to offer us in explanatory power, for it extends the critique of multifaceted oppressions with sexism to include nature, the key to so much of women's past and present oppression[29] and shows how this is related to other dominations. As the women interviewed in this chapter show, however, ecofeminism is more than a critique. Ecofeminism also works for the reconstruction of more viable social and political forms.[30] It is an especially relevant part of third wave feminism today in a world in which women, people of color, third world people, and the natural environment are suffering. The natural resources that make life possible on our planet are being polluted or depleted at an alarming rate, largely through human activity.[31] The relevance of ecological concerns to feminism is increasingly self-evident. There is a growing awareness that as we entered the twenty-first century, human beings faced environmental challenges unprecedented in the history of the planet.[32] Globally, people's struggles for clean water, clean air, and sustainable agriculture have already directly affected a tremendous number of people.[33] Thus the ecofeminist project—exploring the interconnections between the subjugation of women, other subjugated people, and nonhuman nature—is a crucial endeavor.

Third wave feminism generally will continue the importance of feminism to women. In our era of increasing globalization, this feminism is linking local and global concerns important to women's lives. Women in particular are affected by development projects,[34] both by the destruction of resources on which they depend, and by (though not discussed in this chapter) the dislocation of immigration. Women, from the vantage point of their particular locations, understand the costs of "maldevelopment," how these cost are occurring, and are most often the ones in the forefront of actions to stop this damage.[35] Important areas of research in the future for feminists, ecofeminists, and third wave feminists generally, are with these third world women, both in the developed and the developing world. These women have much to tell us.

NOTES

1. Stephanie Lahar, "Ecofeminist Theory and Grassroots Politics," *Hypatia* 6 (Winter 1991): 28–45.
2. Nancy Fraser and Linda Nicholson, "Social Criticism without Philosophy: An Encounter between Feminism and Postmodernism," in *Feminism/Postmodernism*, ed. Linda Nicholson (New York: Routledge, 1990), 19–38. Some credit the coining of the term *intersectionality* to Cathy Cohen, Kathleen B. Jones, and Joan C. Tronto, "Introduction," in *Women Transforming Politics: An Alternative Reader*, ed. Cathy Cohen, Kathleen B. Jones, and Joan C. Tronto (New York: New York University Press, 1997), 7.

3. Val Plumwood, "Beyond the Dualistic Assumptions of Women, Men, and Nature," *The Ecologists* 22 (January 1992): 8–13.

4. Barbara Arniel, *Politics and Feminism* (Oxford: Blackwell, 1999), 186.

5. Rebecca Walker, ed., *To Be Real: Telling the Truth and Changing the Face of Feminism* (New York: Doubleday, 1995).

6. Uma Narayan and Sandra Harding, eds., "Introduction," in "Border Crossings: Multicultural and Postcolonial Feminist Challenges to Philosophy" (part 1), *Hypatia* 13 (Spring 1998): 1–6.

7. Noel Sturgeon, *Ecofeminist Natures: Race, Gender, Feminist Theory and Political Action* (New York: Routledge, 1997), 27.

8. Arneil.

9. Wendy Brown, *Manhood and Politics: A Feminist Reading in Political Theory* (Totowa, NJ: Rowman and Littlefield, 1988).

10. Maria Mies and Vandana Shiva, *Ecofeminism* (London: Zed Books 1993), 13.

11. Irene Diamond and Gloria Feman Orenstein, eds., *Reweaving the World: The Emergence of Ecofeminism* (San Francisco: Sierra Club Books, 1990); Judith Plant, ed., *Healing the Wounds: The Promise of Ecofeminism* (Philadelphia: New Society Publishers, 1989); Vandana Shiva, *Staying Alive: Women, Ecology and Development* (Delhi/London: Zed Books, 1989).

12. Arniel.

13. Karen J. Warren, *Ecofeminist Philosophy: A Western Perspective on What It Is and Why It Matters* (Lanham, MD: Rowman and Littlefield, 2000).

14. Val Plumwood, "Nature, Self, and Gender: Feminism, Environmental Philosophy, and the Critique of Rationalism," in *Ecological Feminist Philosophies*, ed. Karen J. Warren (Bloomington: Indiana University Press, 1996), 155–180.

15. Lahar.

16. Carol Gilligan, *In a Different Voice: Psychological Theory and Women's Development* (Cambridge, MA and London: Harvard University Press, 1982).

17. See Lin Nelson, "The Place of Women in Polluted Places," in *Reweaving the World: The Emergence of Ecofeminism*, eds. Irene Diamond and Gloria Feman Orenstein (San Francisco: Sierra Club 1990), 173–188. Also, Ann Bookman and Sandra Morgen, eds., in their pivotal work on women's activism, *Women and the Politics of Empowerment* (Philadelphia: Temple University Press, 1988) tell us that most of the articles in their work describe campaigns comprised and led primarily by working-class women who did not identify their struggles as feminist. Frances T. Farenthold, "Introduction," in *Women Activists: Challenging the Abuse of Power*, ed. Ann Witte Garland (New York: The Feminist Press, CUNY, 1988), xxiii, tells us the women activists in Garland's book, whether they specifically articulate ecofeminism or not, seem to be spokeswomen of this evolving feminism.

18. Paula Gunn Allen, *The Sacred Hoop: Recording the Feminine in American Indian Traditions* (Old Westbury, NY: The Feminist Press, 1986), 30.

19. K. Tsianina Lomanwaima, in her work *They Called It Prairie Light: The Story of a Chilicco Indian School* (Lincoln: University of Nebraska Press, 1994), describes how the Bureau of Indian Affairs, U.S. Department of Interior, set up boarding schools in the eighteenth and nineteenth centuries to offer vocational training to students from tribes. School officials were determined to control their students, and drastically limited students' contact with their families. From the moment the children entered the institution, strict age and gender segregation split siblings apart. Students might stay at the school for as long as five years without seeing their parents, the monthly letters they sent home were written in class and read by their teachers. Lomanwaima is Creek and Cherokee.

20. Diamond and Orenstein, xii.

21. Sustainable practices can be described in today's economic terms as living off your interest rather than your principle.

22. Mies and Shiva.

23. Diamond and Orenstein; Leonie Caldecott and Stephanie Leland, eds., *Reclaim the Earth: Women Speak Out for Life on Earth* (London: The Women's Press, 1983).

24. Judith Plant, "Searching for Common Ground: Ecofeminism and Bioregionalism," in *Reweaving the World: The Emergence of Ecofeminism,* eds. Irene Diamond and Gloria Feman Orenstein (San Francisco: Sierra Club Press, 1990), 155–161.

25. Bioregions would be organized (socially, politically, and economically) around ecosystems instead of today's cartography, which most often did not take natural systems into account when its political boundaries were drawn.

26. See Carolyn Merchant Brown, *The Death of Nature: Women, Ecology, and the Scientific Revolution* (San Francisco: Harper and Row, 1989).

27. Warren, 198.

28. Diamond and Orenstein, xi.

29. Plumwood, 13.

30. Lahar, 42–43.

31. Joseph R. Des Jardins, *Environmental Ethics: An Introduction to Environmental Philosophy* (Belmont, CA: Wadsworth, 2001), 5.

32. Lester Brown et al., *Vital Signs 2001: The Trends that Are Shaping Our Future* (The Worldwatch Institute, in Cooperation with the United Nations Environment Program, New York: W.W. Norton, 2001).

33. Diamond and Orenstein, xi.

34. Greta Gaard, *Ecological Politics: Ecofeminists and the Greens* (Philadelphia: Temple University Press, 1998), 34.

35. Robert Gottlieb, *Forcing the Spring: The Transformation of the American Environmental Movement* (Washington, DC: Island Press, 1993); Guilda West and Rhoda L. Blumberg, eds., *Women and Social Protest* (New York: Oxford University Press, 1990).

Part IV

Into The Future:
Implications of a Third Wave

12

CONFRONTING THE FUTURE, LEARNING FROM THE PAST: FEMINIST PRAXIS IN THE TWENTY-FIRST CENTURY

Nancy A. Naples

In April 1979, Cherríe Moraga and Gloria Anzaldúa wrote a letter to feminists of color soliciting contributions for a new anthology.

> We want to express to all women—especially to white middle-class women—the experiences which divide us as feminists; we want to examine incidents of intolerance, prejudice and denial of differences within the feminist movement. We intend to explore the causes and sources of, and solutions to these division. We want to create a definition that explains what "feminist" means to us.[1]

This Bridge Called My Back still speaks to feminists across many different political generations and offers a caution to us as we consider the debates between and among different generations of feminists.[2] In this chapter, I revisit the question of what can count as feminism and argue for a broad view of feminism that incorporates the feminist political strategies and analysis of women from diverse racial, ethnic, and cultural backgrounds. In doing so, I hope to provide another vantage point from which to understand the limits and possibilities of viewing feminist activism as a series of historical waves of activism.

The distinction between the second and third waves of the women's movement was conceptualized based on visible waves of protest.[3] Scholars of the women's movement have defined the suffrage movement as the first wave and the struggles against rigidly defined gender roles and for equal rights that occurred during the late 1960s and early 1970s as the second wave. However, a wave of protest linked specifically to women's movement activism does not demarcate the third wave.[4] Self-defined third wave activist Jo Trigilio argues that, "Third wave feminism seems to be more of an academic construction, used to market the development of postmodernist critiques of second wave feminism."[5] Yet, the conceptualization of the third wave has provided an important organizing framework and identity for contemporary feminist activists. In this chapter, I explore the continuity and divergence between feminist activists of the so-called second wave and those associated with the third wave of feminism. In doing so, I examine which actors and forms of activism have been marginalized in certain accounts of the second wave and how women of color and working-class women's activism serve as models for contemporary feminist third wave activism. While the significance of women of color and working-class women's contribution to contemporary feminist activism has been noted by other feminist scholars and activists,[6] I extend this effort by examining whose political practice is left out of different formulations of movement activism in order to broaden the political lessons that can help inspire a more inclusive form of feminist practice.

Some feminist scholars have found Sartre's conceptualization of *praxis* to provide a useful tool for examining the diverse investments of contemporary feminist activism. Building on Sartre's notion, Sonia Kruks argues that praxis or "the specific characteristics of human practical activity must be the point of departure in accounting for the possibility of human knowledge and reason. It is in *doing* (rather than in seeing, or contemplating) that we come (at least initially) to generate forms of knowledge."[7] Kruks stresses that through "the study of one's own situated praxis, ever wider sets of social and historical processes may be made intelligible."[8] I share Kruks's goal of opening up to and understanding the experiences of others "whose worlds and experiences are not our own" in order to enhance the possibility "of respectful solidarity among otherwise different women."[9] In this chapter, I argue that by examining whose political practice is left out of different formulations of movement activism and which political lessons are centralized in dominant discourse on feminist activism, it becomes possible to revisit what counts as feminism and feminist activism.

The political is inherently personal and my critique of the wave metaphor has an unavoidably personal dimension.[10] Although I was born in 1951, due to a series of diverse political investments and experiences, most notably while working as a social worker in New York City during the 1970s, I did not self-define as a feminist until the early 1980s. Although I was employed by a women's organization, the YWCA of New York City, and advocated on behalf of pregnant teens and teen mothers as part of my professional and political commitments during that decade, I did not conceptualize this work as feminist at that time. Therefore, in terms of the political generational view of feminism, I am neither second nor third wave. Consequently, I find myself in the awkward position of being an outsider to my own historical feminist generation and to the generational labels created in the context of efforts to historicize feminisms and women's movement politics.

My analysis, therefore, is by necessity an *interested one* that starts from my investment in feminist praxis as a form of political analysis and struggle that I believe has a great deal to offer contemporary movements for social justice. It has been my privilege since 1980 to work with and chronicle the political insights and political practice of women from diverse racial-ethnic, class, and cultural backgrounds. As a result of my examination of low income and working-class women's community activism, I identified a broad-based notion of "'doing politics' that included any struggle to gain control over definitions of self and community, to augment personal and communal empowerment, to create alternative institutions and organizational processes, and to increase the power and resources of" poor and working-class communities.[11] In my view, the definition of feminism should be broad enough to include the diversity of women's political analyses and strategies for social and economic justice. Historical categorizations that fail to define feminism broadly will inevitably also fail to provide the analytical framework for effective coalition building across the diversity of differences that shape women's identities and experiences.

Despite this assertion, I also want to pose the following question: In order for contemporary feminist theory and practice to contribute to diverse movements for social justice is it necessary to claim that every struggle is a feminist one? As feminist philosopher Nancy Fraser argues, maybe there are issues or struggles that are "bigger than feminism."[12] Anticapitalist globalization movements and democratic practice are clearly bigger than feminism. In other words, need feminism be "the master label for everything"? Surely, as Fraser and other feminist scholars[13] argue, there are "gender dimensions" to all struggles for social justice, and "feminists better be in these struggles and bring out those dimensions because certainly nobody else will."[14] Gendered and racialized exclusions undergird capitalist expansion. Furthermore, economic globalization exacerbates existing gender and racial inequalities.[15] However, even broader left movements have yet to incorporate the ways that gender and race inequalities constitute the foundation for many of these economic and political projects.

By incorporating the perspectives and political practice of women who are usually left out of our historical record, I believe that we can discover new analyses and political strategies that could help us reinvent progressive movements in more inclusive and relevant ways.[16] In contrast to this goal, the wave categorization of the U.S. women's movement offers a narrow conceptualization of what counts as feminism and who can be defined as legitimate participants in the women's movement. For example, the socialist feminist organizing of progressive activists during the progressive era is rarely incorporated into accounts of the first wave.[17] The activism of poor women of color in the National Welfare Rights Movement is typically not included in the definition of the second wave of the women's movement.[18] As Sherna Gluck and her coauthors point out:

> For the most part, the early history of feminist activism among women of color and/or working class and poor women remains, at best, particular and separate and does not challenge the accepted paradigm of "second wave" feminism. It is only when autonomous groups like the National Black Feminist Organization ... and the Combahee River Collective ... came out with statements that explicitly allied them with "the women's movement," that at least some women of color become incorporated into the master narrative.[19]

Furthermore, the periodization of the U.S. women's movement in terms of waves of activism also "obscures the historical role of race in feminist organizing."[20] As Springer explains:

> If we consider the first wave as that moment of organizing encompassing woman suffrage and the second wave as the women's liberation/women's rights activism of the late 1960s, we effectively disregard the race-based movements before them that served as precursors, or windows of political opportunity, for gender activism.[21]

However, rather than abandon the wave model, Springer argues for its reconceptualization to include "women of color's resistance to gender violence."[22]

Antiracism and struggles for racial justice are core commitments for feminist activism and therefore should be incorporated into conceptualizations of feminist waves of protest. This takes on even greater significance as we consider the original constructions of the "third wave." The term was first used by Barbara Smith, founder of Kitchen Table: Women of Color Press in a book on racism.[23] Furthermore, self-defined third wave feminists Leslie Heywood and Jennifer Drake argue that third wave feminism owes a debt to third world feminists for providing the "definitional moment" that led to the development of third wave feminism.[24] Catherine Orr finds their analysis to be "the most satisfying account of the emergence of the third wave."[25] According to Heywood and Drake:

> [T]he contradictory character of the third wave emerged not from the generational divides between second wavers and their daughters, but from critiques by Cherríe Moraga and Gloria Anzaldúa, bell hooks, Chela Sandoval, Audre Lorde, Maxine Hong Kingston and many other feminists of color who called for a "new subjectivity" in what was, up to that point, white, middle-class, first world feminisms.[26]

Despite these efforts to develop an analysis of the third wave of the U.S. women's movement that acknowledges and incorporates the contributions of women of color, I believe that we need to move beyond the wave metaphor of protest in order to capture the complexity of feminist activism and feminist identities in the contemporary era.

One strategy may be to differentiate between waves of protest and political generations. Nancy Whittier argues that "women who entered the women's movement together, at a particular point in the movement's history, came to share an understanding of what it meant to be a feminist."[27] She describes the political practice and feminist perspective of "micro-cohorts" who enter the women's movement at two-year intervals (in contrast to analyses of cohorts defined by ten- or even twenty-year intervals). With an eye to the nuances of changing political practice from the 1960s to the 1990s, Whittier notes how subtle shifts in feminist identity over time can lead to conflict as well as continuity among feminist activists. Her study is based on analysis of feminist organizations and interviews with activists of different generations in Columbus, Ohio. She demonstrates the significance of community-based collectives such as feminist bookstores and rape crisis centers as well as cultural activities such as women's music festivals for keeping feminist consciousness and activism alive, especially during periods of movement quiescence.[28] However, her analysis does not include the diversity of political activities that feminists might also have participated in during the period she studies. It is important to consider the continuity and changes within organizations such as Women Against Rape, Fan the Flames Bookstore, the Ohio ERA Task Force, and NOW, but I believe it is equally important to explore feminist contributions to other campaigns for social justice such as antiracism, welfare reform, prison reform, and environmental justice among others.

Political generations interact, learn from each other, and in the process contribute to transformations in political analyses and strategies. Political generations are also not bounded by particular movements. For examples, feminists are involved in diverse movements for social, economic, and political justice, including struggles against economic globalization campaigns, colonialism, militarism, poverty, and environmental degradation. Feminists who are active in these campaigns range in age, racial-ethnic background, class background, and understanding of feminism. Using Whittier's definition of feminist generations, contemporary feminist activists include those who came into feminist consciousness through participation in the second wave of the women's movement and those who entered feminism at a later date; those who came to feminism as young women and those who did not identify with feminism until much later in their lives; those who came to feminism through personal and community-based struggles and those who were introduced to feminism in women's studies classes and women's organizations. It is possible to differentiate between historical waves of protest based on some circumscribed goals, but given the diversity of contemporary feminist activism and social protest, it is more difficult to situate individual feminist activists in one wave or another. Here, Nancy Whittier's notion of "micro-cohorts" could offer a corrective. However, given the diversity of feminist practices in different geographic areas and among feminists of different cultural, class, and racial backgrounds, I remain concerned that historical frameworks which specify, in advance of more nuanced analysis, the boundaries of feminist political practice will define many activists and forms of political struggle outside the frame.

In contrast to the definition of waves as periods of large-scale protest, many authors use the mother–daughter metaphor to describe the relationship between second and third wave feminists.[29] This metaphor often takes the form of, on the one hand, complaints about a petulant daughter who does not appreciate what her foremother has sacrificed for her freedom versus a controlling mother who judges her daughter's approach to feminism as ineffectual and self-absorbed. For example, some second wave feminists are angered by what they see as an individualist focus of younger feminists.[30] In her discussion of texts written by third wave feminists, Catherine Orr is concerned that third wave authors' "new style of rebellion [is] based on a mis-remembered, or at least extremely narrow, version of history."[31] For their part, younger feminists express resentment that their perspectives on and practices of feminism are discredited by feminists associated with the second wave. This personalization of waves complicates the view of feminist activism by reducing the difference between waves to personal intergenerational struggles over definitions of feminism.

CONTINUITY AND DISCONTINUITY IN FEMINIST ACTIVISM

Many of my students also find the notion of generations problematic for somewhat different reasons. For example, feminists in my women's studies courses who came of age in the 1990s have found some of the key texts associated with the so-called second wave and third wave to be filled with an anger and marked by generational boundaries that did not speak to them.[32] As women's studies student Natalie Peluso[33] explains:

> I find such a focus on feminist "waves" to be both counterintuitive and counterproductive. These divisions seem to foster feelings of competition, and skepticism, rather than unity and trust. As older feminists witness the seemed de-politicization of Women's Studies programs and Women's Centers around the country, feelings of disappointment in and disillusionment with younger feminists may arise. Conversely, younger feminists may feel as though feminists from past generations under appreciate them, and therefore, they have little to learn from these women.[34]

Peluso also expressed concern that firm generational distinctions "exclude those both on the fringe of the movement, such as queer activists, and those who have simply been left out of the movement altogether, such as women of color."[35] By defining the second wave primarily through reproductive rights and antipornography, Peluso argues, "this creates the illusion that feminism is for 'white,' American-born, young, upper-middle class, heterosexual women."[36] She believes that "If one were to surpass such restrictive divides (in other words, to read between the theoretical lines), one would likely discover that feminists are a truly cross-generational, cross-cultural mix of individuals working towards the liberation of all women."[37]

However, Peluso and many of my other women's studies students, regardless of racial, ethnic, or class background, were more receptive to the analyses offered by women of color associated with both waves of the women's movement.[38] In fact, in her final paper for the Women's Studies Senior Seminar in Spring 2003, Bonnie Durgin explained why, as a white Jewish heterosexual woman, she found that of all the many feminisms she was introduced to in her women's studies courses, black feminist thought spoke most directly to her. She explained: "I apply it to my sense of feminism because as I understand it, [black feminist thought] appears to be the only specification of feminism that does not force those who ascribe to it, to apply some unilateral metatheory to their beliefs about the nature of sexist oppression."[39] Durgin argues that "Black feminism is a truly all-inclusive, action based theory of feminism, that enforces coalition building and acknowledges the unending interconnectedness of oppressive forces. These issues, specifically, action and inclusivity, are central to my feminist politics."

In addition to my students' reactions, I also explore some of the links I have found between the political analysis and activism of working-class women of color who came to political consciousness before and during the second wave of the U.S. women's movement and those women of diverse racial-ethnic backgrounds whose political consciousness was shaped in the context of the third wave. This analysis of the continuity and discontinuity in feminist activism complicates the firm differentiation between the waves of movement activism that has dominated recent feminist discourse.

The women community activists I worked with throughout the 1970s and 1980s, and from whom I learned what it meant to be a feminist, were also striving to ensure the continuity of community activism and progressive analyses by educating others in their community about successful strategies to achieve social and economic justice. These grassroots activists mobilized through the intimate connections of their everyday lives to strengthen the grounds for community action and social change, and through these rich encounters create new political analyses.[40] They did not see women's issues as separate from broad-based struggles for social justice and economic security. While not necessarily working on gender-based issues, they often challenged deeply held patriarchal and heterosexist traditions and confronted the limits of democracy for poor and working class people in the U.S. They fought against corporate poisoning of their neighborhoods and police harassment, against homophobia and racism, against the abuse of women and children, and for people-centered economic development, immigrants' rights, access to healthcare, educational equity, and adequate wages. Many had engaged in such struggles for most of their lives and continue to do so despite the decline in the wider society's support for a progressive social agenda.

In this regard, their political praxis resonates with that envisioned by many of my women's studies students who are thirty to fifty years younger than the women whose political practice I document. For example, the following definition of feminism was offered to me by a women's studies student who recently graduated from the University of Connecticut. In defining what feminism meant to her, Nikki McGary wrote:

> To me, feminism is the promotion of open-mindedness. It is the reflection of the hope in equality. It is the desire to raise consciousness and critique social barriers and inequalities. It is the knowledge that things can improve. It is the understanding that there are silenced whispers in our history and society that should be heard and shared.... It is the desire to listen to the silenced voices and promote change that can improve the lives of the oppressed. Feminism allows me to critique with an open mind and find my voice so that I can promote improvement and share my perspectives. Feminism challenges ignorance, encourages empowerment, and embraces diversity.[41]

Like many twenty-first century women's studies students, McGary demonstrates her feminist commitment through a broad range of organizing efforts. She participated in the War Resisters League, organized on behalf of Justice for Janitors linked with the Students Against Sweatshops movement, organized workshops on tolerance and antiracism, and one summer worked with the Sexual Assault/Domestic Violence Taskforce as Coordinator for the LGBTQ Community in Connecticut. McGary's organizing efforts illustrate the point raised by Kaplana Krishnamurthy, who codirected the Third Wave Foundation, that for contemporary feminist activists, "The traditional issues of pay equity and reproductive health have been expanded to school reform, environmental justice, reproductive health including issues of sexual health and safety, globalization,... [and] prisons."[42]

Self-defined third wave feminists take their feminist practice into diverse struggles for progressive economic and social change. Ironically, some feminists who identify with the second wave women's movement mistrust the diverse political commitments of third wave feminist activists and express concern that the issues that were central to second wave feminism have receded from contemporary feminist activism. Some participants in the second wave women's movement in the United States also mourn the loss of what they saw as a "collectivist drive that defined the feminist movement during the second wave."[43] Instead, they fear that an "individualist attitude" is the dominant mode of engagement for young women of the so-called third wave. As Jennifer Friedlin reports, several feminist activists of the 1960s and 1970s at the Veteran Feminists of America conference held at Barnard College in 2002 "spoke of the transition from a movement based on the 'we' to today's sea of disparate 'I's,' fighting for individual gains without a thought about the past, present or future of the feminist cause."[44] Ironically, this charge was also leveled against many of the white, middle-class feminists of the second wave by the working-class community activists in New York City and Philadelphia I interviewed in the 1980s.[45] Furthermore, as mentioned earlier, the campaigns for social and economic justice that drew the political energies of these working-class activists were seldom defined as central to the second wave women's movement.

While the working-class activists of color struggled against sexism and other forms of gender oppression in their everyday lives, their political activism was shaped by a deeply intersectional understanding of the problems that faced their communities. They did not view their struggles against racist educational systems or for adequate health care and housing as a form of activism that was separate from their struggles to improve the lives of women and girls in their communities. The activists who fought for welfare rights and civil rights and against colonialism and environmental racism, among other concerns, also defined these political battles as crucial for protecting and promoting women's rights. Many of the struggles that were central to the African-American and Puerto-Rican women community activists whose political practice I have documented, are now significant aspects of third wave feminist activism.[46] Consequently, third wave feminist activists engage in diverse campaigns for social and economic justice, they broaden what counts as feminism and feminist activism that, in many ways, speaks to the concerns of poor women and women of color in this country and beyond.

Yet, few of the women activists working in poor communities I interviewed defined themselves as feminists.[47] For many of these women, resisting the self-definition of feminist related to their perception that the women's movement did not speak to their concerns as working-class women of color. The politics of political identity is especially contentious in the context of the coalition-building efforts. For example, if activists require participants to take up labels that may not be of their own choosing, we might be unable to build certain kinds of progressive alliances. Another challenge to feminist activism occurs when feminism is broadened to such an extent that it is defined as "something individual to each feminist."[48] On the one hand, this open-ended definition could serve to broaden the base for social protest in this so-called postfeminist age. On the other hand, under this open-ended definition, feminism would no longer signify any particular political practice or analysis. What do we lose when the definition of feminism is so open-ended that any concern can be defined as a feminist issue?

Feminists organizing and writing in the latter part of the 1960s and throughout the 1970s convincingly argued that feminism encompassed more than a concern with "women's issues." They argued that capitalism, militarization, colonialism, poverty, environmental degradation, among other oppressions, must be understand through a gendered lens.[49] Feminists convincingly demonstrated that women's social location placed them into particularly vulnerable positions with regard to the problems that result from large scale economic, political, and social processes like global economic restructuring.[50] They simultaneously argued that those issues associated with women such as child care, reproductive rights, and food security, have profound effects on all members of households and communities regardless of gender.[51]

While recognizing the importance of broadening what counts as a feminist issue and feminist activism for enhanced political and theoretical power, a number of scholars have also cautioned that there needs to be a distinction between women's organizing for their own benefit (e.g., for equal rights) versus organizing on behalf of others in their households or communities.[52] For example, historian Temma Kaplan employs the term *female consciousness* to describe women who make political claims on the basis of their gender roles and subsequently participate in radical political action.[53] Obviously, this distinction often breaks down upon examination of individual women's activism. Furthermore, not all women who make claims through their gender ideology do so on behalf of women-identified issues like equal rights or reproductive choice. In trying to understand the different ways women define political issues, Maxine Molyneux differentiates between "practical gender issues" and "strategic gender issues" to capture the way women activists organize around their practical everyday needs for food, housing, daycare, versus organizing around their gender-specific identities.[54]

Kaplan argues that since grassroots women activists do not construct their activism primarily as feminists they can play with gender stereotypes in a way that those who center their identities as feminists may not. For example, in their efforts to confront corporate and government officials, Lois Gibbs and the other women involved in protesting the environmental dangers of Love Canal permitted themselves to be depicted as comedic figures and as victims, two modes of display that self-defined feminists would resist. As Kaplan explains, "Had the women been feminists, they could have undercut their demands to be treated as full citizens by such actions. But the homeowners were desperate to save their community from disaster; they were willing to compromise their own dignity to survive."[55] The fact that these women did not define themselves as feminists, however, does not mean that they did not recognize sexism in the organizations and movements in which they participated.

Those of us who chronicle the political analyses and strategies of women grassroots activists demonstrate the influence of other social movements in shaping the activists' political analyses and political networks.[56] For example, Dollie Burwell, who has been in the forefront of the fight against environmental racism in the United States, drew on lessons from the U.S. civil rights movement, and South African organizers Regina Ntongana and Josette Cole tied their activism to the antiapartheid movement. Through their activism, they contributed to the larger movement for social justice in South Africa. As Kaplan explains, "Women like Regina Ntongana, by their struggle to establish homes in the cities, helped undermine apartheid and contributed to the view that housing has some relationship to social justice."[57] This dialogic and intergenerational view of activism offers a powerful analytic framework in which to view the interdependence of movements for social justice and the continuity and transformation of political practice.

Building on the lessons of the past and transforming these lessons to meet contemporary challenges has been a hallmark of black and Chicana feminist praxis.[58] As Springer notes:

> Far from reinventing the feminist wheel, young Black feminists are building on the legacy left by nineteenth-century abolitionists, anti-lynching crusaders, club women, Civil Rights organizers, Black Nationalist revolutionaries, and 1970s Black feminists. They are not inserting themselves into the third-wave paradigm as much as they are continuing the work of a history of Black race women concerned with gender issues.[59]

Feminists of color powerfully demonstrate how political conscious-ness and political practice are readily tied to the material of their lives. For example, the Combahee River Collective explained how their sensi-tivity to the complex relationship between race-ethnicity, class, and gender enabled them to go "beyond white women's revelations because we are dealing with the implications of race and class as well as sex."[60] Writing from a historical materialist perspective, Angela Davis demon-strated how the material conditions of black women's lives as women, as blacks, and as working-class people historically shaped their oppres-sion and resistance.[61] Chicana feminists also argue that an intersec-tional understanding of their lives derives from the context in which it is lived, experienced, felt, embraced, and resisted.[62] Many contempo-rary feminist activists also exhibit an intersectional understanding of feminism and feminist practice. They have learned from feminist activ-ists and scholars of the second wave that "women" is a complex cate-gory and that it is necessary to acknowledge and work across the many differences that shape women's lives.

BUILDING ON AND TRANSFORMING FEMINIST PRAXIS

Feminist consciousness and political practice has transformed the minds and hearts of a new generation of activists through experiences that differ, for the most part, from the experiences that shaped feminist praxis of the previous generation of activists. As Amy Schriefer points out, "The third wave marks a return to personal consciousness raising, but it has been rendered different due to postmodern and multicultural ideas of multiplicity and difference.[63] According to Schriefer, women graduating from college in the 1990s were "the first generation to grow up with feminism as part of our cultural and political wallpaper, and in striving to form our own feminist identity, naming and navigating feminism's contradictions has become a primary theme of the third wave."[64]

In contrast to my experience growing up in a household with firm gender roles, class of 2003 women's studies graduate Bonnie Durgin explains how her father and her brother influenced her development as a feminist. She recalled how her father instructed her in the proper use of power tools:

> Standing beside my own father's basement workbench and hear-ing all about the ins and outs of table saws. I was a very thin kid until I was about thirteen, so that weight of his power tools and

push mower in my tiny hands was always of great concern to him. Even so, my dad brought me outside with my older brother, on the same day, to learn how to safely operate our green punch lawnmower, although I wouldn't be big enough to manipulate its bulk until almost a year later.[65]

Durgin describes being raised "in an environment where we could observe and be shaped by shared responsibility."[66] Both she and her brother were told "that no household chore was one person's job, but the entire family's."[67] Durgin and her brother shared the tasks of lawn mowing and doing the dishes. Because both her parents worked full time outside of the home, Durgin "had no conception of their significantly different incomes until my young adulthood, because they never acknowledged any inequalities between them."[68] Durgin's experience may not be specific to her historical generation and others in her generation may have grown up in households with more traditional gender roles. However, she and her brother were more open to feminism as a consequence of their egalitarian upbringing and feminism was alive and well on the campuses of the colleges they attended, so they were drawn to feminist events and quickly took up the feminist identity once they were introduced to it. Ironically, Durgin first heard of the word *feminist* from her brother, who returned from college one winter break

wearing a bright blue T-shirt that proclaimed, "Feminist Chicks Dig Me." He had been working as the web development coordinator with a women's activist group at Castleton College. They had purchased the shirt for him as a "thank you" for all he had done for them. His shirt led to a very brief discussion about feminism, an ideology to which he self-identifies, that served as a wonderful prelude to the introductory women's studies course I was about to begin in the coming semester.[69]

Once she started taking women's studies courses, Durgin found herself "doing feminism everyday."[70] "Doing feminism everyday," reflects the sentiment of many of my students, but it also captures the pervasiveness of feminist praxis in the many movements for social justice that engage the energies of feminists regardless of wave.

In the late twentieth century, feminists along with other activists with diverse political agendas experimented with new forms of activism. Cultural politics and cyberactivism have proven to be two of the most effective forms of organizing that contest, respectively, distinctions between culture and politics and between local and global organizing. Cultural politics expanded as a form of activism in the 1980s and 1990s as exemplified by the Guerrilla Girls and Lesbian Avengers. The Lesbian Avengers drew on the lessons of ACT-UP and created spectacles such as eating fire to creatively challenge homophobia and work toward lesbian visibility—"The fire will not consume us—We take it and make it our own." First started in 1992 in New York City, Lesbian Avengers chapters are now thriving in a number of cities across the United States.[71]

The Guerrilla Girls, a group of art activists who identify themselves through names of deceased women artists, "have been reinventing the F word—feminism" since 1985.[72] Wearing gorilla masks in public, they have generated a series of provocative posters and "actions that expose sexism and racism in politics, the art world, film and the culture at large."[73] As they explain on their website:

We use humor to convey information, provoke discussion, and show that feminists can be funny. We wear gorilla masks to focus on the issues rather than our personalities. Dubbing ourselves the conscience of culture, we declare ourselves feminist counterparts to the mostly male tradition of anonymous dogooders like Robin Hood, Batman, and the Lone Ranger. Our work has been passed around the world by kindred spirits who we are proud to have as supporters. The mystery surrounding our identities has attracted attention. We could be anyone; we are everywhere.[74]

Many of my students have been drawn to the creative performative and "in-the-streets" form of activism modeled by the Guerrilla Girls. While much of the Guerrilla Girls' political performances are unique innovations, their use of spectacles and alternative modes of communication has precedents in the 1960s and early 1970s. For example, Hannah Wilke and Eleanor Antin and other radical feminist performance artists used spectacle, ritual, and their own bodies to challenge sexism and the patriarchal art world.

The expansion of access to media and information through cable television and the Internet has facilitated a wide range of activist efforts and has proven a significant resource for the development of feminist organizing. Over the last decade, we have witnessed the power of cyber-activism in fighting the globalization of capitalism and the U.S. wars against Afghanistan and Iraq, as well as promoting domestic legislative lobbying and fundraising for diverse political causes. I was especially impressed by the work of MoveOn[75] which organized a Virtual March on Washington, a creative organizing strategy that included sending faxes throughout the day to U.S. senators and representatives urging them to oppose the war on Iraq. Of particular note is the diversity of groups that endorsed the "March." Signing on in support of the Virtual March were American Friends, Greenpeace, NAACP, National Council of Churches, National Gay and Lesbian Task Force, National Organization for Women, Rainbow/Push Coalition, Service Employees International Union, Veterans for Common Sense, and Women's Action for New Directions. Despite the diversity of groups and individuals who can access the Internet, it remains a privileged tool that few women can afford and few grassroots organizations can access.

My students and I are especially enthusiastic about the growth and development of transnational feminist organizing, even as we recognize that this form of activism is more difficult to enact than local community-based activism. The processes by which feminists and other progressive actors in different parts of the world can link their resistance strategies across boundaries remains the greatest challenge for contemporary progressive movements. Despite these challenges, I expect that feminists will become increasingly more sophisticated in understanding processes of racialization and globalization and will be better equipped to build coalitions across constituencies, different issues, diverse constituencies, and national borders. Remaining aware of feminism as a work-in-progress that is generated and rejuvenated through reflective dialogue and intergenerational practice will strengthen the power of feminist praxis for social justice and progressive social change.

CONCLUSION

Feminist theory and political strategies have been developed in the context of diverse struggles for social justice.[76] Feminist praxis is transformed in the course of interaction among and between activists of diverse political generations and racial and class backgrounds who are committed to multiple political goals. Through painful lessons from past organizing efforts as well as ongoing struggles to create a more inclusive movement, feminist praxis offers many insights into how to create democratic structures at all levels of organization. Feminist praxis provides a vibrant foundation for coalition-building efforts and democratic process that is essential for progressive social change. There were the calls for social, economic, and political citizenship that marked the first wave of the women's movement in the United States.[77] There were consciousness-raising and politicization strategies developed in the second wave of the women's movement. These developments were coupled with the political lessons offered by feminists of color over past decades, and there have been the more recent efforts to organize across borders, regions, and religions. Furthermore, by building broader coalitions we can broaden our political analyses which, in turn, enables us to build broader coalitions.

Understood as ongoing reflective and dialogic practice, feminism is transformed as well as sustained in the context of widening the constituencies and political insights for action. Finally, and perhaps most importantly, feminist praxis contains crucial insights into how to sustain activist engagement over the long haul. Activist networks established in and through local struggles for social and economic justice provide one of the primary means by which feminists and other activists sustain and promote progressive analyses and alternative political strategies during times of political quiescence and backlash.[78] Women's social networks, in particular, are powerful resources for promoting resistance strategies, especially for those most marginalized in contemporary society.

The wave construction of feminist activism that builds upon a limited view of what counts as feminism reduces feminist political projects to a narrow set of goals. While the struggles for suffrage during the first wave of the U.S. women's movement or the struggles for women's equal rights continue to be important goals for feminist praxis, they cannot be achieved in isolation, nor can their achievement be enjoyed across race, class, and cultures, without feminist engagement in broader social and economic justice movements. By extending our historical, cultural, and geographic angle of vision on feminist praxis, I believe that we are in a better position to generate political analyses that can support effective organizing across cultures, borders, and generations.

NOTES

1.   Cherríe Moraga and Gloria Anzaldúa, eds., "Introduction," in *This Bridge Called My Back: Writings by Radical Women of Color* (Berkeley, CA: Kitchen Table: Women of Color Press, 1981), xxiii–xxvi.

2.   *This Bridge Called My Back* is now in its third edition (2002).

3.   Jo Freeman and Victoria Johnson, eds., *Waves of Protest: Social Movements since the Sixties* (Lanham, MD: Rowman and Littlefield, 1999), ix.

4.   Rita Alfonso and Jo Trigilio, "Surfing the Third Wave: A Dialogue Between Two Third Wave Feminists," *Hypatia* 12, no. 3 (1997): 7.

5.   Alfonso and Trigilio, 7.

6.   See, for example, Kimberly Springer, "Third Wave Black Feminism?" *Signs: A Journal of Women in Culture and Society* 27, no. 4 (2002): 1059–82; See also Springer, chapter 1; Catherine M. Orr, "Charting the Currents of the Third Wave," *Hypatia* 12, no. 3 (1997): 29–45.

7. Sonia Kruks, *Retrieving Experience: Subjectivity and Recognition in Feminist Politics* (Ithica, NY: Cornell University Press, 2001), 119.

8. Ibid., 119.

9. Ibid., 22. I also draw on Kruks's discussion of praxis for my analysis of materialist feminism in *Feminism and Method: Ethnography, Discourse Analysis, and Activist Research* (New York: Routledge, 2003).

10. See Maivân Clech Lam, "Feeling Foreign in Feminism," *Signs: A Journal of Women in Culture and Society* 19 (1994): 864–93.

11. Nancy A. Naples, *Grassroots Warriors: Activist Mothering, Community Work, and the War on Poverty* (New York, Routledge, 1998), 180.

12. Nancy Fraser and Nancy A. Naples, "To Interpret the World and to Change It: An Interview with Nancy Fraser," *Signs: A Journal of Women in Culture and Society* 29, no. 4 (Summer 2004): 1103–24.

13. Patricia Ticineto Clough, *Feminist Thought: Desire, Power, and Academic Discourse* (Cambridge, MA: Blackwell, 1999); Sandra Harding, *The Science Question in Feminism* (Ithaca, NY: Cornell University Press, 1986); Myra Marx Ferree and Beth B. Hess, *Controversy and Coalition: The New Feminist Movement Across Three Decades of Change* (New York: Routledge, 2000).

14. Fraser and Naples, 1121.

15. Debra Liebowitz, "Can You Dance with a 'Neo-liberal' Partner? Questions for Feminist Anti-Globalization Activism" (paper presented at the Sustainable Feminisms Conference, Macalaster College, St. Paul, Minnesota, 2003).

16. Nancy A. Naples, 2003.

17. Wendy Sarvasy, "Social Citizenship from a Feminist Perspective," *Hypatia* 12, no. 4 (1997): 54–73.

18. Sherna Gluck, with Maylei Blackwell, Sharon Cotrell, and Karen Harper, "Whose Feminism, Whose History? Reflections on Excavating the History of (the) U.S. Women's Movement(s)," in *Community Activism and Feminist Politics: Organizing Across Race, Class, and Gender,* ed. Nancy A. Naples (New York: Routledge, 1998), 31–56.

19. Gluck et al., 32.

20. Springer, "Third Wave," 1061.

21. Ibid. Also see Orr.

22. Ibid., 1063–64.

23. As cited in Springer, "Third Wave," 1062–63.

24. Leslie Heywood and Jennifer Drake, eds., *Third Wave Agenda: Being Feminist, Doing Feminism* (Minneapolis: University of Minnesota Press, 1997).

25. Orr, 39.

26. Heywood and Drake as cited in Orr, 37.

27. Nancy Whittier, *Feminist Generations: The Persistence of the Radical Women's Movement* (Philadelphia, PA: Temple University Press, 1999), 15. Also see Beth Schneider, "Political Generations in the Contemporary Women's Movement," *Sociological Inquiry* 58, no. 1 (1988): 4–21.

28. Also see Verta Taylor and Leila J. Rupp, "Women's Culture and Lesbian Feminist Activism: A Reconsideration of Cultural Feminism," in *Community Activism and Feminist Politics: Organizing Across Race, Class, and Gender,* ed. Nancy A. Naples (New York: Routledge, 1998), 57–79; Verta Taylor, "Social Movement Continuity: The Women's Movement in Abeyance," *American Sociological Review* 54 (1989): 761–75.

29. Tamara Straus, "Lipstick Feministas," *MetroActive Features/Third Wave Feminism,* June 10, 2003, http://www.metroactive.com/papers/cruz/11.29.00/femijsims-0048.html (accessed August 11, 2004).

30. This concern was raised at the Veteran Feminists of America conference held in New York in 2002. See Jennifer Friedlin, "A Clash of Waves: Second and Third Wave

Feminists Clash over the Future," *Women's ENews*, May 26, 2002. http://www.vfa.us/Clash.htm (accessed August 9, 2004), 1.

31. Orr, 32. See also Henry, chapter 5.

32. See Alice Echols, *Daring to Be Bad: Radical Feminism in America, 1967–1995* (Minneapolis: University of Minnesota Press, 1989); and Barbara Findlen, ed., *Listen Up: Voices From the Next Feminist Generation* (Seattle, WA: Seal Press, 1995). Second wave feminists have also expressed their anger at what they see as a more individualist focus of younger feminists, see Friedlin, 1.

33. Natalie M. Peluso, "Lives Lived, Feminisms Found" (unpublished paper, Women's Studies Program, University of Connecticut, 2003).

34. Peluso, 1.

35. Peluso, 1. Also see Jenny Morris, ed., *Encounters with Strangers: Feminism and Disability* (London: The Women's Press, 1996).

36. Peluso, 1.

37. Ibid.

38. For example, my students responded positively and with enthusiasm to the authors in Moraga and Anzaldúa, and Daisy Hernández and Bushra Rehman, eds., *Colonize This! Young Women of Color on Today's Feminism* (New York: Seal Press, 2002).

39. Bonnie Durgin, "Being a Feminist in the 21st Century" (unpublished paper, Women's Studies Program, University of Connecticut, 2003).

40. Also see Susan Cavin, "The Invisible Army of Women: Lesbian Social Protests, 1969–1988," in *Women and Social Protest*, eds. Guida West and Rhoda Lois Blumberg (New York: Oxford University Press, 1990), 321–32; Arlene Stein, ed., *Sisters, Sexperts, Queers: Beyond the Lesbian Nation* (New York: Plume, 1993); Nancy A. Naples, ed., *Community Activism*; Ann Bookman and Sandra Morgen, eds., *Women and the Politics of Empowerment* (Philadelphia, PA: Temple University Press, 1988); Barbara Omolade, *The Rising Song of African American Women* (New York: Routledge, 1994); Rayna Green, "American Indian Women: Diverse Leadership for Social Change," in *Bridges of Power: Women's Multicultural Alliances*, eds. Lisa Albrecht and Rose Brewer (Philadelphia, PA: New Society Publishers, 1990), 61–73; Karin Aguilar-San Juan, *The State of Asian America: Activism and Resistance in the 1990s* (Boston, MA: South End Press, 1994); Mary Pardo, *Mexican American Women Activists: Identity and Resistance in Two Los Angeles Neighborhoods* (Philadelphia, PA: Temple University Press, 1998).

41. Nikki McGary, "The Evolution of a Feminist Consciousness" (unpublished manuscript, Women's Studies Program, University of Connecticut, 2003).

42. Kaplana Kishnamurthy, codirector, Third Wave Foundation in 2002, http://www.thirdwavefoundation.org.

43. Friedlin, 1.

44. Ibid.

45. Naples, *Grassroots Warriors*.

46. Ibid., Also see Naples, ed., *Community Activism*.

47. With many pundits declaring this the age of postfeminism, the politics of identity poses a central challenge to feminist praxis. Judith Stacey ["Sexism by a Subtler Name? Postindustrial Conditions and Postfeminist Consciousness in Silicon Valley," *Socialist Review* 96 (1987)] defined postfeminism as "the simultaneous incorporation, revision and depoliticization of many of the central goals of second wave feminism" (339). Also see Mary F. Rogers and C. D. Garrett, *Who's Afraid of Women's Studies? Feminisms in Everyday Life* (Walnut Creek, CA: AltaMira Press, 2002).

48. For example, Jennifer Baumgardner defines third wave feminism as any issue that is important to a third wave feminist in Tamara Straus, "A Manifesto for Third Wave Feminism," *Alternet.org*, October 24, 2000, http://www.alternet.org/story/9986 (accessed August 11, 2004), 1.

49. See, for example, Julie Peters and Andrea Wolper, eds., *Women's Rights, Human Rights: International Feminist Perspectives* (New York: Routledge, 1995); Cynthia Enloe, *Maneuvers: The International Politics of Militarizing Women's Lives* (Berkeley, CA: University of California Press, 2000); Kaplan, 1997; Inderpal Grewal and Caren Kaplan, eds., *Scattered Hegemonies: Postmodernity and Transnational Feminist Practices* (Minneapolis, MN: University of Minneapolis Press, 1994); Carolyn Sachs, *Gendered Fields: Rural Women, Agriculture and Environment* (Boulder, CO: Westview, 1996); Catherine Eschle, *Global Democracy, Social Movements, and Feminism* (Boulder, CO: Westview Press, 2001); Nancy J. Hirschmann and Christine DiStefano, eds., *Revisioning the Political: Feminist Reconstructions of Traditional Concepts in Western Political Theory* (Boulder, CO: Westview Press, 1996); Robin Lee Zeff et al., eds., *Empowering Ourself: Women and Toxics Organizing* (Arlington, VA: Citizens Clearinghouse for Hazardous Wastes, 1989).

50. Sheila Rowbotham and Swasti Mitter, eds., *Dignity and Daily Bread: New Forms of Economic Organizing among Poor Women in the Third World and the First* (London: Routledge, 1994); Lourdes Beneria and Shelly Feldman, eds., *Unequal Burden: Economic Crises, Persistent Poverty, and Women's Work* (Boulder, CO: Westview Press, 1992).

51. Linda Stout, *Bridging the Class Divide and Other Lessons for Grassroots Organizing* (Boston, MA: Beacon Press, 1990); Ida Susser, *Norman Street: Poverty and Politics in an Urban Neighborhood* (New York: Oxford University Press, 1982).

52. See, for example, Myra Marx Ferree and Patricia Yancey Martin, eds., *Feminist Organizations: Harvest of the New Women's Movement* (Philadelphia, PA: Temple University Press, 1995).

53. Temma Kaplan, "Female Consciousness and Collective Action: The Case of Barcelona, 1910–1918," *Signs: A Journal of Women in Culture and Society* 7, no. 3 (1982): 545–566.

54. Maxine Molyneux, "Mobilization Without Emancipation: Women's Interests, the State and Revolution in Nicaragua," *Feminist Studies* 11(1985): 227–54.

55. Temma Kaplan, *Crazy for Democracy: Women in Grassroots Movements* (New York: Routledge, 1997), 30.

56. Nancy A. Naples and Manisha Desai, eds., *Women's Activism and Globalization: Linking Local Struggles and Transnational Politics* (New York: Routledge, 2002); Kaplan, *Crazy for Democracy*; Naples, ed., *Community Activism*; Karen Brodkin Sacks, "Gender and Grassroots Leadership," in *Women and the Policies of Empowerment*, eds. Ann Bookman and Sandra Morgen (Philadelphia, PA: Temple University Press, 1988), 77–94.

57. Kaplan, *Crazy for Democracy*, 128.

58. Patricia Hill Collins, *Black Feminist Thought: Knowledge, Consciousness, and the Politics of Empowerment* (New York: Routledge, 2000).

59. Springer, 1079.

60. Combahee River Collective, "A Black Feminist Statement," in *All the Women are White, All the Blacks Are Men But Some of Us Are Brave*, eds. Gloria T Hull, Patricia Bell Scott, and Barbara Smith (Old Westbury, NY: The Feminist Press, 1982), 17.

61. Angela Davis, *Women, Race, and Class* (New York: Random House, 1981).

62. Moraga and Anzaldúa (3rd ed.).

63. Amy Schriefer, "We've Only Just Begun: Translating Third Wave Theory into Third Wave Activism," *The Laughing Medusa*, Opinion, 2003, http://www.gwu.edu/~medusa/thirdwave.html (accessed August 11, 2004), 4.

64. Schriefer, 2.

65. Durgin, 11.

66. Ibid.

67. Ibid.

68. Ibid., 11–12.

69. Ibid., 13.

70. Ibid., 22.

71. For example, there are chapters in Chicago (http://www.lesbian.org/chicago_avengers/); San Francisco (http://www.lesbian.org/sfavengers/); Cincinnati (http://www.geocities.com/cinci_avengers/); Rochester (http://www.frontiernet.net/~billijo/avengers.htm).

72. Guerilla Girls, Home Page, 2004, http://www.guerrillagirls.com (accessed August 11, 2004).

73. Ibid.

74. Ibid.

75. MoveOn.org was established as an advocacy effort to protest the impeachment proceedings against President Bill Clinton. Since that time, it has raised $1,500,000 for a large number of candidates. According to their website, over half of the donations were under $50. MoveOn.org, "About MoveOn.Org," 2004, http.//www.move-on.org/about/documentation.html.

76. Feminist perspectives include the political frameworks of liberal, Marxist, and socialist feminism; the historical categorizations such as psychoanalytic feminism, existential feminism, black feminism, multicultural feminism, and global feminism. In their various formulations, feminist theories emphasize the need to contest sexism, racism, homophobia, colonialism, class, and other forms of inequalities.

77. Sarvasy, 1997. Also see Estelle B. Freedman, *No Turning Back: The History of Feminism and the Future of Women* (New York: Ballantine Books, 2002).

78. Taylor, "Social Movement Continuity."

13

ARE WE ON A WAVELENGTH YET?
ON FEMINIST OCEANOGRAPHY, RADIOS,
AND THIRD WAVE FEMINISM

Ednie Kaeh Garrison

While much of what is called third wave feminism is still forming
its own generational and historical distinctions, the metaphor of a
wave allows us to shape a space that has both continuity and discontinuity with the past.[1]

The summer 1997 issue of the feminist philosophy journal *Hypatia* is
dedicated to the topic of "Third Wave Feminisms." Waves are referred to
consistently throughout the articles, and with an unusual self-awareness,
the authors make some effort to explain the context and historical relevance of the metaphor. The articles in the first section claim to be
"Charting the Currents of the Third Wave,"[2] to be "Surfing the Third
Wave,"[3] to be "Making Waves and Drawing Lines."[4] In the section's final
essay, Deborah Siegel coins the phrase "feminist oceanography" and
uses the *Oxford English Dictionary*'s definitions of "wave" as epigraphs
three times.[5] These images invoked by the authors in this special issue
are consistent with the ways in which women's and feminist movement
formations are conceptualized, organized, categorized, and historicized
in hegemonic (i.e., dominant) feminist narratives. Their use conforms

to the implications often presumed in the name *third wave feminism,* that we have passed through a period of low activity and now a "new" wave of feminist activity is upon us.

In this collection of essays a "feminist oceanographer," then, is one who "charts," "surfs," and possibly "makes" and "draws" the boundaries around what counts as the third wave. All these authors are invested in determining what it constitutes and to do so they draw upon images, analogies, metaphors, and strategies preferred by their predecessors. The third wave of feminism is not the same as the second, but the third is perceived, like the second, as an ocean wave.[6] As Flora Davis explains in her 1991 history, *Moving the Mountain: The Women's Movement in America Since 1960:*

> The wave analogy is helpful because it underscores the fact that the women's movement didn't die after 1920, though it did lose much of its momentum. The analogy also reminds us that major social changes tend to happen in waves. First, there's a lot of intense activity and some aspects of life are transformed; then, when the public has absorbed as much as it can stand, reaction sets in. Stability reigns for a while, and if there's a strong backlash, some of the changes may be undone. Eventually, if vital issues remain unresolved, another wave of activism arises.[7]

This conception of women's movement formations, especially as a means to distinguish a third wave from a second wave of feminism, is strangely comforting, at least within the United States, not only because of the visceral effect of undulating waves, but also because it allows us to see how things happen cyclically and chronologically at one and the same time. Furthermore, it fits well with conventional sociological explanations of social movements.[8] It is certainly not an unfair analysis of what motivates people to continually return to activism.

Missing in these invocations of the feminist movement as ocean waves are the internal changes and shifts that alter feminism's meanings and constituencies. For example, in Davis's explanation women's movements arise from external forces. But how, in this model of reactionary movement activity, are differing perspectives on the meaning of feminism and the category "women" incorporated? A primary problem with the oceanic metaphor is that it limits our ability to recognize difference and to adequately represent shifts in feminist ideological and movement formations over the last half of the twentieth century. Perhaps the most important contributions to feminist movement over the past thirty-five years have been the conflicts and confrontations among feminist advocates who have not had the privilege of seeing themselves as women only. The expansion of feminism to encompass broader conceptualizations of gender that incorporate the intersecting, compounded subjectivities constituted from sexuality, race, class, nation, ability, age, and culture have blown asunder all certainty about the subject of feminism. In the ocean wave model, the specificities of compounded subjectivity are often elided by the popular perception that who and what counts as women is self-evident and universal. Feminists are assumed "naturally" to be women who are presumed "naturally" to be aligned as a singular collectivity. The imperative to know that women share some kernel of experience in common, and that this is the basis for speaking of/for "all women," bears consequences for what and who can count within feminism.

In the United States the wave metaphor as an analogy for ocean waves constructs certain kinds of historical narratives of women's movements and feminism, narratives which continue to reproduce exclusions and obfuscations. Developing a self-conscious and critical perspective on the linguistic turn third wave feminism will make a huge difference in whether it becomes confined to the same exclusions and obfuscations, or whether it can be utilized to signify the potent challenges, reconfigurations, and epistemological effects that have altered the registers upon which feminist ideology and movement formations can be read. Without relinquishing the discursive power of the wave metaphor, I propose a resignification of meaning so that different narratives, histories, and voices are made visible as constitutive parts rather than addenda attached at the end of some generic, singular version of feminism. This resignified metaphor privileges, for example, Barbara Smith's definition of feminism as both a deconstructive critique of exclusionary feminism and a moment of paradigmatic rupture.[9] Such moments of paradigmatic rupture have played too significant a role in shaping feminist consciousness in the early twenty-first century to be so completely absorbed within the already existing structures of meaning.

As a way to position such moments in their constitutive context, this essay tinkers with the idea that the "waves" in "waves of feminism" are the technologically harnessed electromagnetic wavelengths we call radio waves. The difference in this analogy resides in the technological rhetorics of radio wave transmission and reception, and in its capacity to reorganize the ways consciousness of feminism, history, and movement can be comprehended. Since language has the power to shape consciousness, how might a wave metaphor that registers different, multiple, and simultaneous wave frequencies change our understandings of feminism and the ways it signifies culturally?

PROBLEMS WITH FEMINIST OCEANOGRAPHY

The language we use, including metaphors, impacts the ways we can think and know. In the case of the oceanic metaphor, the impact on feminist consciousness is that the meaning of "feminism" and the ideas we can hold about the feminist movement are shaped by the logic of the metaphorical association. The notion of the modern feminist movement as a "wave" coincided with the coining of the emerging movement in the late 1960s and early 1970s as "the second wave." Its adoption to explain the growth in popularity of the women's liberation movement was intentional, and yet only after the fact reflected upon. The metaphor was already part of the repertoire of discursive tools and the cultural logic behind the metaphor shaped the way history, constituencies, politics, and ideology could be comprehended.[10]

In conjunction with the contemporary feminist movement, the wave as an oceanic metaphor helped make *women's movement* and *feminism/feminist movement* become interchangeable terms; only certain cohorts and constituencies are recognizable as feminist; so that some generations, classes, races, and constituencies are left out of feminist genealogies and historiographies; and certain feminist theories are claimed/reclaimed by cohorts under the wave marker (also see Springer, chapter 1, and Naples, chapter 12). For example, *This Bridge Called My Back*[11] is eagerly claimed now as an important (second wave) feminist text, although at the time its publication was a rather sharp retort by a coalition of constituencies who'd been excluded and marginalized within the movement. Moreover, this important movement anthology produced a political constituency—radical women of color—as it renamed the dominant feminist movement "the white women's movement." Within the logic of the oceanic metaphor, it was preferable to genealogically submerge the distinct contributions of Chicana, African-American, Native American, and Asian-American feminists in order to name the dominant interests within U.S. feminism, even though this move both homogenized the second wave and resulted in delayed attention to the contributions of nondominant feminists.

To frame the relationship between second wave and third wave, the metaphor and image is deployed as a political/aesthetic strategy in at least two ways: it assumes the third wave is a new full-fledged social movement that is like or parallel to the first and second; and it draws affinities between what gets named "third wave" and what gets named "second wave." The same strategy was employed by feminists in the 1960s and 1970s to construct parallels and draw affinities between what has become known as the "first wave" of feminism (the series of "woman" and "women's" movements between the 1840s and 1920) and what, consequently, became the "second wave" (those series of cohorts who constituted the "women's liberation movement" of which feminists in the 1960s and 1970s became a part).[12] This strategy legitimates as movements many disparate collectivities and cohorts, suggests historical continuity between collectivities and cohorts constituted as "social movements," and proclaims discontinuity by naming each "movement" differently. Each movement is apparently distinct because more than forty years separated the historical events identified as marking the end of one wave and the founding of the other (the passage of the Nineteenth Amendment in the first case, and both the formation of the National Organization for Women and the separation of women's liberationists from the New Left in the second).

Historically locating and specifying the "first wave" allowed those who recognized themselves as the "second wave" to draw specific boundaries around themselves and consequently to argue for their viability as a legitimate social movement. What enabled hegemonic feminists in the second wave to construct "their" movement as the "second wave of feminism" and the movements between 1848 and 1920 as the "first wave of feminism" was not only the fact that these were both periods of increased "women's movement" activity, but also the introduction of the term *feminism* at the turn of the last century. After 1910, the "vocabulary of feminism"[13] influenced the kinds of "women's movement" activity that counted for "feminists." What is really interesting here is the way the period between 1920 and the 1960s is viewed as having been a low-activity era. Barbara Deckard, Barbara Ryan, Verta Taylor and Leila Rupp, and Nancy Cott, among others, have all studied this period to understand why the women's/feminist movement was in "abeyance"[14]; however, except for Cott, none adequately address the effects of the cultural consciousness of feminism on the ability to see or recognize feminist activity outside of those groups and individuals who already claimed the name *feminism* for themselves.[15] The "first wave" includes as feminist those who never heard the term, and who by contemporary definitions might not be regarded as feminists. Following the emergence of the first wave, to be recognized as feminist required calling oneself or one's group "feminist"; that is, until the "second wave" when feminism became synonymous with "women's issues." Chandra Mohanty has called this slippage the "feminist osmosis thesis"—the assumption that women are feminists by virtue of their experiences as women.[16] Early in the second wave this assumption was exploited to link the movement emerging in the late sixties, specifically, to the suffrage campaign.

Understandably, dominant feminist histories of the "doldrums"[17] become trapped in a desire for lines of continuity between "first wave" and "second wave" through the term *feminism*, and since a very small group of privileged, elite, and (mostly) white women counted as "the feminists" throughout these years of "abeyance," their stories are the only ones that tend to get recognized. So we hear about the National Woman's Party (providing a line of continuity through the Equal Rights Amendment drive), the National Federation of Business and Professional Women's Clubs, and the National League for Women Voters, but very little about groups or individuals not directly associated with "feminism." Even when other feminist activity is recognized by historians (i.e., "Rosie the Riveter," black women's community work, trade union organizing, women's peace and antinuclear activism), it is not considered sufficient enough to constitute a "movement," or more specifically, a "feminist movement," although often these little movements are assumed to be tied to other (read: not feminist) social movements. When the first wave is construed to have culminated in the suffrage campaign as its pinnacle act, all "feminist" activity within the first wave is forced to fall within the purview of that campaign.[18] The second wave, then, was construed to represent the step *beyond* the vote: What happens to women within patriarchy after the franchise? In this relationship, the second wave is different from the first by radically altering the feminist project to question the very ways women are forced to conform to patriarchal norms, while the first wave, embodied in the fight for suffrage, could only achieve recognition within "rights" discourse as already culturally established. This differentiation is invoked when second wave feminists explain that the first wave was a movement for "social and legal identity" and the second wave a movement for "social and legal equality."[19]

These specifications and boundaries are reinforced by means of "feminist oceanography," Siegel's term for the ways in which the feminist movement has been historicized and distinguished as a series of interconnected "waves."[20] This "oceanography of the feminist movement" is consistent with dominant cultural interpretations of social movement existence and success, which tend to assume that collective protest and resistance becomes a "movement" when it reaches a certain level of saturation or gains a certain level of popular and political recognition and has mobilized sufficient numbers and resources. In the United States at least, the popular perception is that social movements must have national recognition and be universal in scope in order to speak to/for the largest, most general population. The pressure for nationwide social movements to have a "universal" scope helps to explain why suffrage becomes the defining first wave issue rather than, say, trade unionism or the anti-lynching campaign spearheaded by Ida B. Wells. The perception that suffrage constitutes a national or universal issue, whereas anti-lynching is too specific and localized, speaks directly to the ease with which dominant feminists adopt dominant cultural values (of course suffrage is a "pure" feminist issue because it deals with "universal women's experience"; antilynching, however, confuses the clarity of the movement by tainting it with issues of race and racism).

It is not that "feminist oceanography" is not viable, it is just that as an epistemological tool it sets limits on the ways we can articulate feminist history, consciousness, and praxis. While the name *third wave* draws from this epistemic version of a feminist movement as a tension and a desire, in the nineties when it first gained popular recognition (a period arguably still in the "second wave"), we must view its emergence as differently strategic. Even now, a few years into the twenty-first century, we still want and desire another "wave" of activism like the 1960s and 1970s (this desire is part of the cultural predicament of feminist consciousness in the United States), and yet we really can't reproduce that historical moment or cultural milieu. In part, this is because those very movements altered our thinking about identity, politics, and social justice. However, although U.S. feminists today have for the most part abandoned the dream of unity through sameness, our metaphors reveal a stubborn inability to give up the desire for sameness-as-identification.

METAPHORICAL RETUNINGS: INTERLUDE ON A WAVELENGTH

So, what is the difference between ocean waves and radio waves? Both are naturally occurring movements involving oscillation, undulation, fluttering, signaling. It is not enough that ocean waves and radio waves are named such because they are similar forms of motion; what matters is the medium through which the motion is utilized and our relative engagement with them. Both kinds of waves are forms of movement that happen despite human intervention. As well, in both cases it is possible for human intervention to alter, shift, redirect, and manipulate waves, but only radio wave technology can harness radio waves as a carrier current transmitting and receiving information and sound. Ocean waves can move objects—kinds of information—but radio waves can be used to communicate information in the form of ideas, words, narrative, consciousness, knowledge. As an analogy, ocean waves infer a movement that carries us along, we get caught up in the action and movement, and come to see later that we have been part of some massive influx and reflux. Radio waves, on the other hand, infer a kind of intentionality and purposefulness. This means that the very ability to see ourselves inside radio waves requires, first, that we know they exist, and second, that we have the means to make use of them. This is why I want to think about the waves in "third wave feminism" as radio waves—it appeals to me in the same way the concept *technologics* (my term for the ways in which technology and the rhetorics of technology infiltrate our consciousness) does.[21] Moreover, conceptualizing multiple waves existing at the same time—sometimes fading and dissolving, other times interrupted or appropriated or colonized, oftentimes overlooked because we can't hear or perceive a signal we haven't got an ear for—disrupts the chronologically and evolutionarily rendered narratives of feminist movements. For example, unlike the oceanographic analogy, a radio technology analogy is not as susceptible to the romantic narrative of the family or of nature, in which primogeniture reigns and even mothers and daughters can be substituted in the Oedipal drama.

Radios comprise a broadcasting technology for distributing cultural information.[22] I like to think of our culture, or even feminism, as a radio both fixed in space (the radio that sits in my living room) and capable of moving through space and time (the radio in a moving car or a walkman/Discman or a boom box). I also like to think of political-cultural-historical consciousness affected by and affecting our interactions and engagement with our radios, of carrier waves dialectically transmitting and receiving information, ideology, meaning, sound, and noise by transmitters equally and differently situated within the technological networks that link receivers to sites of dissemination (such that transmitters and receivers both sometimes become each other[23]). Issues of access and power still register here since, for example, the politics of the FCC regulating who can transmit, how and where and what, plays a central role in determining what gets heard and the strategies and tactics of those who pirate into the airwaves at frequencies below 100 watts.

This metaphor permits us to think differently—more multiply and complexly—about modes of consciousness, power, ideology, and knowledge. But, to talk about radio waves we must employ the rhetoric of technology developed to harness radio electromagnetic wavelengths as a means of communication. This rhetoric is appealing because the power of the logics of technology is such that our very consciousness, our ways of knowing, and being in the world, are increasingly filtered through the language of technical systems. Since we were first invited to think of the human brain as a computer, and even earlier when bureau-cratic systems were developed to efficiently collect, label, and categorize everything from geological systems, to political systems, to human behavioral systems, technological rhetorics have played a key role in shaping and structuring our thinking. To begin to unpack the rhetoric of radio wavelengths, let us look briefly at some of its vocabulary.

Radio waves occur in the spectrum of electromagnetic radiation (or waves) on the bandwidth that falls between the highest audio fre-quency and the shortest infrared waves. A bandwidth consists of a range of frequencies within a radiation band required to transmit a particular kind of signal. Radio frequencies are used for different kinds of telecommunications, and within this technical system radios func-tion as both receivers of sound and as transmitters. Radio wavelengths are harnessed for communication by manipulating carrier waves using various forms of wave modulation. The broadcasting systems we know as AM (amplitude modulation) and FM (frequency modulation) refer to the various ways by which carrier waves transmitting a particular signal are deployed. Another form of modulation involves phase varia-tions. When a carrier wave is measured by the distance between its wave crests, the space between the crests is called a "phase" cycle. Producing a variation of the phase cycles will result in different kinds of transmissions. These forms of wave modulation are examples of ways in which radio waves have been technologically harnessed to carry sound transmissions through space. While they rely on the same nar-row band of electromagnetic radiation, the different ways they can be used to manipulate individual frequency ranges makes it possible to recognize and value the potentially infinite (to us) malleability of waves.

This foray into radio modulation technologies may seem a bit abstract, but a feminist transliteration of the language of modulation can allow us to move beyond the primarily discursive claim that there has been a proliferation of feminisms to the enactment of a paradigm shift in how we comprehend and experience the effects of this prolifer-ation. Chela Sandoval has adopted this metaphorical terminology to describe the praxis of differential consciousness, which she describes as a "kaleidoscopic activity," wherein dominant modes of consciousness in opposition (equal rights, revolutionary, supremacist, and separatist) are reconfigured as tools (technologies) rather than ends in themselves. As she writes:

> Differential consciousness re-cognizes and works upon other modes of consciousness in opposition to transfigure their meanings: they

convert into repositories within which subjugated citizens either occupy or throw off subjectivity; a process that simultaneously enacts yet decolonizes their various relations to their real conditions of existence. This *dialectical modulation* between forms of consciousness permits functioning within, yet beyond, the demands of dominant ideology while also speaking in and from within ideology. The differential form of consciousness thus is composed of narrative worked self-consciously.[24]

The metaphor Sandoval adopts to help the reader visualize this dialectical modulation of oppositional consciousness is a car clutch. The differential mode of oppositional praxis utilized by U.S. third world feminists is the gear shift; the "technologies of oppositional consciousness" are the gears.[25] As a metaphor, the images and mechanics of a car clutch assists Sandoval in explaining how differential consciousness is a methodology that enables what she calls "tactical subjectivity." This technological metaphor is effective because it is easier for contemporary readers to grasp than the more abstract language of "tactical subjectivity." A question her work leads to is: What would the feminist movement and the production of feminist identities and histories look like if we really, seriously started from such modes of praxis? How would history, consciousness, and movement register differently from such a shift?

One way to see the difference this shift registers can be witnessed in the example of Linda Nicholson's edited volume, *The Second Wave: A Reader in Feminist Theory*.[26] Unlike many texts that adopt wave references, Nicholson opens the introduction to *The Second Wave* with a brief comment about scholars questioning the "first wave/second wave" distinction for "organizing the history of feminism." However, this invitation to discuss the matter is truncated by her claim: "I believe that something important occurred in the 1960s that is still spinning itself out. That occurrence was a new intensity in many societies in the degree of reflection given to gender relations."[27] I agree with Nicholson, but it is telling that she invites a discussion she then neglects to develop. Especially revealing in this move is the abandonment of three vital questions she knows are important: "Is 'the second wave' a useful concept? What activities and what social groups are excluded by this distinction? What countries does it or does it not apply to?"[28] On the surface, Nicholson presents her subject in a way symptomatic of much hegemonic U.S. feminist praxis: she recognizes omissions and admits them, but she does not actually shift perspective because that would cause the analysis to become messy and unstable. I point this out not to condemn

Nicholson or this book. Rather, I want to suggest that the text is in fact structurally "second wave," and as such a kind of historical archive. What helps to situate it thus is the final paragraph of the introduction:

> If one accepts that feminism should not attempt to base itself on the supposedly pre-given, but should recognize its own meaning as evolving out of the multiple input of actors who are diversely situated, what are the conditions in which such input should be made? How can we avoid, or at least minimize, existing inequalities of power in the construction of the very meaning of feminism? How do we conceptualize the meaning of such other constructions of identity as race, nation, or class to allow for meaningful understandings of the ways in which "woman" is multiply constituted? And, finally, how do we forge political movements capable of addressing the complex ways imbalances of wealth, dignity, power, and love are reproduced? These, I believe, are the questions now facing us.[29]

Indeed. And yet, Nicholson *concludes* the introduction with these questions. The discussion of the articles collected in this volume leads to these questions, rather than begins from them. It is not so much the readings that makes this a "second wave" reader, but the ways in which they are read, or tuned in to. By setting the essays up in "rough" chronological order, the text is made to appear as a kind of progression. This privileges a particular perspective, a particular way of comprehending history, a particular way of conceiving the production of knowledge and meaning. This is not the wrong way to read these essays; I am simply asserting that this way of reading is specific to second wave epistemology, and it prevents certain other readings and perspectives from being able to guide surveys of history and knowledge production. I would not ask her to rework the book; its value is due largely to the fact that it *is* a second wave reader in feminist theory. I would, however, contest that other structurings are possible. For instance, to read the essays with the questions Nicholson closes with as one's starting point modulates them all differently. This different modulation produces different effects in terms of knowledge, historical, constituent, and movement formations that matter in the construction of feminist consciousness. Although cognizant about challenges, debates, and conflicts among and between feminists, Nicholson still avoids the challenge of reconceiving feminist theory (in this case) to start elsewhere so that the power dynamics in the production of the meaning of feminism itself can be made more visible.

Without reconceptualizing the wave metaphor, feminists will likely continue to reproduce this avoidance strategy, despite best intentions. This goes as well for those who claim the name *third wave*, for, although the name powerfully marks a difference from the second wave, it also invokes shared tropes, contexts, histories, and political intents. For third wave feminism to be understood as a strategy/position that refuses to avoid such challenges, we must consider carefully the differences that distinguish second wave from third. For example, "third wave" doesn't so much constitute a "new generation" (either in terms of age cohorts or Beth Schneider's concept of "political generations"[30]) so much as it constitutes a different orientation to the multiplicity and shifting constructions of feminism. I think this ironic name can be understood as a reconceptualization of what a reference to "waves" means in the context of the formation of feminist ideology, political identity, collective action, and movement. This difference is rhetorical, political, conceptual, and epistemological. To be a "third waver" might mean to be on a wavelength in the sense of seeing something in the same way as someone else, but it might also mean to be on a wavelength in the sense of being between—to be in translation or in process or a state of liminality, which doesn't necessarily have to be a lull or "doldrums" if we understand a wave frequency as an undulating carrier current through which we transmit and receive, synthesize and morph, network and coalesce. In this sense radio waves are both a wavelength on the spectrum of electromagnetic waves, and are comprised of multiple (possibly infinite) wavelengths or frequencies within its own bandwidth. What has been learned is that it matters who accesses, attends to, and tunes into the bandwidth.

THIRD WAVE AS MODULATION, NOT CURRENT

If there's no good reception for me
Then tune me out, 'cause honey
Who needs the static
It hurts the head
And you wind up cracking
("You Turn Me On, I'm a Radio," Joni Mitchell)[31]

Despite considerable ambivalence about the existence of a third wave (as movement, identity, or age cohort), I am still committed enough to engage in my own little contest for meaning. I agree with Deborah Siegel that:

[T]he invocation of "third wave feminism" signals a rejection of scripts that assume that the gains forged by the second wave have so completely invaded all tiers of social existence that feminists themselves have become obsolete. When used in this context, "third wave" becomes a stance of political resistance to popular pronouncements of a moratorium on feminism and feminists, a sound bite to counter the now infamous refrain "I'm not a feminist, but. ..."[32]

More recently, Amanda Lotz has suggested that women who echo this almost iconic refrain "express their alienation not from feminism, but from a perception that feminism provides a singular agenda from which one cannot vary."[33] While the "third wave" may not be a "wave" of feminism in the sense assumed by social movement scholars, the strategic invocation of the name as "political resistance" to the vocabulary of postfeminism is significant. As such, claiming to be a "third wave feminist" intentionally establishes distinctions between a "feminism" that signifies something particularly related to the historical dominance of the early second wave desire for unity (sisterhood) among women, and "feminisms" that emerge in resistance to the erasures of differences such unity imposes.

Still, invocations of third wave feminism are not simply or only reactionary articulations in resistance to the popular vocabulary of postfeminism. Even Rebecca Walker's 1992 declaration, "I am not a postfeminism feminist. I am the third wave,"[34] is no uncomplicated proposition. In addition to Walker's well-known *Ms.* article, a cursory survey of early invocations of the concept reveal its strategic power as resistance within the feminist movement more so than resistance to popular proclamations of feminism's demise. First, in the late 1980s, Kitchen Table: Women of Color Press was working to publish an anthology, *The Third Wave: Feminist Perspectives on Racism*, before the press folded. Although this book never materialized, the desire for it is such that people do speak as though it exists, and at least one U.S. university library had the book on permanent order through 1998. The proposed title of this feminist praxis anthology speaks to another meaning for third wave feminism.

Second, in 1991 Lynn Chancer published a short piece in the *Village Voice* called "Third Wave Feminism,"[35] in which she articulates a need "for a revitalized radical feminist offensive, a 'third wave' of feminism" that comes not from a rejection of the "second wave" or a rejection of "second wave feminists," but rather as a response to her own passivity and inclination to wait for those women who led the movement in the

1960s and 1970s to take the lead in the 1990s in combating the anti-feminist backlash so pervasive in the United States. She asks: "But I wonder now at the passivity implied: why wait for others to do what one could begin to think about oneself? And in any event, would a third wave of feminism do no more than continue where a second had left off?" In response she suggests that, "Ideally, a third wave would have to ... [synthesize] the various feminisms, which are trying to refine, revise, or alter the original feminist paradigm."[36] The "original feminist paradigm" is the concept of unity; the new paradigm is difference and coalition. This third wave feminism hinges upon a paradigm shift, rather than a simple cohort formation.

Third, in the same year, Chela Sandoval's oft-cited article, "U.S. Third World Feminism: The Theory and Method of Oppositional Consciousness in the Postmodern World," was published in the academic feminist journal *Genders*. While generally an overlooked claim, Sandoval declares early in the essay that:

> The recognition of differential consciousness is vital to the generation of a next "third wave" women's movement and provides grounds for alliance with other decolonizing movements for emancipation. My answer to the perennial question asked by hegemonic feminist theorists throughout the 1980s is that yes, there is a specific U.S. third world feminism: it is that which provides the theoretical and methodological approach, the "standpoint" if you will, from which this evocation of a theory of oppositional consciousness is summoned.[37]

Initially, when I happened upon the idea of a third wave, it was by means of these various utterances. And, at the time, I found them full of hope and promise because they appeared to advocate disruption from the status quo. However, it is not this feminist history, consciousness, or praxis that is elaborated in most popular accounts of third wave feminism. Instead, the differences tuned into are an age and generation cohort and a "feminist" who is opposed to the mythological "militant, anti-sex, anti-male feminist."[38] In fact, these two distinctions between third wave and second wave are grafted together in truly disturbing ways. Because "the oceanography of feminist movement" relies on a particular kind of historical movement (a linear, chronological model), age and generation boundaries make a lot of sense. And besides, age and generational specificities do matter, as does historical locality. Still, I find the demarcation of an age cohort as *the* third wave insufficient because it eliminates from the picture multitudes of feminists who came of age in and after the second wave, but who are part of the contemporary feminist landscape, and whose feminist politics are also directly caught up in the cultural predicament of feminist consciousness in the fin-de-siècle United States (see Naples, chapter 12). This demarcation also imposes an identity and presumes an embodied nature to "third wave feminism" that distinguishes it from ideology and politics. Third wave feminism, to be a movement, cannot be mistaken for an identity group; a more productive meaning would be as a name for spaces where multiple and complex identities can be represented, articulated, complicated, and mobilized.

The persuasiveness of the age cohort version is discursive rather than empirical or pragmatic, much in the way of contests for power. In this case, the contest names a particular problem (ageism, cut in both directions) as a divide-and-conquer tactic that also, and importantly, shifts attention away from differences that are vital collectively to the project of feminism as a transformational politics.[39] I sometimes think of the cry of young feminists—many of them white and middle class, and not fully politically informed—for a voice in feminist communities today as a complaint poorly articulated. I view the complaints of older feminists—many of them white and middle class, and scarred by experience—that they are being relegated to a dead past in much the same way. They are complaints to have their differences from one another acknowledged and valued, and at the same time they are desperate appeals to an empowered agency that simultaneously submerges the privileges which grant them the sense of entitlement to voice their complaints in the first place. On both sides there is a struggle over the modulation of the meaning of feminism as a single frequency, even as there is also a struggle over which frequencies are better to tune in to. At one moment the contest feels like a battle over one radio station, a struggle between two factions over who will control programming and content. At other moments, it feels like two different but nearly identical radio stations battling over control of a single market. In the process, these contesting cohorts miss the vibrant and conflicted alternative frequencies registering below or outside signal ranges whose strength is enhanced by incessant repetition and dominant cultural validation.

One important lesson learned from midcentury civil rights movements is that attention only to one single issue or identity results not in revolution, but in narrow and one-dimensional politics. The weakness of singularly oriented movements is the elision of differences (driven by a desire to get at the essence of some supposedly universal quality/ aspect/experience shared by all who bear the markers of femaleness,

maleness, whiteness, blackness, etc.). Increasing attention to differences has enabled the production of "new" knowledge about individual and collective identity and the construction of broad coalition politics. Iris Marion Young[40] argues that rather than "pretending that group differences do not matter," we need instead to understand "precisely how they do matter."[41] She provides a powerful, culturally relevant example to illustrate her point:

> Despite the dominant rhetoric in this country that depicts poor people as a group of lazy and irresponsible black single mothers, the real circumstances of poverty are variable, and analyses from social-group perspectives are important for understanding that variability. Latino and Asian movements and groups can explain and interpret one face of poverty, feminist analysis shows another, a rural perspective another, African-American experiences of racist exclusion another, reservation Indians another, older working-class white men in the former industrial heartland yet another. If each of these constituencies does not communicate its specific situations to the others, then the ruling powers can continue to co-opt one by using another as scapegoat.[42]

Besides illustrating the Combahee River Collective's argument about the intersectionality of identities, this example also reveals both the difficulty of and the desperate need for coalition politics among groups with multi-valenced relationships to large, social issues (in this case, poverty). And, it makes Young's final claim that much more comprehensible: "We need to wake up to the challenge of understanding across difference rather than keep on dreaming about common dreams."[43] The impossibility of Adrienne Rich's "dream of a common language" is exposed in Audre Lorde's "house of difference."

The name *third wave feminism* could suggest a shift in this direction within feminist politics and consciousness. In fact, it did at one point, as discussed above. The interesting question is, what happened to make this shift less primary? Rather than a "new wave" in the sense invoked by the paradigm of oceanography, this "wave" is much more about shifts in how the term *feminism* is understood and how those who identify as feminists practice feminist politics. It signifies multiplicity and complexity as requisites for and by-products of coalition and networking, and the subsequent commitment to these sometimes pleasurable and sometimes painful combinings, reconfigurings, and confrontations. In the language of radio technology, this wave is a frequency, or better yet, a series of networked radio frequencies patched together by lines of alliance, crossover politics, shared resources, tools (conceptual and physical), people, political goals, ideological apparatuses, and sometimes aesthetic pleasures. One interesting thing about radio wave frequencies is that they aren't typically conceived of as overlapping and fractured, but they do overlap, they do fracture—especially when there is interference—something gets in the way, something disturbs the frequency (like mountains, storms, telephone or electrical lines, other electromagnetic waves).[44] Interference also can occur when two or more frequencies encounter one another or are so close together as to be nearly indistinguishable (for instance, tuning into a particular radio station can be difficult if other stations use frequencies located nearby and any or all of the signals are more or less strong). As well, when two identical signals meet at the place where their broadcast ranges end, interference will occur because of overlapping boundaries.

To extend reach and create lines of communication across broadcast ranges, transformers are used as networking nodes. In terms of feminist history, consciousness, and praxis, transformers (translators) can take the form of encounters between constituencies who must learn to listen and hear through difference; those individuals who find themselves working as bridges between constituencies (think of Donna Kate Rushin's "The Bridge Poem"[45] and the entire life of Gloria Anzaldúa); or the work of coalition building among groups and issues that are not usually aligned with one another. These modes of networking form the weaving together of commitments to expanding the scope of what and who constitutes feminist politics. Because there is so much crossover, ideological and constituent "purity" is not possible—as if "purity," like its ideological companion "unity," should be the goal. Often what we accept as a sign of "purity" is the ability to mark out boundaries (hence, the efforts throughout the 1980s of historians of feminist consciousness to clarify the distinctions between different feminisms such as liberal, Marxist, cultural, radical, socialist, and the myriad of others that do and don't overlap these categories). Since I believe in impurity (pollution, mixtures, mestizas), working to make the boundaries of third wave feminism clear and distinct is particularly unsatisfying.

The rhetoric of radios, radio waves, and radio broadcasting can be a discursive technology for mapping different feminist frequencies that exist simultaneously, transmitting and becoming silent, heard only if we tune in to them—assuming we have the tools and that we know how to tune in—traveling through and across and between geographies and movements and cultural sites of resistance. Metaphors are themselves technologies, after all. This technological analogy hails a conceptualization of feminist history, consciousness, and praxis that can reflect the multiplicity of locations, experiences, and ideologies shaping the production of meaning today. Its rhetoric is playful and serious. It is playful because it doesn't demand blind allegiance and can accommodate other perspectives; but, it is serious because we desperately need to incorporate into our analyses of the cultural predicament of feminist consciousness in the United States at the turn of the century a discursive thread attuned to the "cultural repertoire of discourses, objects, ideas and modes of resistance"[46] that break with seamless narratives of history and knowledge that exclude the nonnormative and nondominant. I hope this proposal is read in the spirit of expanding and opening up space for coalition and critical consciousness. Personally, I can't imagine a truly transformative, revolutionary feminist future until we begin from those places of disruption and confrontation where our sense of certitude and the desire for sameness have been rendered incomprehensible. To that end, I offer this form of serious play not as a simple argument to replace one modulation of the wave metaphor with another, but rather as an opportunity to hold both in view (and tension) at the same time so that multiple cultural-historical phenomena can coincide together. I invite others to join me in exploring its epistemological implications.

NOTES

1. Jacquelyn Zita, "Third Wave Feminisms: An Introduction," *Hypatia* 12, no. 3 (Summer 1997): 6.

2. Catherine M. Orr, "Charting the Currents of the Third Wave," *Hypatia* 12, no. 3 (Summer 1997): 29–45.

3. Rita Alfonso and Jo Triglio, "Surfing the Third Wave: A Dialogue Between Two Third Wave Feminists," *Hypatia* 12, no. 3 (Summer 1997): 7–16.

4. Cathryn Bailey, "Making Waves and Drawing Lines: The Politics of Defining the Vicissitudes of Feminism," *Hypatia* 12, no. 3 (Summer 1997): 17–28.

5. Deborah Siegel, "The Legacy of the Personal: Generating Theory in Feminism's Third Wave," *Hypatia* 12, no. 3 (Summer 1997): 46–75.

6. The one exception is the section "Third Frequencies," which focuses on bisexuality.

7. Flora Davis, *Moving the Mountain: The Women's Movement in America Since 1960* (New York: Simon and Schuster, 1991), 11.

8. For examples, see Sydney Tarrow, "Cycles of Protest," in *Social Movements: Perspectives and Issues*, eds. Steven M Buechler and F. Kurt Cylke, Jr. (Mountain View, CA: Mayfield, 1994/1997), 441–56; Doug McAdam, *Political Process and the Development of Black Insurgency, 1930–1970* (Chicago: University of Chicago Press, 1982); Jo Freeman, *The Politics of Women's Liberation* (New York: Longman, 1975); Verta Taylor, "Social Movement Continuity: The Women's Movement in Abeyance," *American Sociological Review* 54 (October 1989): 761–75; David A. Snow and Robert D. Benford, "Master Frames and Cycles of Protest," in *Social Movements: Perspectives and Issues*, 456–72.

9. Barbara Smith, "Racism and Women's Studies," in *All the Women Are White, All the Blacks Are Men, But Some of Us Are Brave: Black Women's Studies*, eds. Gloria T. Hull, Patricia Bell Scott, and Barbara Smith (Old Westbury, NY: The Feminist Press, 1982), 48–51.

10. I haven't found any one origin for this coining, but claims have been made as to its earliest articulations. In 1999 a discussion of the topic commenced on WMST-L during which several contributors shared early references. Some of these include: a Boston women's journal, *The Second Wave* (1970–71); an article, Gerda Lerner, "New Approaches to the Study of Women in American History," *The Journal of Social History* 4 (1969): 33–56; Joan Didion's 1972 essay, "The Women's Movement," republished in *The White Album* (New York: Simon and Schuster, 1979); and, both Shirley Frank and Marge Piercy, both of whom lived in Boston at the time, testified that the term was popular in the Northeast by 1970. Additionally, in *Daring to Be Bad: Radical Feminism in America, 1967–1975* (Minneapolis: University of Minnesota Press, 1989), 302, Alice Echols credits Martha Weinman Lear with the first use of the phrase "the second wave of feminism" in a 1968 *New York Times Magazine* article. More recently, Carole R. McCann and Seung-Kyung Kim identify Kate Millett's book *Sexual Politics* as containing the earliest usage of the term. See their *Feminist Theory Reader: Local and Global Perspectives* (New York: Routledge, 2003): 8.

11. *Gloria Anzaldúa and Cherríe Moraga*, eds., *This Bridge Called My Back: Writings by Radical Women of Color* (Watertown, MA: Persephone, 1981; Latham, NY: Kitchen Table: Women of Color Press, 1983).

12. Among others, these affinities are invoked in: Judith Hole and Ellen Levine, *Rebirth of Feminism* (New York: Quadrangle Books, 1971); Freeman; Davis; Barbara Ryan, *Feminism and the Women's Movement: Dynamics of Change in Social Movement Ideology and Activism* (New York: Routledge, 1992).

13. Nancy Cott, *The Grounding of Modern Feminism* (New Haven, CT: Yale University Press, 1987).

14. Taylor, "Social Movement Continuity."

15. Barbara Deckard, *The Women's Movement: Political, Socioeconomic, and Psychological Issues* (New York: Harper and Row, 1975; 3rd ed. Reading, MA: Addison-Wesley, 1983); Ryan; Verta Taylor and Leila J. Rupp, "Women's Culture and Lesbian Feminist Activism: A Reconsideration of Cultural Feminism," *Signs: A Journal of Women in Culture and Society* 19, no. 1 (Autumn 1993): 32–61; Cott; for Taylor and Rupp's contrasting view of their work, see Foreword.

16. Chandra Mohanty, "Feminist Encounters: Locating the Politics of Experience," *Copyright* 1 (Fall 1987): 30–44.

17. Taylor and Rupp.

18. Many historians have problematized both the emphasis on suffrage and the preoccupation with elite women's issues in the production of first wave histories.

19. This is a fairly standard schemata, but two helpful articulations are Gloria Steinem, "Looking to the Future," *Ms. Magazine* 16, no. 1 (July/August 1987): 55–57 and Catherine Stimpson, "Women's Studies and Its Discontents." *Dissent* 43, no. 1 (Winter 1996): 67–75.

20. Siegel, 52.

21. The term *technologics* includes the discursive moves of many feminist and cultural theorists to apply technological rhetorics to the production of knowledge about language, power, and movements.

22. See Bertolt Brecht, "Radio as an Apparatus for Communication," in *Video Culture: A Critical Investigation*, ed. John G. Hanhardt (Layton, UT: Gibbs M. Smith / Peregrine Smith Books, 1986), 53–55; and Hans Magnus Enzenberger, "Constituents of a Theory of the Media," trans. Stuart Hood, in *Video Culture*, 96–123.

23. An example, my stereo consists of separate components fulfilling distinct functions. However, the component that links all the separate components together and transmits the sounds from the CD player and the tape deck to the speakers, and which also contains the radio unit, is called the "stereo receiver," despite the fact that I would get no sound from the other components if my "stereo receiver" could not transmit and relay messages to and from the stereo speakers and the CD player and tape deck. This simultaneous function is also replicated in the fact that my tape deck recording capabilities are completely facilitated through the receiver unit.

24. Emphasis added. Chela Sandoval, *Methodology of the Oppressed* (Minneapolis: University of Minnesota Press, 2000), 63.

25. Chela Sandoval, "U.S. Third World Feminism: The Theory and Method of Oppositional Consciousness in the Postmodern World," *Genders* 10 (Spring 1991): 1–24.

26. Linda Nicholson, ed., *The Second Wave: A Reader in Feminist Theory* (New York: Routledge, 1997).

27. Nicholson, 1.

28. Ibid.

29. Ibid., 5.

30. Beth Schneider, "Political Generations and the Contemporary Women's Movement," *Sociological Inquiry* 58, no. 1 (Winter 1988): 4–21.

31. Joni Mitchell, "You Turn Me On I'm a Radio," For the Roses, Electra, 1972.

32. Siegel, 52.

33. Amanda Lotz, "Communicating Third-Wave Feminism and New Social Movements: Challenges for the Next Century of Feminist Endeavor," *Women and Language* 26, no. 1 (Spring 2003) (accessed October 23, 2003, from ProQuest Co. Database).

34. Rebecca Walker, "Becoming the Third Wave," in *Testimony: Young African-Americans on Self-Discovery and Black Identity*, ed. Natasha Tarpley (Boston: Beacon Press, 1995): 215–218. First published in *Ms. Magazine* (January/February 1992).

35. Lynn Chancer, "Third Wave Feminism," *Village Voice* 36, no. 21 (May 21, 1991): 28.

36. Chancer.

37. Sandoval, "U.S. Third World Feminism," 4.

38. See Ednie Kaeh Garrison, "Contests for the Meaning of 'Third Wave Feminism': Feminism and Popular Consciousness," in *Third Wave Feminism: A Critical Exploration*, eds. Stacy Gillis, Gillian Howie, and Rebecca Munford (New York: Palgrave Macmillan, 2004).

39. bell hooks, "Feminism: A Transformational Politic," in *Talking Back: Thinking Feminist, Thinking Black* (Boston: South End Press, 1989): 19–27.

40. Iris Marion Young, "The Complexities of Coalition." *Dissent* 44, no. 1 (Winter 1997): 64–69.

41. Young, 69.

42. Ibid., 68–69.

43. Ibid., 69.

44. Interestingly, I understand that water doesn't disturb radio wave transmission.

45. Donna Kate Rushin, "The Bridge Poem," *This Bridge Called My Back*, xxi–xxii.

46. Ednie Kaeh Garrison, "U.S. Feminism—Grrrl Style! Youth (Sub)Cultures and the Technologics of the Third Wave," *Feminist Studies* 26, no. 1 (Spring 2000): 150.

DIFFERENT WAVELENGTHS:
A BIBLIOGRAPHY

Julie Voelck

This bibliography is a selective but extensive list of books, book chapters, articles, and special issues of journals, published from 1991 to the present. The resources selected for inclusion are significant, influential, or unique contributions to the literature on the third wave of feminism. With few exceptions, they are limited to U.S. publications, and, aside from some important essays in popular periodicals, the articles are from academic and scholarly journals. Because the topic is extraordinarily multidisciplinary, dozens of research and bibliographic databases covering all disciplines were searched to gather these citations.

The bibliography is arranged first by format, with the journal article section organized by topics that roughly coincide with the themes of this book: Issues of Diversity; Second and Third Waves; and Tactics of the Third Wave. Many of the cited works could be listed under more than one theme, but to avoid repetition they are not. In addition to the three major themes, each citation is followed by one or more keywords to help further identify the content of the work.

BOOKS

Baumgardner, Jennifer, and Amy Richards. 2000. *Manifesta: Young Women, Feminism and the Future.* New York: Farrar, Straus and Giroux.
Keywords: Feminist Generations/Feminist History/Issues of Third Wave/Second to Third Wave

Bondoc, Anna, and Meg Daly, eds. 1999. *Letters of Intent: Women Cross the Generations to Talk About Family, Work, Sex, Love and the Future of Feminism.* New York: The Free Press.
Keywords: Anthology/Feminist Generations/Feminist History/Second to Third Wave

Chancer, Lynn S. 1998. *Reconcilable Differences: Confronting Beauty, Pornography, and the Future of Feminism.* Berkeley: University of California Press.
Keywords: Pornography/Second to Third Wave/Sexuality

Dicker, Rory C., and Alison Piepmeier, eds. 2003. *Catching a Wave: Reclaiming Feminism for the 21st Century.* Boston: Northeastern University Press.
Keywords: Anthology/Diversity and Inclusivity/Issues of Third Wave/Second to Third Wave

Enns, Carolyn Z. 2004. *Feminist Theories and Feminist Psychotherapies: Origins, Themes, and Diversity.* 2nd ed. New York: Haworth Press.
Note: When this bibliography was being compiled, this book was forthcoming and not yet available for review.

Evans, Sara M. 2003. *Tidal Wave: How Women Changed America at Century's End.* New York: The Free Press.
Keywords: Feminist History/Second to Third Wave

Findlen, Barbara, ed. 2001. *Listen Up: Voices From the Next Feminist Generation.* 2nd ed. Emeryville, CA: Seal Press.
Keywords: Anthology/Diversity and Inclusivity/First-Person Essays and Personal Narrative/Issues of Third Wave

Gillis, Stacy, Gillian Howie, and Rebecca Munford. 2005. *Third Wave Feminism: A Critical Exploration.* New York: Palgrave Macmillan.
Note: When this bibliography was being compiled, this book was forthcoming and not yet available for review.

Glickman, Rose L. 1993. *Daughters of Feminists.* New York: St. Martin's Press.
Keywords: Feminist Generations/Interviews/Second to Third Wave

Henry, Astrid. 2004. *Not My Mother's Sister: Generational Conflict and Third Wave Feminism.* Bloomington: Indiana University Press.
Note: When this bibliography was being compiled, this book was forthcoming and not yet available for review.

Hernandez, Daisy, and Bushra Rehman, eds. 2002. *Colonize This! Young Women of Color on Today's Feminism.* New York: Seal Press.

Keywords: Diversity and Inclusivity/First-Person Essays and Personal Narrative/Issues of Third Wave

Heywood, Leslie, and Jennifer Drake, eds. 1997. *Third Wave Agenda: Being Feminist, Doing Feminism.* Minneapolis: University of Minnesota Press.
Keywords: Anthology/Issues of Third Wave

Johnson, Merri L., ed. 2002. *Jane Sexes It Up: True Confessions of Feminist Desire.* New York: Four Walls Eight Windows.
Keywords: Anthology/Diversity and Inclusivity/First-Person Essays and Personal Narrative/Sexuality

Kamen, Paula. 1991. *Feminist Fatale: Voices from the "Twentysomething" Generation Explore the Future of the "Women's Movement".* New York: Donald I. Fine.
Keywords: Interviews/Issues of Third Wave/Second to Third Wave

Karaian, Lara, Lisa B. Rundle, and Allyson Mitchell, eds. 2001. *Turbo Chicks: Talking Young Feminisms.* Toronto: Sumach Press.
Keywords: Anthology/Diversity and Inclusivity/First-Person Essays and Personal Narrative/Issues of Third Wave

Karp, Marcelle, and Debbie Stoller, eds. 1999. *The Bust Guide to the New Girl Order.* New York: Penguin Books.
Keywords: Anthology/Issues of Third Wave/Zines

Kaschak, Ellyn, ed. 2001. *The Next Generation: Third Wave Feminist Psychotherapy.* New York: Haworth Press.
Keywords: Anthology/Feminist Psychotherapy/Issues of Third Wave/Second to Third Wave
Note: Copublished simultaneously as *Women and Therapy,* Volume 23, no. 2 (2001).

Labaton, Vivien, and Dawn L. Martin, eds. 2004. *The Fire This Time: Young Activists and the New Feminism.* New York: Anchor Books.
Keywords: Activism/Anthology/Diversity and Inclusivity/Issues of Third Wave

Looser, Devoney, and E. Ann. Kaplan, eds. 1997. *Generations: Academic Feminists in Dialogue.* Minneapolis: University of Minnesota Press.
Keywords: Anthology/Second to Third Wave

O'Barr, Jean F., and Mary Wyer, eds. 1992. *Engaging Feminism: Students Speak Up and Speak Out.* Charlottesville, VA.: University Press of Virginia.

Keywords: Anthology/Diversity and Inclusivity/First-Person Essays and Personal Narrative/Second to Third Wave

Taormino, Tristan, and Karen Green, eds. 1997. *A Girl's Guide to Taking Over the World: Writings from the Girl Zine Revolution.* New York: St. Martin's Press.
Keywords: Anthology/Diversity and Inclusivity/Issues of Third Wave/ Zines

Vale, V., ed. 1996. *Zines!* Volume 1. San Francisco: V/Search.
Keywords: Anthology/Diversity and Inclusivity/Interviews/Issues of Third Wave/Zines
Note: Not all the zines featured in this volume and volume 2 (see below) were produced by feminists or cover feminist themes. In this volume, see: "Housewife Turned Assassin," "Meat Hook," "Mystery Date," "Outpunk," and "Fatgirl."

————, ed. 1997. *Zines!* Volume 2. San Francisco: V/Search.
Keywords: Anthology/Diversity and Inclusivity/Interviews/Issues of Third Wave/Zines

Walker, Rebecca, ed. 1995. *To Be Real: Telling the Truth and Changing the Face of Feminism.* New York: Anchor Books.
Keywords: Anthology/Diversity and Inclusivity/Issues of Third Wave

Whittier, Nancy. 1995. *Feminist Generations: The Persistence of the Radical Women's Movement.* Philadelphia: Temple University Press.
Keywords: Content Analysis/Feminist Generations/Interviews/Second to Third Wave
Note: See especially chapter 7: "The Next Wave," 225–44.

Wolf, Naomi. 1993. *Fire With Fire: The New Female Power and How It Will Change the 21st Century.* New York: Random House.
Keywords: "Anti-victim Feminism"/Issues of Third Wave/Second to Third Wave

BOOK CHAPTERS

Baker, Christina. "Telling Our Stories: Feminist Mothers and Daughters." In *Mothers and Daughters: Connection, Empowerment, and Transformation,* edited by Andrea O'Reilly and Sharon Abbey, 203–12. Lanham, MD: Rowman and Littlefield, 2000.
Keywords: Feminist Generations/Second to Third Wave

Cateforis, Theo, and Elena Humphreys. "Constructing Communities and Identities: Riot Grrrl New York City." In *Musics of Multicul-*

tural America: A Study of Twelve Musical Communities, edited by Kip Lornell and Anne K. Rasmussen, 317–42. New York: Schirmer Books, 1997.
Keywords: Issue of Third Wave/Riot Grrrl

Drake, Jennifer. "The Mis/Education of Righteous Babes: Popular Culture and Third-Wave Feminism." In *Growing Up Postmodern: Neoliberalism and the War on the Young*, edited by Ronald Strickland, 181–203. Lanham, MD: Rowman and Littlefield, 2002.
Keywords: "Anti-victim Feminism"—critique of/Mass Media/Second to Third Wave/Wave Model

Gottlieb, Joanne, and Gayle Wald. "Smells Like Teen Spirit: Riot Grrrls, Revolution and Women in Independent Rock." In *Microphone Fiends: Youth Music and Culture*, edited by Andrew Ross and Tricia Rose, 250–74. New York: Routledge, 1994.
Keyword: Riot Grrrl

Hanna, Kathleen. "Gen X Survivor: From Riot Grrrl Rock Star to Feminist Artist." In *Sisterhood Is Forever: The Women's Anthology for a New Millennium*, edited by Robin Morgan, 131–37. New York: Washington Square Press, 2003.
Keywords: First-Person Essay and Personal Narrative/Riot Grrrl/Second to Third Wave

Henry, Astrid. "Biting the Hand that Feeds You: Feminism as 'Bad Mother.'" In *Mothers and Daughters: Connection, Empowerment, and Transformation*, edited by Andrea O'Reilly and Sharon Abbey, 213–24. Lanham, MD: Rowman and Littlefield, 2000.
Keywords: "Anti-victim Feminism"/Feminist Generations/Second to Third Wave

Kaminer, Wendy. "Feminism's Third Wave: What Do Young Women Want?" In *True Love Waits: Essays and Criticism*, Wendy Kaminer, 39–50. Reading, MA: Addison-Wesley, 1996.
Keywords: "Anti-victim Feminism"/"Anti-Victim Feminism"—critique of/Issues of Third Wave
Note: Originally appeared in *New York Times Book Review*, 100 (June 4, 1995): 3+.

Kearney, Mary C. "'Don't Need You': Rethinking Identity Politics and Separatism From a Grrrl Perspective." In *Youth Culture: Identity in a Postmodern World*, edited by Jonathon S. Epstein, 148–88. Malden, MA: Blackwell, 1998.
Keywords: Riot Grrrl/Subcultures

Nehring, Neil. "The Riot Grrrls and Carnival." In *Popular Music, Gender, and Postmodernism*, edited by Neil Nehring, 150–93. Thousand Oaks, CA: Sage, 1997.
Keyword: Riot Grrrl
Note: Also published as a chapter in Dettmar, Kevin J. H., and William Richey, eds. *Reading Rock & Roll: Authenticity, Appropriation, Aesthetics.* New York: Columbia University Press, 1999, 209–35.

Pearce, Kimber C. "Third Wave Feminism and Cybersexuality: The Cultural Backlash of the New Girl Order." In *Sexual Rhetoric: Media Perspectives on Sexuality, Gender, and Identity*, edited by Meta G. Carstarphen and Susan C. Zavoina, 271–81. Westport, CT: Greenwood Press, 1999.
Keywords: Issues of Third Wave/Second to Third Wave/Technologies

Richards, Amy and Marianne Schnall. "Cyberfeminism: Networking the Net." In *Sisterhood Is Forever: The Women's Anthology for a New Millennium*, edited by Robin Morgan, 517–25. New York: Washington Square Press, 2003.
Keywords: Issues of Third Wave/Technologies

Schilt, Kristen. "'Riot Grrrl Is …': The Contestation Over Meaning in a Music Scene." In *Music Scenes: Local, Translocal, and Virtual*, edited by Andy Bennett and Richard A. Peterson, 115–30. Nashville, TN: Vanderbilt University Press, 2004.
Keywords: Interviews/Riot Grrrl/Zines

ARTICLES

Issues of Diversity

Diaz, Angeli R. "Postcolonial Theory and the Third Wave Agenda." *Women and Language* 26, no. 1 (2003): 10–17.
Keywords: Feminist Theory/Issues of Third Wave

Fregoso, Rosa L. "On the Road With Angela Davis." *Cultural Studies* 13, no. 2 (1999): 211–22.
Keywords: Feminist Theory/Issues of Third Wave

Guy-Sheftall, Beverly. "Response From a 'Second Waver' to Kimberly Springer's 'Third Wave Black Feminism?'" *Signs: Journal of Women in Culture and Society* 27, no. 4 (2002): 1091–94.
Keywords: Black Feminism/Diversity and Inclusivity/Wave Model

Radford-Hill, Sheila. "Keepin' It Real: A Generational Commentary on Kimberly Springer's 'Third Wave Black Feminism?'" *Signs: Journal of Women in Culture and Society* 27, no. 4 (2002): 1083–89.
Keywords: Black Feminism/Diversity and Inclusivity/Wave Model

Springer, Kimberly. "Third Wave Black Feminism." *Signs: Journal of Women in Culture and Society* 27, no. 4 (2002): 1059–82.
Keywords: Black Feminism/Diversity and Inclusivity/Wave Model

Stryker, Susan and Marysia Zalewski. "A Conversation with Susan Stryker." *International Feminist Journal of Politics* 5, no. 1 (2003): 118–25.
Keywords: Diversity and Inclusivity/Second to Third Wave

Taylor, Ula Y. "Making Waves: The Theory and Practice of Black Feminism." *Black Scholar* 28, no. 2 (1998): 8–28.
Keywords: Black Feminism/Diversity and Inclusivity/Feminist Theory

SECOND AND THIRD WAVES

Armstrong, Elisabeth. "Contingency Plans for the Feminist Revolution." *Science and Society* 65, no. 1 (2001): 39–71.
Keywords: Feminist History/Feminist Theory

Bailey, Cathryn. "Unpacking the Mother/Daughter Baggage: Reassessing Second- and Third-Wave Tensions." *Women's Studies Quarterly* 30, no. 3/4, (2002): 138–54.
Keyword: Feminist Generations

Beggan, James K., and Scott T. Allison. "The Playboy Playmate Paradox: The Case Against the Objectification of Women." *Advances in Gender Research* 6 (2002): 103–56.
Keywords: Content Analysis/Pornography

Braithwaite, Ann. "The Personal, the Political, Third-Wave and Post-feminisms." *Feminist Theory* 3, no. 3 (2002): 335–44.
Keywords: Feminist Theory/Issues of Third Wave

Bulbeck, Chilla. "Simone De Beauvoir and Generations of Feminists." *Hecate* 25, no. 2 (1999): 5–21.
Keyword: Feminist History

Buszek, Maria-Elena. "Waving Not Drowning: Thinking about Third Wave Feminism in the U.S." *Make: The Magazine of Women's Art* 86 (1999/2000): 38–39.
Keywords: Feminist Art/Issues of Third Wave

Chancer, Lynne. "Third Wave Feminism." *Village Voice* 36, no. 21 (1991): 28.
Keywords: Diversity and Inclusivity/Issues of Third Wave/Sexuality
Note: This article, along with Walker's 1992 essay in *Ms. Magazine* (see below), has been credited with being one of the first to present the concept of a third wave of feminism.

Chancer, Lynn S. "From Pornography to Sadomasochism: Reconciling Feminist Differences." *Annals of the American Academy of Political and Social Science* 571, no. 1 (2000): 77–88.
Keywords: Pornography/Sexuality

Cole, Alyson M. "Victims No More (?)." *Feminist Review* 64 (2000): 135–38.
Keyword: "Anti-victim Feminism"—critique of

Drake, Jennifer. "Third Wave Feminisms." *Feminist Studies* 23, no. 1 (1997): 97–108.
Keywords: Review Essay/Wave Model

Faludi, Susan. "'I'm Not a Feminist but I Play One on TV." *Ms. Magazine* 5, no. 5 (1995): 30–39.
Keyword: "Anti-victim Feminism"—critique of

Gilmore, Stephanie. 2001. "Looking Back, Thinking Ahead: Third Wave Feminism in the United States." *Journal of Women's History* 12, no. 4 (2001): 215–21.
Keywords: Review Essay/Issues of Third Wave

Hogeland, Lisa M. "Against Generational Thinking, or, Some Things that 'Third Wave' Feminism Isn't." Pt. 1. *Women's Studies in Communication* 24(2001): 107–21.
Keywords: Consciousness Raising/Wave Model

Howry, Allison L. and Julia T. Wood. 2001. "Something Old, Something New, Something Borrowed: Themes in the Voices of a New Generation of Feminists." *Southern Communication Journal* 66, no. 4(2001): 323–36.
Keyword: Issues of Third Wave

Johnson, Amy. 2003. "Seeking Sisterhood: A Voice From the Third Wave." *off our backs* 33, no. 9/10(2003): 22–25.
Keyword: First-Person Essay and Personal Narrative

Kruckemeyer, Kate. "Making Room for Teen Voices: Feminist Discourse in Magazines by and for Girls." *Iris: A Journal About Women* 44 (2002): 46–52.

Keyword: Mass Media

Larson, Jane E. "Symposium Introduction: Third Wave—Can Feminists Use the Law to Effect Social Change in the 1990s?" *Northwestern University Law Review* 87 (1993): 1252–301.
Keyword: Legal Theory

Lotz, Amanda D. "Communicating Third Wave Feminism and New Social Movements: Challenges for the Next Century of Feminist Endeavor." *Women and Language* 26, no. 1 (2003): 2–9.
Keywords: Feminist Theory/Wave Model

Mandle, Joan D. "Sisterly Critics." *NWSA Journal* 11, no. 1(1999): 97–109.
Keyword: "Anti-victim Feminism"—critique of
Note: See also in this issue Alyson M. Cole's "'Are There Sisters in the Class?' A Response to 'Sisterly Critics',"110–14; Mandle's "A Response to 'There are No Victims in this Class',"114–16; and Cole's "Response to Response,"114.

Pillow, Wanda S. "Gender Matters: Feminist Research in Educational Evaluation." *New Directions for Evaluation* 96 (2002): 9–26.
Keywords: Education/Feminist Theory

Renegar, Valerie R., and Stacey K. Sowards. 2003. "Liberal Irony, Rhetoric, and Feminist Thought: A Unifying Third Wave Feminist Theory." *Philosophy and Rhetoric* 36, no. 4 (2003): 330–52.
Keyword: Feminist Theory

Roberts, Tomi-Ann. 2002. "The Woman in the Body." *Feminism and Psychology* 12, no. 3 (2002): 324–29.
Keyword: Nonverbal Communications

Ruffino, Joan. "Questions of Identity for the Third Wave: Evidence of an Evolving Feminist Movement." *West Virginia University Philological Papers* 46 (2000): 35–45.
Keywords: Developmental Psychology/Feminist Theory

Sabbarwal, Sherry. "The Changing Face of Feminism: Dilemmas of the Feminist Academic." *Sociological Bulletin* 49, no. 2 (2000): 267–77.
Keywords: Feminist History/Women's Studies

Sapiro, Virginia. "Feminism: A Generation Later." *Annals of the American Academy of Political and Social Science* 515 (1991): 10–22.
Keyword: Politics

Sharpe, Sue. "Going for It: Young Women Face the Future." *Feminism and Psychology* 11, no. 2 (2001): 177–81.
Keywords: Interviews/Issues of Third Wave

Shaw, Rhonda. "'Our Bodies, Ourselves,' Technology, and Questions of Ethics: Cyberfeminism and the Lived Body." *Australian Feminist Studies* 18, no. 40 (2003): 45–55.
Keywords: Feminist Theory/Technologies

Sherry, Ann. 2000. "Building the Bridge: Taking Feminism into the Twenty-First Century." *Australian Feminist Studies* 15, no. 32 (2000): 221–26.
Keywords: Feminist Theory/Wave Model

Shugart, Helene A. "Isn't It Ironic? The Intersection of Third-Wave Feminism and Generation X." *Women's Studies in Communication* 24, no. 2 (2001): 131–68.
Keywords: Issues of Third Wave/Wave Model

Shugart, Helene A., Catherine E. Waggoner, and D. L. O. Hallstein. "Mediating Third-Wave Feminism: Appropriation As Postmodern Media Practice." *Critical Studies in Media Communication* 18, no. 2 (2001): 194–210.
Keywords: Commodification/Content Analysis/Mass Media

Spencer, Nancy E. "Reading between the Lines: A Discursive Analysis of the Billie Jean King vs. Bobby Riggs 'Battle of the Sexes'." *Sociology of Sport Journal* 17, no. 4(2000): 386–402.
Keyword: Women in Sports

Stimpson, Catharine R. 1996. "Women's Studies and Its Discontents." *Dissent* 43, no. 1(1996): 67–75.
Keywords: Wave Model/Women's Studies

Walker, Rebecca. "Becoming the Third Wave." *Ms. Magazine* 2, no. 4(1992): 39–41.
Keywords: Issues of Third Wave/Wave Model
Note: This article, along with Chancer's 1991 essay in the *Village Voice* (see above), has been credited with being one of the first to present the concept of a third wave of feminism.

Yob, Iris M. "Feminism in the Schools in a Postfeminist Age." *Educational Theory* 50, no. 3 (2000): 383–403.
Keyword: Education

TACTICS OF THE THIRD WAVE

Aikau, Hokulani, Karla Erickson, and Wendy L. Moore. "Three Women Writing/Riding Feminism's Third Wave." *Qualitative Sociology* 26, no. 3 (2003): 397–425.
Keywords: First-Person Essays and Personal Narrative/Wave Model

Baumgardner, Jennifer. "Third Wave: A Multicultural Feminist Group Gets Organized, Modernized and Mobilized." *Hues* 4, no. 3 (1998): 20–22.
Keywords: Issues of Third Wave/Mobilization

Bell, Brandi Leigh-Ann. "Riding the Third Wave: Women-Produced Zines and Feminisms." *Resources for Feminist Research* 29, no. 3/4 (2002): 187–98.
Keywords: Content Analysis/Riot Grrrl/Zines

Comstock, Michelle. "Grrrl Zine Networks: Re-Composing Spaces of Authority, Gender, and Culture." *JAC: A Journal of Composition Theory* 21, no. 2 (2001): 383–409.
Keywords: Riot Grrrl/Zines

Driscoll, Catherine. "Girl Culture, Revenge and Global Capitalism: Cybergirls, Riot Grrls, Spice Girls." *Australian Feminist Studies* 14, no. 29 (1999): 173–93.
Keywords: Riot Grrrl/Zines

Fraser, M. L. "Zine and Heard: Fringe Feminism and the Zines of the Third Wave." *Feminist Collections: A Quarterly of Women's Studies Resources* 23, no. 4 (2002): 6–10.
Keywords: Riot Grrrl/Zines

Frey, Hillary. "Kathleen Hanna's Fire." *Nation* 276 (2003): 27–28.
Keywords: Issues of Third Wave/Riot Grrrl

Garrison, Ednie K. "U.S. Feminism—Grrrl Style! Youth (Sub)Cultures and the Technologies of the Third Wave." *Feminist Studies* 26, no. 1(2000): 141–70.
Keywords: Riot Grrrl/Technologies

Halberstam, Judith. "What's That Smell?: Queer Temporalities and Subcultural Lives." *International Journal of Cultural Studies* 6, no. 3 (2003): 313–33.
Keywords: Riot Grrrl/Subcultures

Harris, Anita. "Revisiting Bedroom Culture: New Spaces for Young Women's Politics." *Hecate* 27, no. 1 (2001): 128–38.

Keywords: Interviews/Riot Grrrl/Zines

Isaksen, Judy. "Identity and Agency: Riot Grrrls' Jouissance." *Encultura-tion: A Journal for Rhetoric, Writing, and Culture* 2, no. 2 (1999): No pagination. See http://enculturation.gmu.edu/2_2/isaksen.
Keywords: Riot Grrrl/Zines

Johnson, Angela. "Start a Fucking Riot: Riot Grrrl D.C." *off our backs* 23, no. 5 (1993): 6.
Keywords: Interviews/Riot Grrrl

Riordan, Ellen. "Commodified Agents and Empowered Girls: Consum-ing and Producing Feminism." *Journal of Communication Inquiry* 25, no. 3 (2001): 279–97.
Keywords: Commodification/Riot Grrrl

Sparks, Anne. "What TLC and Riot Grrrls Tell Us about the Feminiza-tion of Poverty." *Crosscurrents: The Journal of Graduate Research in Anthropology* 8 (1996): 69–72.
Keywords: Feminization of Poverty/Hip Hop/Riot Grrrl

Zobl, Elke. 2003. "Let's Smash Patriarchy! Zine Grrrls and Ladies at Work." *off our backs* 33, no. 3/4(2003): 60–61.
Keywords: Riot Grrrl/Zines

SPECIAL ISSUES

Bhavnani, Kum-Kum, Kathryn R. Kent, and France W. Twine, eds. "Feminisms and Youth Cultures." Special issue, *Signs: Journal of Women in Culture and Society* 23, no. 3 (1998).

Bhavnani, Kum-Kum, Kathryn R. Kent, and France W. Twine. "Editorial": 575–83.

Wald, Gayle. "Just a Girl? Rock Music, Feminism, and the Cul-tural Construction of Female Youth": 585–610.

O'Neill, Kelly. "No Adults Are Pulling the Stings and We Like It That Way": 611–18.

Porter, Mary A. "Resisting Uniformity at Mwana Kupona Girls' School: Cultural Productions in an Educational Setting": 619–43.

Esquibel, Catriona R. "Memories of Girlhood: Chicana Lesbian Fictions": 645–82.

Venkatesh, Sudhir A. "Gender and Outlaw Capitalism: A His-torical Account of the Black Sisters United 'Girl Gang'": 683–709.

Byers, Michele. "Gender/Sexuality/Desire: Subversion of Difference and Construction of Loss in the Adolescent Drama of 'My So-Called Life'": 711–34.

Bing-Canar, Jennifer, and Mary Zerkel. "Reading the Media and Myself: Experiences in Critical Media Literacy with Young Arab-American Women": 735–43.

Carter, Mia. "The Politics of Pleasure: Cross-Cultural Autobiographic Performance in the Video Works of Sadie Benning": 745–69.

Projansky, Sarah. "Girls Who Act Like Women Who Fly: Jessica Dubroff as Cultural Troublemaker": 771–807.

Rosenberg, Jessica, and Gitana Garafalo. "Riot Grrrl: Revolutions from Within": 809–41.

Gillis, Stacy and Rebecca Munford, eds. "Harvesting Our Strengths: Third Wave Feminism and Women's Studies." Special issue, *Journal of International Women's Studies* 4 no. 2 (2003).

Gillis, Stacy, and Rebecca Munford. "Harvesting Our Strengths: Third Wave Feminism and Women's Studies": 1–6.

Altman, Meryl. "Beyond Trashiness: The Sexual Language of 1970s Feminist Fiction": 7–19.

Denney, Colleen. "Mothers of Future Kings: The Madonna Redux Phenomenon": 20–30.

Dias, Karen. "The ANA Sanctuary: Women's Pro-Anorexia Narratives in Cyberspace": 31–45.

Kaplan, E. Ann. "Feminist Futures: Trauma, the Post-9/11 World and a Fourth Feminism?": 46–59.

Grace, Daphne. "Women's Space 'Inside the Haveli': Incarceration or Insurrection?": 60–75.

Woodhull, Winnie. "Global Feminisms, Transnational Political Economies, Third World Cultural Production": 76–90.

Harris, Ashleigh. "From Suffragist to Apologist: The Loss of Feminist Politics in a Politically Correct Patriarchy": 91–99.

Graff, Agnieszka. "Lost between the Waves: The Paradoxes of Feminist Chronology and Activism in Contemporary Poland": 100–116.

Zalewski, Marysia. "Is Women's Studies Dead?": 117–33.

Zita, Jacquelyn N., ed. "Third Wave Feminisms." Special issue, *Hypatia: A Journal of Feminist Philosophy* 12, no. 3(1997).

Jacquelyn N. "Third Wave Feminisms: An Introduction": 1–6.

Alfonso, Rita, and Jo Trigilio. "Surfing the Third Wave: A Dialogue between Two Third Wave Feminists": 7–16.

CONTRIBUTOR BIOGRAPHIES

Dawn Bates is a doctoral candidate in the Clinical Psychology Program at Indiana University of Pennsylvania (IUP). As a third wave feminist, she was the campus organizer for V-Day IUP, and works with the Health AWAREness Office, the Women's Studies program, and the Center for Counseling and Psychological Services. She is a zinester herself (*I Was Raised by Wolves*) and has presented on zines nationally (Association for Death Education and Counseling; Association for Women in Psychology); regionally (Women's Consortium, Pennsylvania; Women's Undergraduate Leadership Institute, Pennsylvania); and on campus (women's studies classes). Her dissertation involves a discourse analysis of zines.

Susanne Beechey is a doctoral candidate in gender and social policy at the George Washington University School of Public Policy and Public Administration, where she is also an adjunct instructor in the Women's Studies program. She has worked in a national women's policy organization, and authored an undergraduate thesis on third wave feminism at Macalester College.

Barbara Duncan is currently teaching at the University of Kentucky and working on her dissertation on third wave feminism and computer literacy from the University of Illinois. She has published articles on various aspects of technology in relation to education, and her main interests center around young adult literacy as it relates to generational transitions and popular culture.

Ednie Kaeh Garrison is Visiting Assistant Professor of Women's Studies at Wells College in Aurora, New York. She has published articles on third wave feminism in *Feminist Studies* (Spring 2000) and *Third Wave Feminism: A Critical Exploration* (New York: Palgrave, 2004). Resisting the commodification of third wave feminist meaning keeps her on a disgruntled edge as she tunes in to submerged movement and ideological wavelengths. Within the grips of an image-based culture, she foolishly begs people to listen.

Stephanie Gilmore is Assistant Professor of Women's History at the University of Toledo, She completed her dissertation on National Organization for Women chapters in Memphis, Columbus, and San Francisco, a study that examines the role of location and reconsiders the liberal/radical divide in second wave U.S. feminism while holding a 2004–2005 Presidential Fellowship from Ohio State University. She is also the editor of the forthcoming collection, *Feminist Coalitions: Historical Perspectives on Second-Wave Feminism in the United States* (Champaign, IL: University of Illinois Press).

Astrid Henry is Assistant Professor of Women's Studies and English at Saint Mary's College in Indiana. She is the author of *Not My Mother's Sister: Generational Conflict and Third-Wave Feminism* (Bloomington: Indiana University Press, 2004). Her essays on third wave feminism have appeared in *Reading "Sex and the City"* (London: I. B. Tauris, 2004), *Catching a Wave: Reclaiming Feminism for the 21st Century* (Boston: Northeastern University Press, 2003), and *Mothers and Daughters: Connection, Empowerment and Transformation* (Lanham, MD: Rowman and Littlefield, 2000).

Sally Hines teaches sociology and cultural studies at the Open University in the United Kingdom. She has recently completed doctoral research on transgender identities, intimate relationships, and practices of care. Her publications include contributions to *Sexuality: The Essential Glossary* (2004). She is currently writing articles on transgender practices of intimacy and care, and on tran(s)sexualities.

Florence Maätita is Assistant Professor in Sociology and Criminal Justice at Southern Illinois University, Edwardsville. She received her Ph.D. from the University of Connecticut in 2003. Her chapter on Chicana feminism stems from her master's thesis, "That's How I Came to Voice: Negotiating the Meaning of Chicana Feminism." Currently, her research interests include gender, race-ethnicity, and the social construction of motherhood.

Colleen Mack-Canty is an Assistant Professor in the Political Science department at the University of Idaho. She holds a Ph.D. in political science, with an emphasis on feminist theory, from the University of Oregon. Her research and publishing are in the areas of ecofeminism, third wave feminism, and feminist families. Her publications include two journal articles: "Third Wave Feminism and the Need to Reweave the Nature/Culture Duality" in *NWSA Journal* (2004) and "Feminist Family Values: Bridging Third Wave Feminism and Feminist Families" in *Journal of Family Issues* (2004), coauthored with Sue M. Wright.

Maureen C. McHugh is a Professor of Psychology at Indiana University of Pennsylvania where she teaches graduate and undergraduate courses in gender and in diversity. She has been teaching Psychology of Women and Human Sexuality since 1975, and has published chapters in many psychology of women texts on violence against women, and on research methods. A special issue of *Psychology of Women Quarterly* on measures of sex role attitudes that she coedited with Irene Frieze received the Distinguished Publication Award from the Association for Women in Psychology. Maureen was also awarded the Christine Ladd Franklin Award for her contributions to feminist psychology.

Nancy A. Naples is Professor of Sociology and Women's Studies at the University of Connecticut. She is author of *Feminism and Method: Ethnography, Discourse Analysis and Feminist Research* (New York: Routledge, 2003) and *Grassroots Warriors: Activist Mothering, Community Work, and the War on Poverty* (New York: Routledge, 1998). Her edited books include *Community Activism and Feminist Politics: Organizing Across Race, Class, and Gender* (New York: Routledge, 1998); *Women's Activism and Globalization: Linking Local Struggles with Transnational Politics*, coedited with Manisha Desai (New York: Routledge, 2002), and *Teaching Feminist Activism*, coedited with Karen Bojar (New York: Routledge, 2002). Her work also appears in *Signs: Journal of Women and Culture*, *Gender & Society*, *Feminist Economics*, and *Women and Politics*, among other journals and books.

Jo Reger is an Assistant Professor of Sociology at Oakland University in Michigan where she teaches classes in gender, social movements, and feminist theory. Her research examines social movement organizations, and communities and their influence on the construction of activist identities. She is currently studying the contemporary women's movement. Her work on the National Organization for Women has appeared in journals such as *Gender & Society* and *Qualitative Sociology* and she has authored book chapters on the subject.

Leila J. Rupp is Professor and Chair of Women's Studies at the University of California, Santa Barbara. She is coauthor with Verta Taylor of *Drag Queens at the 801 Cabaret* (2003) and *Survival in the Doldrums: The American Women's Rights Movement, 1945 to the 1960s* (1987) and author of *A Desired Past: A Short History of Same-Sex Sexuality in America* (1999), *Worlds of Women: The Making of an International Women's Movement* (1997), and *Mobilizing Women for War: German and American Propaganda, 1939–1945* (1978).

Kristen Schilt is a graduate student in sociology at the University of California, Los Angeles. She has published articles on Riot Grrrl and zine making in *Youth and Society* and *Popular Music and Society*. She is currently working on her dissertation, which focuses on the workplace experiences of female-to-male transsexuals.

Kimberly Springer teaches American studies at Kings College, London. She is the author of *Living for the Revolution: Black Feminist Organizations, 1968–1980* (Durham, NC: Duke University Press, 2005) and editor of *Still Lifting, Still Climbing: African-American Women's Contemporary Activism* (New York: New York University Press, 1999).

Lacey Story graduated from Oakland University with degrees in women's studies and sociology. She is the cofounder of the feminist student organization on campus and has been doing research on *The Vagina Monologues* and its impact on third wave feminism on college campuses since 2002. She is currently getting ready to attend graduate school in women's studies and her new area of research interest is the women's health movement and its impact on third wave feminism.

Verta Taylor is Professor of Sociology at the University of California, Santa Barbara. She is coauthor with Leila J. Rupp of *Drag Queens at the 801 Cabaret* (University of Chicago Press) and *Survival in the Doldrums: The American Women's Rights Movement, 1945 to the 1960s* (Oxford University Press); coeditor with Laurel Richardson and Nancy Whittier of *Feminist Frontiers VI* (McGraw-Hill); and author of *Rock-a-by Baby: Feminism, Self-Help and Postpartum Depression* (Routledge). Her articles on the women's movement, the gay and lesbian movement, and social movement theory have appeared in journals such as *The American Sociological Review, Signs, Social Problems, Mobilization, Gender & Society, Qualitative Sociology, Journal of Women's History,* and *Journal of Homosexuality.*

Julie Voelck is the Associate Dean of the Library at Oakland University in Rochester, Michigan. In addition to working in administration, her twenty-plus years of experience as an academic librarian include serving as women's studies bibliographer, developing a diversity film series, and creating one of the first library websites devoted to the support of feminist, multicultural, and diversity-related research. In her heart and in action she will always be a riot librarrrian—building feminist and LGBTQ library collections, supporting socially engaged campus programs, and sharing CDs by Le Tigre, Sleater-Kinney, and Kim Gordon. An article describing her research on gender-based differences in management styles was published in the July 2003 issue of *portal: Libraries and the Academy.*

DIFFERENT WAVELENGTHS: INDEX

Wallace, Michele, 6, 10, 15
Wave model, 216; see also Second wave; Third wave; Women's movement
    comparison of metaphors, 243–245
    continuity between, 97–112
    critique of, xi, xxii, 24, 158, 215–231, 237–254
    radio waves, 239, 243–245, 252–254
    role of women of color, 218–219, 239, 240
    use of, 237–239
WEAL, see Women's Equity Action League
Weigand, Kate, xxii
Western political theory, 196, 197, 198
When Chickenheads Come Home to Roost, see Morgan, Joan
White Women, Race Matters, see Frankenberg, Ruth
Whiteness, 41–42; see also Dyer, Richard; Frankenberg, Ruth
    white racism, 48
    "white solipsism," 45–46
    "whitewashing," xix,
    zines, see Zines
Whittier, Nancy, 144, 157, 158, 219–220; see also Micro-cohorts; Political generations
Wolf, Naomi, xx, 84, 89
    power feminism, xx, 84
        critique of, 84
    victim feminism, xx
Woman
    as fixed category, 69, 82
        fracturing of, 73
    as identity, 70–71,
    as universal category, 238–239
    women-born-women, 69; see also Trans woman
Womanist, 86
Women's Equity Action League, 100
Women's Movement; see also Feminism; Second Wave; Third Wave; Wave model
    abeyance, xi, xxii, 241, 242, 248
    doldrums, see abeyance
    exclusion of women of color, 29, 39, 42; see also Intersectionality; Third Wave
    generational approach, xii, 24, 81–94, 157, 215, 217
        critique of, 134–135, 248
    terms for, 240
    universal "womanhood," 40
    "whiteness," 28–30,

Women of color; see also African-American women; Black feminism; Chicana feminism; Chicana woman; Native American women
    third wave origins, xxiii, 86
    writings by, 86–87
Women's organizations, 117, 118; see also National women's policy organizations
Wright, Fred, 181
Working class women, 217; see also Low income women

X

Xicanista, 30, 31

Z

Zines, 39–56, 179–192
    and punk music, 181; see also Punk music
    as feminist tactic, 179, 180
    class, 41
    compilation zines, 52
        Evolution of a Race Riot, 52
        Yello Kitty, 53
    definition, 179–180
    fanzines, 181
    "feminist awakenings," 45–47, 53–54
    generational stances, 189–190
    girl zines, 181
        and fashion, 187
        as community, 190–191
        as creativity and voice, 182–184
        as healing, 188–189
        as resistance, 184–188
        BITCH DYKE WHORE, 189
        brainscan, 18, 184
        Death of Psyche, 188
        Fixing Her Hair, 183
        Glamour Queen, 183
        make me numb, 12, 187
        No, I Don't Think So, 188
        personal and political, 189–190
        Satan's Panties, 188
        Skirt, 186
        Soots and Stars, 187
        Triplicate and File, 186
        voice, 183–184
    girls' empowerment movement, 179
    history, 180–181
    language, 187